The Kongolese Saint Anthony

This book describes the Christian religious movement led by Dona Beatriz Kimpa Vita in the Kingdom of Kongo, from her birth in 1684 until her death, by burning at the stake, in 1706, only two years after the movement had started. Beatriz, a young woman, claimed to be possessed by Saint Anthony, argued that Jesus was a Kongolese, and criticized Italian Capuchin missionaries in her country for not supporting black saints. The movement was largely a peace movement, with a following among the common people, attempting to stop the devastating cycle of civil wars between contenders for the Kongolese throne that fed the growing Atlantic slave trade.

Thornton supplies background information on the Kingdom of Kongo, the development of Catholicism in Kongo since 1491, the nature and role of local warfare in the Atlantic slave trade, and contemporary everyday life, as well as sketching the lives of some local personalities.

John Thornton is Professor of History at Millersville University of Pennsylvania. He has taught at the University of Zambia, Allegheny College, and the University of Virginia. His other works include: *Africa and Africans in the Making of the Atlantic World, 1400–1800*, now in its second edition (Cambridge University Press, 1998), and *The Kingdom of Kongo*.

The Kongolese Saint Anthony

Dona Beatriz Kimpa Vita and the
Antonian Movement, 1684–1706

JOHN K. THORNTON

CAMBRIDGE
UNIVERSITY PRESS

CAMBRIDGE UNIVERSITY PRESS
Cambridge, New York, Melbourne, Madrid, Cape Town, Singapore,
São Paulo, Delhi, Dubai, Tokyo, Mexico City

Cambridge University Press
32 Avenue of the Americas, New York NY 10013-2473, USA

www.cambridge.org
Information on this title: www.cambridge.org/9780521596497

© John K. Thornton 1998

First published 1998
11th printing 2009

A catalogue record for this publication is available from the British Library

ISBN 978-0-521-59370-0 Hardback
ISBN 978-0-521-59649-7 Paperback

To the women in my life:

Mary Elizabeth
Linda
Amara and Amanda
Betsy, Alix, and Salli

Contents

Illustrations

Introduction

IN THE EIGHTEENTH CENTURY, a Kongolese woman possessed by Saint Anthony led a mass movement to restore the Kingdom of Kongo. The movement was violently suppressed by the religious and political authorities of the country, and she was burned at the stake as a witch and heretic in 1706 – but not before she had drawn thousands of people to her in the ruins of the country's ancient capital.

Dona Beatriz Kimpa Vita's religious and political movement is surprisingly little known outside narrow academic circles. Even though the movement has been discussed quite widely by Africanists since the 1960s, its full implications for the history of Africa and the slave trade to America have not been explored in popular history. Dona Beatriz' movement, although primarily aimed at ending a long-lasting civil war and reestablishing a broken monarchy, can also be seen as a popular movement directed against the slave trade in Africa at the time of the export slave trade. Yet up to the present, it has not fired much popular knowledge.

This neglect may be partly because West Africa is still regarded in the United States as the principal place of origin of African Americans, even though recent research shows that as many as one-quarter of all African Americans ultimately derive from central African (and mostly Kongolese) roots. Then, too, Dona Beatriz' movement, with its possessed saint and Christian ideology, often seems too embarrassingly bizarre or too atypical of African culture to appeal to American conceptions. Although most Americans are comfortable with the idea of Muslim Africans in the slave trade period, they seem much less comfortable with Christian Africans. A literate elite, dressing partially in European clothes, bearing Portuguese names, and professing Catholicism seems somehow out of place in the popular image of precolonial Africa.

In spite of this image, however, Kongo was an important contributor to the population of the Americas, thanks to the civil wars which Dona Beatriz' movement sought to end. Although the great burst of slaves from Kongo directed to North America (and particularly South Carolina) lay about fifteen years later than Dona Beatriz' death, the issues raised in her day were very much a part of the much less well-known period that followed. The Stono Rebellion of South Carolina in 1739, led by Catholic Kongolese slaves, marked the end of the burst and may have involved the working out of some of the issues raised by Dona Beatriz, as did the Haitian revolution in even greater force a half-century later.[1]

Whereas Americans might find Dona Beatriz' movement interesting because of its implications for the population of the New World, Dona Beatriz and her followers were not thinking primarily about the slave trade. For them, war spawned many problems besides the slave trade – only one of a host of possibly damaging outcomes to conflict. The problems of war – displaced people, intransigent elites, and the absence of popular checks on rulers – remain with Africa today, even if the specific threat of the slave trade is no longer present. In this way, Dona Beatriz prefigures modern African democracy movements as much as she can be seen as an antislavery figure.

The years of Dona Beatriz' movement are some of the best-documented in Kongo's history, which itself is probably the best described country in Atlantic Africa in the period. This documentation is a product of the convergence of Italian Capuchin mis-

---

[1] John Thornton, "African Roots of the Stono Rebellion," *American Historical Review* 96 (1991): 1101–13; " 'I am the Subject of the King of Congo': African Political Ideology and the Haitian Revolution," *Journal of World History* 4 (1993): 181–214.

sionaries on the eastern part of Kongo and their production of lengthy and detailed diaries of their lives there. Luca da Caltanisetta and especially Marcellino d'Atri produced two long (more than 500 pages together) diary-type accounts of the earlier periods of Dona Beatriz' life. The two were often independent witnesses to the same events as they frequently served together. When they left in 1701–2, Bernardo da Gallo and Lorenzo da Lucca, who left briefer but nevertheless detailed accounts, took their places. Dona Beatriz' own movement is described in da Gallo's report to the Propaganda Fide, written in 1710, and da Lucca's annual letters to the Capuchin province of Tuscany of 1706 and 1707. In addition to this eyewitness documentation, the archives contain a number of shorter documents that illuminate the period, one of the most important being the report of the Jesuit priest Pedro Mendes written in 1710 and giving historical background from 1665.

In all this mass of documentation, however, there is not a very strong Kongolese contribution. While some periods, notably the first half of the sixteenth century, are almost wholly presented in documents written by Kongolese, only one letter, written by Pedro IV and included in da Gallo's report, survives from a Kongolese author and deals directly with the period of the crisis.

Yet the Kongolese elite was literate, and the Capuchin accounts frequently mention their correspondence and even their recourse to archives. But this material may not have survived, and if it has, at present its location is not known. Eva Sebastyén's discovery of numerous seventeenth- and eighteenth-century documents in private hands and in local archives in the Dembos regions of Angola (just south of Kongo) in 1987–8 gives us hope that there are documents of eighteenth-century date still to be found in northern Angola that might remedy this situation. At present, however, we learn of the movement mostly through Italian priests.

The Capuchin priests were not impartial observers of the Kongolese scene, and indeed their actions helped to precipitate the movement itself. In the current situation, though, the modern scholar has little choice but to try to read between the lines and hope that the Kongolese viewpoint can be surmised. Sometimes it has been necessary to make use of modern observation and documentation to interpret or expand what the Capuchins tell us. Ever since the missionaries of the late nineteenth century began teaching literacy in Kikongo, the Kongolese have produced no small number of self-ethnographies, most notably the thousands of pages produced for the Swedish missionary Karl Laman in the early twentieth century, and more modern work by such Kongolese writers as Bahelele Ndimansa, Simon Bockie, and Fu-kiau Bunseki.[2] Unfortunately, most of these writers came from regions within the Kikongo-speaking world that had never been a part of the Kingdom of Kongo.

Students of Catholic missionaries, especially Jesuits and Redemptorists, often from within the boundaries of the old kingdom, have produced works on local history and early-twentieth-century customs. Of this smaller corpus, the most influential is probably the unpublished account, of 1910, of Mpetelo Boka, whose work underlies much of the ethnographic and traditional accounts of the missionary-historian Jean Cuvelier.[3]

Kongolese writers since the early twentieth century have recorded in writing, usually in Kikongo, historical information that was once transmitted orally. Along with their long tradition of literacy, the Kongolese maintained an oral tradition with historical implications, particularly the histories of families and clans. Cuvelier collected and published hundreds of these accounts, both from Kongolese texts and from his own interviews in the 1920s and 1930s.[4] The traditions that he and others recorded,

---

[2] Bahelele Ndimansa, *Lusansu ye fu mu Kongo tekila mvu 1900* (Kinshasa, (1977); *Kizonzi ye ntekolo andi Makundu*; André Fu-kiau Bunseki, *N'Kongo ye nza yakundilila* (Kinshasa, 1966); Simon Bockie, *Death and the Invisible Powers* (Bloomington, Ind., 1993).

[3] Mpetelo Boka, "Nsosani a Kinguli," 1910 MS, in Archiven der Paters Redemptoren, Leuven, portion was published by Jean Cuvelier in "Mambu ma Kinza Nkulu mu Nsi a Kongo," *Kukiele* 2 (1929): 11–12. A partial French translation appeared in Cuvelier, "Traditions Congolaises," *Congo* 2 (1930–1), and *L'ancien royaume du Congo* (Brussels, 1946; originally published in Flemish in 1941).

[4] In *Nkutama a mvila za makanda* [collection of praise names of clans] (1st ed. Tumba, Congo, 1934; 4th ed. Matadi, Congo, 1972 [revised by Joseph de Munck]. The content of the book first began appearing serially in the missionary newspaper, *Kukiele*, in 1928 under the title "Mambu ma Kinza

however, do not tell us much about life in Kongo before about 1800. Moreover, the most intensive collection and publication of traditions related more to Kongo's northern provinces in modern Zaire (renamed Congo in 1997), and less from the region where Dona Beatriz lived and worked as well as from the lands of the great royal families of Kongo that lay in Angola.[5] More may yet be gleaned from such sources when systematic research is again possible in northern Angola.

The Kongolese writers of orally transmitted history and ethnography have been joined by Western writers, primarily missionaries like Cuvelier and by anthropologists like John Janzen and Wyatt MacGaffey, who have mined Kikongo sources and conducted fieldwork. Although much of this work also concerns regions north of the old Kingdom of Kongo, it can still help scholars to understand the ideological world of the eighteenth-century Kongo presented in the Capuchin accounts. By using these studies, one hopes to see beyond the prejudices of the missionary sources.

The book that follows is a narrative based largely on the eyewitness observations of the primary sources. The records of the four principal sources – Marcellino d'Atri, Luca da Caltanisetta, Lorenzo da Lucca, and Bernardo da Gallo – are all arranged chronologically in diary or letter format, so that they lend them-

Nkulu mu Nsi a Kongo" [Matters of the Ancient World of the Land of Kongo] and ran until 1933, but the book was organized differently and contained more information. A supplement, composed of a lengthy clan history called "Nkutama . . ." by a catechist Gustave Nenga, came out in 1935, apparently forming the "2d edition," and a partial "3d edition" was serialized in 1948–9. Cuvelier only rarely stated the sources of the information, although some can be located through study in the Redemptorist Archives. My thanks to the archivist, Father Joseph Roosen, for his help in locating material and his knowledge of the language, environment, and history of the Redemptorists.

[5] Joseph de Munck, however, did visit both the São Salvador region and that around Kibangu expressly to collect oral traditions, some of which he published. They were revealed to be more or less of the same nature as those in *Nkutama* (see de Munck, "Notes sur un voyuage au Kongo dia Ntotila" in *Ngonge* 3 [1960], no. 8, and "Quelques clans bakongo d'Angola," ibid. 4 [1960]). The Kikongo versions of these traditions were added to the 4th edition of *Nkutama*, edited by de Munck, which appeared in 1972.

selves readily to narrative style. They are very rich in details, and even in conversation, for this crucial period of Kongo's history. Because sources of this kind are very rare in eighteenth-century African history, even in the history of Kongo which is already unusually well documented, it is likely this will be a striking narrative for Africanists who are not familiar with these particular sources. Throughout I have followed them very closely, although, at times, interrupting the flow for interpretative passages and presenting the details from a different point of view. The book has very few footnotes, as I have chosen to identify the source from which I have drawn my tale only when it is necessary to switch to another source or make commentary. Readers who wish to consult the original sources will have little difficulty, for all this, in locating the passages I have used. I have made one significant alteration, however, which needs to be noted. Much of the dialogue in this book is presented in the sources as reported speech or after the fact, along the lines of "He said that he would come . . ." which I have altered to "He said, 'I will come . . .' " In all such cases, however, my alterations of the quoted material extend only to changing personal pronouns from third to first person, and to altering verbs from past to present. The effect is a great gain in immediacy without, I think, changes in the material presented in the sources.

The interpretation of this book is not substantially different from the one I presented in 1979,[6] which broke with the then prevalent interpretation of Dona Beatriz' movement as a nationalist one in a "semicolonial" context.[7] In addition to adopting a narrative style, I have been able to add a great deal of detail by consulting d'Atri's account, which was unavailable to me then. Other scholars have touched on the movement since then in a variety of contexts, sometimes not in ways identical to my inter-

[6] In my UCLA Ph.D. thesis, subsequently published as John Thornton, *The Kingdom of Kongo: Civil War and Transition, 1641–1718* (Madison, Wis., 1983). Also see " 'I am the Subject.' "

[7] Georges Balandier, *Daily Life in the Kingdom of the Kongo from the Sixteenth to the Eighteenth Century*, trans. Helen Weaver (New York, 1968 [French original, 1965]); Teobaldo Filesi, *Nazionalismo e religione nel Congo all'inizio del 1700: La setta degli Antoniani* (Rome, 1972).

pretation, but generally not in ones that would cause me to alter the interpretation of my earlier work.[8] Dona Beatriz' movement has inspired some popularization, for example a play by the Ivorian writer Bernard Dadié, a popular story for young readers by Ibrahima Kaké, and even a plea for her canonization by R. Batsikama.[9] The narrative here advances on my and the other scholars' work, primarily in fixing the context of the movement more precisely in time, and proposes a chain of events leading to the immediate crisis in Dona Beatriz' life that led to her mission. My primary goal, however, is not to break new interpretative ground but to present a narrative account of the movement in a way that is accessible to a nonacademic audience.

ORTHOGRAPHY AND PRONUNCIATION

I have written all names and terms in European languages according to modern orthographic rules. This includes the Christian names of the Kongolese, although as is noted in the text, their phonology would not be the same as for Europeans.

There is no standardized modern orthography for Kikongo as the language has several dialects and is spoken in three different modern countries. For this book I have modernized these words

[8] António Custodio Gonçalves, La symbolisation politique: le "prophetisme" Kongo au XVIIIème siècle (Munich, 1980), subsequently developed in Kongo, Le linage contre l'état (Évora, Portugal, 1985); Celestine Goma Foutou, Histoire des civilisations du Congo (Paris, 1981), pp. 305–13; Anne Hilton, The Kingdom of Kongo (Oxford, 1985); Wyatt MacGaffey, Religion and Society in Central Africa: The BaKongo of Lower Zaire (Chicago, 1986). I have followed with interest, but ultimately not accepted, the contention that the present-day cult of Saint Mary in Soyo and the Antonian movement are connected, advanced by Henrique Abranches in his Sobre os Basolongo: Arqueologia da Tradição Oral (Gand, Belgium, 1991), pp. 49–52; 69–75 (also notes on pp. 84–5), using local research; nor the more elaborate contention on Beatriz' origin and itinerary presented fictionally in his Misericórida para o Reino do Kongo! (Lisbon, 1996).

[9] Bernard Dadié, Béatrice du Congo (Paris, 1970); Ibrahima Baba Kaké, Dona Béatrice: La Jeanne d'Arc congolaise (Paris, 1976). I have not been able to locate or consult the plea for her elevation to sainthood proposed by R. Batsikama, Ndona Béatrice: Serait-elle témoin du Christ et de la foi du vieux Congo? (Kinshasa, Congo, 1970).

according to usage in works written by the early-twentieth-century Kongolese writers, the English Baptist missionaries of São Salvador, and the Belgian Redemptorist missionaries whose language corresponds most closely to the modern form of the dialect of Dona Beatriz' home in the Kingdom of Kongo. The dialect, vocabulary, and grammar of this language were first established in the catechism of 1624, prepared by native speakers for use by Jesuit missionaries, but using modified Portuguese orthography. It is possible to demonstrate that some phonological changes (e.g. use of "v" for the bilabial "b") and grammatical changes (loss of singular class prefixes on the some words and loss of the *ku*-class altogether on infinitives of verbs) have taken place since Dona Beatriz' day, but I have used modern forms in all cases.

I have sought most of the historical terms and usages from the material written in Kikongo by the early-twentieth-century Kongolese historians and their missionary compilers and synthesizers such as Cuvelier and de Munck.[10] I have also followed the grammatical rules of the Mbanza Kongo/Zombo dialect in which these texts are written, although I have omitted the use of the articles "o" and "e," which are very common in this dialect and sometimes attached to words.

In presenting Kikongo terms, I have not pluralized according to the rules of Kikongo. Like many other related languages in central and southern Africa, Kikongo pluralizes by changing the prefix of nouns, according to their membership in a number of noun classes. This system is unfamiliar to most readers, so I have adopted a seventeenth-century convention used by both European and Kongolese writers of the time, of pluralizing the singular form of the noun, with its singular class prefix, according to English rules.

[10] Notably in Cuvelier's presentation of Kongo's history in *Kukiele,* "Mambu ma Kinza" and "Lusansu lua Nsi a Kongo" and in Joseph de Munck, *Kinkulu kia nsi eto Kongo* [History of Our Country Kongo] (Tumba, Congo, 1956; 2d edition, Matadi, Congo, 1971). I have also read Diawaku dia Nseyila, *Bimfumu Biankulu bia Nzanza* (Kinshasa, 1986), an abridgment and paraphrased translation of Jan Vansina, *Kingdoms of the Savanna* (Madison, Wis., 1966; original French, 1965), but have not followed his usage, which reflects a more northern dialect.

I have also followed these rules in giving ethnonyms, so that the inhabitants of the Kingdom of Kongo are Kongolese, not, as would be correct in their language, Esikongo or Besikongo (singular Mwisikongo). In this case, I have dropped class prefixes and used English rules for creating ethnonyms from the resulting root.

Readers unfamiliar with Kikongo might consider the following for pronunciation: the consonants are all pronounced more or less as in English, and the vowels all have the "Italian" values, that is, *a* as "a" in "father," *e* as the "ay" in "hay," *i* as the "ea" in "peach," *o* as the "o" in "phone," and *u* as the "u" in "glue."

Nasal clusters like "nz," "nk," or "mb" give nonspeakers the most trouble, since the tendency is to try to pronounce the "n" and then the following letter. Usually this creates something like "imbanza" or "inkisi" (for *mbanza* and *nkisi*), which are less correct than if one simply treats the initial "m" or "n" as if it were silent, as in "banza" for *mbanza* or "kisi" for *nkisi*. In regular spoken Kikongo the initial sound is often not pronounced or is pronounced so softly and quickly that it almost disappears. However, it is frequently quite noticeable when it occurs after a final vowel in whole Kikongo sentences, where it elides to produce something like "ganga ankisi" (*nganga a nkisi*) meaning "priest" or after a definite article as in "onganga ankisi" (*o nganga a nkisi*) meaning "the priest." For purposes of reading this text, however, one is rarely called upon to produce sentences, and so it is best to leave it unpronounced.

1

A Land in Turmoil

IN AUGUST OF 1704, DONA BEATRIZ KIMPA VITA, a twenty-year-old Kongolese woman, lay deathly ill upon her bed. For seven days she had been sick. Sweat poured from her feverish body and wild visions flashed in her head. She knew now she was dying. Then, suddenly, she became calm, and a clear vision appeared to her. It was a man dressed in the simple blue hooded habit of a Capuchin monk, so real that he seemed to be standing in the room with her. She turned to him, transfixed.

"I am Saint Anthony, firstborn son of the Faith and of Saint Francis," he told her, "I have been sent from God to your head to preach to the people. You are to move the restoration of the Kingdom of Kongo forward, and you must tell all who threaten you that dire punishments from God await them." He told her he had tried for a long time to help Kongo, going from one province to another. "First I had gone into the head of a woman who was in Nseto, but I had to leave as the people there did not receive me well. Then I left Nseto and went to Soyo where I entered the head of an old man. But there was a Reverend Father stationed there, and the people wanted to beat me, so again I fled. Then I went to Bula, and the same thing happened again. I am trying once more, this time in Kibangu, and I have chosen you to do this."

With those words, the vision of the saint moved toward her, entered into her head and merged with her. She felt herself recover. Her strength returned. In fact, she felt in vibrant good health, strong and in good spirits. She rose from her bed, full of

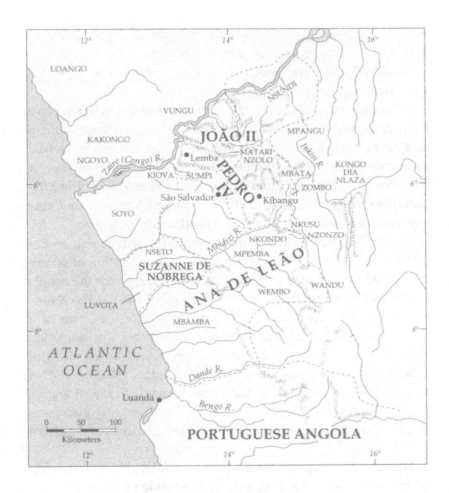

Kongo in 1700. Territories of the major factions.

resolve to complete the mission. Beatriz had been possessed by Saint Anthony.[1]

Dona Beatriz, a spiritual leader in the making, was born on the banks of the Mbidizi River, in the eastern end of the Kingdom of

[1] Bernardo da Gallo, "Relazione dell'ultime Guerre civili del Regno di Congo; della Battaglia data dal Rè D. Pietro Quarto; e della vittoria da lui ottenuta contro i Rebelli. Come anche del scisma nella Fede per via d'una donna, che si fingeva S. Antonio, felicemente superato colla di quella," 17 October 1710, fols. 296–96v, published from the original in the Archivio "de Propaganda Fide," Scritture originali riferite nella Congregazione Generale (hence forward APF:SOCG), vol. 576, in Teobaldo Filesi (ed.), "Nazionalismo e religione nel Congo all'inizio del 1700: La

Kongo. Her native town was in the shadow of the mountain of Kibangu – "fortress" in her native language, Kikongo – and a great sacred place. The peak was often shrouded in clouds, which gave it an air of mystery.

Kibangu was regarded locally with something of religious awe – the birthplace of five rivers that flowed out from the mountain and coursed their way in all directions. The Kongolese viewed rivers as sacred places, the boundary between the everyday of This World and the spiritual realm of the Other World. The Mbidizi, the largest of Kibangu's rivers, emerged from a spring near the mountain's summit that was a particularly holy place.

People thought of the stream as an oracle of Lusunzi, a *nkita* or local deity, its turbulence was seen as an indication of failure in war, while a quiet day augured success. Every year the people made sacrifices of goats and left offerings of food at the river's source. A perfectly shaped spherical stone about the size of a cannonball that had been found long ago near there was regarded as a spiritual token from Lusunzi. It was placed in the midst of a field shaded by a holy *nsanda* tree and surrounded by a great thicket of grass and shrubs that formed a sort of cave. A *kitome*, a special minister of the stone, and the Otherworldly guardians of the mountains, served to coordinate the sacrifices and augury of the place.

Mysterious though it seemed from below, the mountaintop plain was thickly inhabited, and for the residents the mist was a

setta degli Antoniani," *Africa (Roma)* 9 (1971): 276–303, 463–508, 645–68. I have cited the folio numbers of the original (marked in this edition, and the separate edition of the same title, published in Rome, 1972, and in the French translation of Louis Jadin, "Le Congo et la secte des Antoniens. Restauration du royaume sous Pedro IV et la 'Saint Antoine' Congolaise [1694–1718]," *Bulletin, Institute historique belge de Rome* 33 [1961]: 411–615). There is not a specific date given in the sources for her possession. Bernardo da Gallo, our witness, who interviewed her shortly afterward, first heard about the movement after returning from a mission trip in August. No more than about two weeks elapsed between his return to Kibangu and Beatriz' arrival there. Since she stated that she went straight to Kibangu after her possession, it seems likely that the events took place in August or perhaps early September at the latest.

constant nuisance. On the mountaintop there was scarcely a sunny day during the dry season of June to September, and the humidity ruined everything in short order. Local humor said that "morning" in Kibangu was whenever the sun finally broke through the mist, and sometimes morning did not come until noon. The elevation and dampness made it a chilly place in an otherwise tropical climate. But in the rest of the year the climate was delightful, and from the top one had a marvelous view of the countryside below.

Kibangu was at the northern end of the Miongo mia Kanda, the "Mountains of Kanda," which formed a rugged backbone to Kongo's eastern provinces; sheer drops of over a thousand feet separated it from plains to the north and west. The Mbidizi River, most important of the five whose sources were found there, fell with a thundering roar over a spectacular waterfall two hundred feet high to the valley below, sending up a great permanent cloud of mist, the source of constant rainbows as the sun played on it. From the valley floor the Mbidizi flowed westward for about five miles, then turned south and grew rapidly as it was joined by a dozen smaller streams known locally as Mpangi a Mbidizi or Mwana a Mbidizi – the "Brother of the Mbidizi" or the "Child of the Mbidizi." The young river, still growing and carving its way southward, was a turbulent stream during this 30-mile course, before making a final bend and heading off westward toward the ocean some 125 miles away, now a stately and mature river too broad to be bridged.[2]

Dona Beatriz's home, a *mbanza* or small provincial town, was between the two great bends in the broad valley defined by a

[2] See Marcellino d'Atri, "Giornate apostoliche fatte da me Fra M. d'A . . . 1690," in Carlo Toso (ed.), *L'Anarchia Congolese nel sec. XVII. La relazione inedita di Marcellino d'Atri* (Genoa, 1984), pp. 460–2, for the geography of Kibangu, and pp. 483–6, 499 on the religious elements. Fr. Joseph de Munck visited Kibangu in 1960 and reported on the continuing veneration of the rock Lusunzi and its sacred trees: "Quelques clans Bakongo d'Angola," *Ngonge* 4 (December 1960), no. 14. I have called this deity an *nkita* rather than use the term *simbi*, a synonymous term preferred by modern anthropologist Wyatt MacGaffey in describing modern Kongo-

ridge of low hills on the west and the Kanda mountain ranges
that trailed southward from Kibangu on the east. Nearly ten thousand people lived in this valley, in a handful of towns and some
forty villages ruled by a king from his town on the mountaintop.
By Kongolese standards, the valley was thickly inhabited, and the
villages, posted along the banks of the Mbidizi and its "brothers"
and "children," were frequent enough that their lights at night
could guide a traveler along the road.[3]

The small town in which Dona Beatriz was born was not an
important place. Her own family lived in houses typical of the
lesser elite of Kongo, several buildings joined together by walls
and small courtyards, and the whole surrounded outside by a
stout palisade. Buildings were rectangular with walls of wood
and woven grass, and roofs that were thatched with tough
grasses from the open fields nearby. They were built in the same
style and materials as those of the commoners around them,
though the buildings were somewhat larger and more carefully
made.

Intricately woven mats, made from fibers drawn from tree bark
and pounded to reveal threads, formed the decoration of the
walls, which were sometimes planked. Wall hangings such as tap-
estries, upon which were mounted arms, such as a sword and
shield and bow, made up the elite decorations. The cloth, of
which Kongolese were justly proud, was attractive enough that
much was exported to Portuguese Angola, and smaller quantities,
even farther away. The wall hangings and noble weapons like

lese religion, because *nkita* is used in seventeenth- and eighteenth-century
sources, and in this dialect. See *Religion and Society in Central Africa*, pp.
85–8.

[3] On the demography of the region in this time period, see John Thornton,
"Demography and History in the Kingdom of Kongo, 1550–1750," *Journal
of African History* 18 (1977). On village lights guiding a traveler in the
valley, Archivio Provinciale dei Cappuccini da Provincia da Toscana
(Montughi Convent, Florence), Filippo Bernardi da Firenze, "Ragguaglioi
de Congo . . . ," 2 vols. (1714). Lorenzo da Lucca, "Lettera Annua, 1706,"
vol. 2, p. 296 (Jean Cuvelier edited and translated this text in French,
marking the original pagination in *Relations du Congo du P. Laurent de
Lucques* [Brussels, 1954]).

swords and shields were the marks of wealth and distinction that set nobles even of humble estate off from the common folk.

Commoners' and peasants' houses were very simple affairs made rectangular and composed of only one or two rooms, fenced from each other so that they formed lanes that wove through the town. Dona Beatriz' hometown was made up of perhaps two hundred houses, those of a handful of elite families and the rest the poorer buildings of the ordinary people.

The poorer townspeople, as well as the villagers in the many *vatas*, as villages were called in Kikongo, that surrounded the town were mostly farmers. Although men helped clear new fields from forests, once that was accomplished virtually all the agricultural work was done by women. They hoed up their fields in ridges before the rainy season began each September, and then planted them in staggered sessions so the crops would ripen at different times. They planted a variety of crops in the same field, often interplanting them to maximize fertility and minimize total loss from drought or invasions of pests, like locusts. The staggered harvests that resulted from this strategy allowed food to be consumed directly from the fields without having to store crops. By March each year the first plantings were done and a second crop was sown, for final harvests ending when the dry season began in June.

Cooking was done in earthenware pots, and meals consisted of three parts, typically served on three plates. The first was boiled grain, usually corn, which was dried, then pounded, and the flour mixed into boiling water to make *nfundi*, the "daily bread" that the Kongolese asked God to give them each day when they said the Lord's Prayer. The nfundi was cooked until quite stiff, and most people rolled it into bite-size balls to eat it. The second plate contained *mwamba*, which was a stew made up of meat if it was available, or fish and numerous vegetable supplements, in a base of palm oil. Balls of nfundi, dimpled with the thumb to make a small cup, were dipped into the mwamba. In the third plate were vegetables, most commonly *wandu*, probably pigeon peas, which are still called Congo beans in the West Indies today. Fruit was eaten separately and the whole was washed down with water or palm wine drunk from cups made from gourds.

In those days Kongolese would say that women, as farmers, brought the food to dinner and men would bring the wine. Without the men bringing the wine, women would refuse to bring the food; without the women's food, the men would refuse to bring the wine. To make wine, men cultivated trees, just as the women cultivated fields. Various types of palm trees provided sap and nuts which could be used to make oil for cooking and, if fermented, *malafu*, the wine that everyone drank.

Men produced cloth and clothing from bark stripped from special trees and pounded until tough fibers were revealed. These fibers were then woven, using a simple loom, into strips, which in turn were sewn together to make clothing. Wood, leaves, and grasses were the normal materials for building houses. Hunting and fishing, as well as tending to larger animals such as goats and pigs, fell to men and boys.

Commoners wore a simple cloth that went from the waist to the knees, called a *tanga*. Men normally wore one and women wore two, one on top of their bodies and the other below. Unmarried girls often did not cover the tops of their bodies, and young children often went naked. At night the tanga became a blanket, and in the highlands where temperatures in the cold season could approach freezing, it was needed.[4]

The simplicity of the commoners' material culture did not necessarily mean poverty, however. If the weather was good and the wars had spared the crops, there was always enough to eat, for Kongolese agriculture was productive, at least by the standards of the time. Housing, although of simple construction and not intended for use beyond a few years, took a short time to build and was adequate for protection from the rain or the kind of cold encountered in central Africa.

Unlike commoner women, Dona Beatriz' mother did not work in the fields to produce crops and feed her family. Dona Beatriz' family had slaves and clients who managed the household and

---

[4] Thornton, *Kingdom of Kongo*, pp. 28–37.

produced its food for her mother. Some of the slaves were Kongolese, and Christians like their masters, but had been captured in warfare in one or another part of Kongo and then shipped far enough away from home that returning was unlikely. The rest were from the east and north, and while many could speak Kikongo, they were not originally Christian and spoke in distinctly different dialects. The clients were local people serving under conditions similar to those of the slaves: they had to obey orders and could be physically punished by beating or by restraint for disobedience or unauthorized absenteeism. Clients could go from time to time to visit their homes and families, but not without their master's permission and only for set time periods.[5]

Dona Beatriz was born in 1684,[6] and like all Kongolese "*yadia mungwa*" (she ate salt), as they called baptism locally, as soon as a priest passed her town. Baptismal rituals of the time called for the priest to place a small amount of salt on the tongue of the baby when performing the service, hence its name.

Kongolese were proud to call themselves Catholics, and had been so for six generations – nearly two centuries. Christianity set true Kongolese aside from their neighbors, and in their view made them superior to the "heathens," even those to the north and east who spoke dialects of the same Kikongo language. As Kongolese saw it, it was the salt rather than the water that conferred the blessing of baptism, in line with the general belief that evil people or spirits did not like salt and would thus avoid a baptized person.

Priests were scarce, however, so it was not until the vicar Father Luis de Mendonça, a mulatto originally from the Portuguese col-

---

[5] On housing styles, see d'Atri, "Giornate," p. 503. The situation of nobles' slaves is taken from numerous references to the conditions of the household servants of Capuchin missionaries with the assumption that they lived more or less the same way as the elite did. See especially d'Atri, "Giornate," pp. 532, 537–8.

[6] We cannot determine the date of Beatriz' birth exactly; her age at her death was given as between twenty and twenty-two years old. I have opted for an older age simply because she had already done so many things by the time her mission began that there seems to be a need for more time.

ony of Angola, visited her town that Dona Beatriz was actually baptized.[7] Teachers, accompanied by a train of students and acolytes, might come on a yearly basis to perform services and instruct the young, but a priest to perform the sacraments might not come every year. Father Luis, who lived with the king on the mountain of Kibangu, traveled out annually, but his parish was so large that he could not visit all the villages each year.

Dona Beatriz, the name she was given by her parents, was what Kongolese knew as a *zina dia nsantu*, a saint's name. These names were in a Portuguese form and followed Portuguese usage, though a curious local feature was that everyone, even commoners, bore the title "Dom" (if male) and "Dona" (if female), titles which in Portugal were usually reserved for nobility. Local pronunciation also changed them so that Dom João was rendered as "Ndozau" and Dom Pedro as "Ndopetelo," while Dona Isabela would be "Ndona Zabela." Dona Beatriz' own name was probably pronounced "Ndona Betelisi" in Kikongo.[8]

In addition to the saint's name, which all Kongolese carried even if they had not yet been baptized, Dona Beatriz also had Kikongo names. These were sometimes namesakes honoring parents or grandparents, or sometimes reflected events of the day. Occasionally, too, when people underwent changes in life, they might take another name. If Dona Beatriz was named Kimpa Vita – the Kikongo name she later carried – as a child, then Kimpa was her given name and Vita was her father's given name. Nobles who were proud of their lineage might add a grandfather's or even a great-grandfather's given name to the list, but normally even kings had just two. Many noble families also had family names that were passed down through generations, and these

---

[7] This is a speculation; we only know that de Mendonça was active at the time of her birth and that it is likely he baptized her, but no document actually proves it.

[8] A good list of the Kikongo forms of these names, which were still regularly given in the early twentieth century, is in Jean Cuvelier, "Lusansu lua Nsi a Kongo [Knowledge about the country of Kongo]," *Kukiele* [Dawning] 12 (1930): 105–7. Unfortunately, Beatriz is not among the names on the list.

were either typical Portuguese surnames – da Cruz, de Castro, or da Silva – or names that were unique to Kongo, such as Agua Rosada, Pimenta Raposo, or Valle das Lagrimas.[9]

Dona Beatriz' family were members of the highest group of the nobility, the Mwana Kongo or "child of Kongo," although such a background did not necessarily mean either wealth or political importance. Kongolese extended families were part of what was called a *kanda* in Kikongo, a word which might be translated as "clan" or "lineage" in English but which really refers to a very large social group that was related sometimes by blood and descent, and other times simply through clientage and adoption. Even slaves and their children would be part of a kanda. The Mwana Kongo kandas were those who could claim a king of Kongo somewhere in their past. Over the years the royal kanda had subdivided into many branch kandas, so that Beatriz' family's membership in it was more a source of pride than material or political gain.[10]

If Vita was Dona Beatriz' father's given name, then it might have suited the baby Dona Beatriz well, for *vita* means "war" in Kikongo. The year 1684 was one of war at Kibangu and the valley of the Mbidizi, in a period filled with armed turbulence. King João II, a claimant to the throne of Kongo who ruled the district

[9] For a study of seventeenth-century naming practices in Kongo, see John Thornton, "Central African Names and African-American Naming Patterns," *William and Mary Quarterly* 50 (1993): 729–40.

[10] Lorenzo da Lucca gives her ancestry simply as the "highest nobility," which implies membership in the Mwana Kongo. Kongo nobility had three levels: *fidalgos mobatas*, or people descended from ancient village rulers, who were of little larger importance; *fidalgos Moxicongos*, including all whose ancestors had held higher office or were associated with the founding king and his clients; and finally, the *Infantes* or "Mwana Kongo" descended as just described; see the discussion of the mid-seventeenth century in Biblioteca Nacional de Madrid, MS 3533, Antonio de Teruel, "Descripcion Narrativa de la mission serafica de los Padres Capuchinos . . . en el reyno de Congo" (ca. 1664), p. 72; these terms were still in use in the late eighteenth century as well. See Academia das Ciencas de Lisboa, MS Vermelho 296, "Viagem do Congo do Missionario Fr. Raphael de Castello de Vide hoje Bispo de S. Thomé" (MS of 1781–8), p. 202.

of Bula, launched an attack on Kibangu that year, though it was repulsed with heavy losses by the Kibangu's royal claimant, Garcia III.

Wars did not cease with this victory, however, for shortly afterward Garcia III died and was succeeded by André I, who died himself within a year. Manuel Afonso Nzinga Elenke succeeded King André I as ruler of the mountain of Kibangu, but the succession was contested. Two brothers of a former king, Álvaro Afonso Agua Rosada Nimi a Mvemba and Pedro Afonso Agua Rosada Nusamu a Mvemba, refused to accept his power and withdrew from the mountain to the valley where Dona Beatriz' family lived. They won the loyalty of part of the army, a citizen force raised from the villages and serving under local nobles such as Dona Beatriz' father. Using these forces, the brothers made war on Manuel but were defeated and had to retreat back to the valley.

Two years later, in 1688, the brothers raised an army to try again, and as in past conflicts, four-year-old Dona Beatriz' father was probably called to fight. Thanks to support within the king's subjects on Kibangu, the Agua Rosada brothers defeated Manuel and drove him off. The dethroned king fled westward with a body of his followers to Kongo's long disobedient coastal province of Soyo, where he was well received by the prince António II Baretto da Silva.[11]

Having achieved their objective, the older of the two Agua Rosada brothers, Álvaro, succeeded Manuel as king on the mountaintop. He took the title King Álvaro X of Kongo, though in fact he ruled only the mountain of Kibangu and the upper reaches of its five rivers. Were it not for his rivals farther away – the former King Manuel, rebuilding his strength in Soyo, and another king, João Manuel II Nzuzi a Ntamba, who ruled a region called Bula that lay northwest of Kibangu – there might be a lasting peace for the people of the Mbidizi valley. But thanks to these rivals in a still larger civil war that already had clouded Kongo for more

---

[11] On the brothers' war, Pedro Mendes to General of the Jesuit Order, 1710, in Levy Maria Jordão de Pavia Manso (ed.), *História do Congo (Documentos)* (Lisbon, 1877), p. 351.

than a generation, there would be only two years of peace to follow.

Dona Beatriz, by virtue of living in a noble household, grew up hearing about the ins and outs of Kongo's complex politics, as news was discussed and rumor reported. News of wars that did not involve the people of the Mbidizi valley might still find its way there.

She was only six in 1690 when the ex-king Manuel, having gathered support from Soyo, once again laid claim to the kingship. Prince António supplied troops, and with their aid Manuel returned, not to Kibangu to face the Agua Rosadas who had originally dethroned him, but to the ruined and abandoned ancient capital of São Salvador beyond the hills that marked the western side of the Mbidizi valley. There, amid the ruins of the once proud capital, Soyo's officials proclaimed him king. But he was a king with no subjects and after the army from Soyo returned home, he had to withdraw, fearing that one of his rivals would attack him.

These events did not trouble Dona Beatriz' family; but in 1691, when Dona Beatriz was seven, once again her father was called for war. A large army raised by King João II of Bula marched toward Kibangu. An earlier invasion by João had been defeated the year of Dona Beatriz' birth, and the people of Kibangu knew to fear his army, for among his troops were Jagas, dreaded mercenaries from beyond Christendom's northern frontier at the Zaire River.

João's army had been responsible for Manuel's withdrawal from São Salvador the year before, but like Álvaro at Kibangu and Manuel, when he announced his claim to be king of all Kongo in 1688, his real power did not extend much beyond a portion of the country. João had found some support from the Church, although Father Girolamo Merolla, the prefect of the Capuchin mission to Kongo, imposed conditions on him for this recognition, including reoccupying São Salvador and reconciling himself with implacable enemies in Soyo. João was unwilling to

The Prince of Soyo with his army greets a Capuchin priest. (From "Missione in Practica" ca. 1750)

do this, though, because his defeat by Kibangu in 1684 had made him feel too vulnerable. Nevertheless, he decided to take up the title of King.

Bula, King João's territory, lay to the north of Kibangu, tucked into a bend in the great Zaire River. João's brother, King Pedro III, had founded Bula more than twenty years earlier when he fled São Salvador after having been crowned King of Kongo. Driven from the city by his rivals, Pedro had taken refuge at Bula, where the broken country and wooded hills provided strongly fortified positions. On the strongest of these, he built Lemba, his refuge and capital until he could once more occupy the true capital at São Salvador. The temporary refuge had become a more or less permanent home, and Pedro, then João, had built a regular administrative structure over the dozen smaller territories, known as marquisates, which he controlled.

King João and his army from Bula marched out of the Marquisate of Sumpi, his southeasternmost territory, and entered the lands belonging to the mountain of Kibangu. João relied on the reputation of his Jaga allies as much as their numbers to win their victory, and rumors and stories were a part of this. The Jagas were said to have sold human flesh like meat in the public market when Pedro III led them in the final cataclysmic sack of the ancient capital of São Salvador in 1678. They were also unrepetant pagans who sacked, destroyed, and desecrated São Salvador's dozen churches that day, and João's continued association with them gave him an unsavory though largely undeserved reputation as being sacrilegious himself.

To meet this challenge, King Álvaro sent out a royal *bando*, or order, giving prospective soldiers a specified future time to gather at a predetermined assembly point. They were expected to gather fifteen days' food for the campaign in large *ntetes*, or baskets; bring their arms, which might be bows, arrows, or clubs, and, increasingly in this time, also muskets; and report for muster at the mbanza of their area. There they were met by their leaders, among them Dona Beatriz' father, who served as commander in the unit raised from their region. The whole army was therefore divided into regionally based military units, which served together in campaigns under their own flags and with their own local officers.

As an officer, Dona Beatriz' father carried a fine sword with either a straight or a curved blade like a scimitar, and a shield. When the army assembled, Father Luis blessed the weapons of the officers and the army as a whole – a particularly significant gesture in a war against the heathen Jagas. Then, with the fanfare typical of troops departing for war, Dona Beatriz' father was off to battle for King Álvaro.

Her mother, having a small child, remained at home, even though many women also served the army, not as soldiers but as the supply train. They followed husbands, brothers, perhaps even sons to the field, helped locate food, cooked for the forces, and provided what few comforts could be had on campaign.

As the two armies approached each other, the smaller units began harassing and exploratory engagements, operating almost independently from each other, gradually coming together over a period of days for a battle in which the smaller units formed into three or four columns or wings of five to six thousand men each for a major battle, sharp affairs that lasted three or four hours and had heavy casualties.[12]

King Álvaro's forces were completely victorious. King João's soldiers broke and fled before the army of King Álvaro, and the valley was safe again. Dona Beatriz' father once again returned home.

Military victory was followed by political recognition from one of the most important people in Kongo, Queen Ana Afonso de Leão. Queen Ana did not claim to rule the country, but she was the eldest important member of the Kinlaza kanda, the branch of the Mwana Kongo that had supplied the most powerful kings of the earlier part of the century when Kongo was united and strong. Queen Ana was the sister of King Garcia II, the last of the great and powerful seventeenth-century kings, and her husband, Afonso II, had ruled briefly in Kongo in the late 1660s. When he died, she moved to the town of Nkondo at the junction of the Mbidizi and Lukunga rivers just below the great bend in the Mbidizi. There she established direct control over an area, at the Marquisate of Nkondo, in her own name, and elsewhere through her junior relatives, who gave her great loyalty and support. These relatives controlled virtually the rest of the Mbidizi valley, including the large Marquisates of Wembo and Mpemba along the river, the County of Wandu along the valley of the Lukunga River, south of her capital at Mbanza Nkondo, and then the Duchy of Mbamba, the largest of Kongo's provinces along the Mbidizi and the Atlantic coast.

When King Álvaro posted his victory over the army of King João, the queen declared her willingness to recognize him as king. It was welcome news in Kibangu, since it moved Álvaro one step closer to being able to reunite the country. More good news followed when two of the queen's allies, Pedro Valle das Lagrimas,

---

[12] Military details are culled from a number of contemporary sources: d'Atri, "Giornate," pp. 53, 519–21; Luca da Caltanisetta, "Relatione del Viaggio e Missione fatta per me Fra Luca da Caltanisetta . . . ," in Romain Rainero (ed.), *Il Congo agli inizi del settecento nella relazione di P. Luca da Caltanisetta* (Florence, 1974), fols. 8v–9.

Duke of Mbamba, and Alexio, the Marquis of Wembo, sent embassies to Kibangu offering their loyalty.

But King Manuel and his allies in Soyo could not allow his rival to outdo him, and moved strongly against Nkondo. Toward the end of 1691 his armies invaded Nkondo, driving the queen away. Her nephew, Pedro Valle das Lagrimas, brought his army up from Mbamba to try to dislodge Manuel, but the ensuing battle in May 1692 resulted in Pedro's defeat. Manuel granted the Duchy of Mbamba to his cousin Alexio, and to his most successful general, Pedro Constantinho da Silva – known as Kibenga, "the Brave" – he gave the Marquisate of Wembo.

Queen Ana and her entourage, refugees, and the remnants of her army retreated north up the Mbidizi valley to seek asylum in Kibangu. Álvaro welcomed them, and the arrival of the haggard troops and the defiant old queen was grounds for much talk and speculation. She was a striking figure, who often wore the habit of a Capuchin monk in a show of piety – in fact she had received a special dispensation from the order permitting her to do this. As an elderly woman, she had substantial facial hair and had to shave to prevent her seeming bearded. But this strange external appearance could not hide her strong will or belittle her mastery of politics; she was fully in charge behind the scenes among her nominally superior nephews.

King Álvaro gave her the right to settle in the Marquisate of Bonga, establishing a makeshift court at the village of Gando a Suka, in the Mbidizi valley not far to the north of her former capital.[13] From there she and Valle das Lagrimas continued a low-key fight against Manuel, forcing Soyo to keep its army in the field throughout 1692.

Eight-year-old Dona Beatriz might have absorbed the general feeling that the wars had gone on too long and that the motives of the participants had gradually crossed the line from upholding their rights to greed and spitefulness. That feeling was driven

[13] Details on the war of 1691–2 are drawn from Pedro Mendes, pp. 350, 352; da Caltanisetta, "Viaggio," fols. 10–14; d'Atri, "Giornate," pp. 53–5. I have determined the location of this place from the Bonga River on the "Carta da Colónia de Angola" (Luanda, 1944), scale 1:250,000.

home the next year just before Christmas. Acting in a secret plot, Pedro Constantinho da Silva Kibenga and the new Duke of Mbamba, Alexio, rose up and killed Manuel, cutting off his head and sending it to Álvaro. The king put this grisly trophy in front on his palace in the public square in Kibangu. Kibenga followed this up by sending Álvaro the royal insignia that Manuel had taken when he was driven from Kibangu by Álvaro and his brother Pedro.

Then the rumor spread, and was gradually confirmed, that this stroke of good luck for the king of Kibangu had a sinister other side. To win Álvaro's support for the killing of his rival, Kibenga and his colleagues had extracted a promise that Álvaro would murder the elderly Queen Ana. In the end, Álvaro did not carry out his end of the plot, and the queen remained, dignified and defiant, at Gando a Suka.[14]

The scandal of these betrayals and double crosses reached most of the nobles in Kibangu's realm, and for sensitive people like the young Dona Beatriz the telling and retelling of the story helped reinforce the feeling that greed and jealousy had gotten out of hand in Kongo. Manuel's head, which remained fully five years on display at the plaza, served to keep the tale of deceit alive beyond its time and into Dona Beatriz' teenage years. An evolving awareness of these demonstrations of bad faith began to shape a political dimension to her own religious feelings.

At about the time that Manuel was betrayed by his followers, Dona Beatriz began to have visions that would start to establish her personal inclination toward religion. In her vision two children, white in color, came to play with her and gave her gifts. One of their most telling gifts was a beautiful glass rosary that she wore in her vision. To her family and friends these visions were a sign that she was spiritually gifted, and people paid attention to her and treated her as a special person.

The white children of her vision were *nkitas* from the Other World rather than Europeans or racially "white." Kongolese

---

[14] Da Caltanisetta, "Viaggio," fol. 16v; d'Atri, "Giornate," p. 79; Mendes, p. 353.

knew well that the colony of Angola, which bordered Kongo to the south, was held by the European country of Portugal, but Portugal had not been much of a threat since the princes of Soyo crushed an invading force from Angola in 1670. As Christians, Kongolese saw Europeans represented as Jesus, the saints, and the Virgin Mary in religious items. A handful of Italian priests who performed the majority of the sacraments were also European. As she grew older Dona Beatriz became aware of this disparity and it would become important for her, but her earlier companions in the vision were another order of beings.

In Dona Beatriz' day the legend circulated that the first Kongolese to see Europeans thought the Portuguese were riding on whales, and hence they gave them the name *mundele*, derived from the Kikongo word for whale, the only way they could describe their ships. It was their craft and not their skin color that marked them as different, and this is why all Europeans were called by this name and not a variant of *mpembe*, which meant "white."

The color white, mpembe, was the color of the Other World in Kongolese symbolism, just as black was the color of This World, and so Dona Beatriz' childish companions were not simply imaginary children but visitors from the Other World, and the child visionary soon acquired a reputation for saintliness.[15]

During this time, too, Dona Beatriz began to pay more attention to Christian religious life. Aside from Father Luis in Kibangu the nearest priests to her town were far away in Nkusu, where the Italian Capuchin missionaries had a station. But Christianity in Kongo did not depend on priests or missionaries to thrive, because an active laity took their place. At least once a year, a teacher and a group of students would work their way to all the villages and towns under Kibangu's jurisdiction to conduct classes and ensure that everyone learned the rudiments of Christian religion. They could not perform sacraments, but they could answer questions and provide spiritual help.

[15] Da Gallo, "Ultime," fol. 304. For an interpretation of the dream in Kongolese cosmology, see Wyatt MacGaffey, *Religion and Society in Central Africa*, pp. 208–11.

Miguel de Castro, one of Dona Beatriz' relatives and a member of her kanda, was such a teacher but also held an important position in Kibangu, that of royal interpreter and secretary. He was a regular visitor in her town, and came to know her fairly well through her family. At court, he was responsible for the king's correspondence and also for a variety of matters including the introduction of strangers. De Castro could speak Portuguese as well as Kikongo, and wrote in Portuguese, the language of official documents. He, along with a number of other such people, was responsible for teaching noble children to read, write, and speak Portuguese and sometimes Latin. Such education was largely for boys, but noble girls often also received this instruction. The students at de Castro's school also provided him, and other teachers, with an entourage when they traveled about.

Dona Beatriz, however, did not manage to go to school, and although de Castro visited her town, she got not much more of an education than memorizing the critical tenets of the Church and the most important prayers. The basis for learning these was an old catechism, first produced in Portuguese in 1556, translated into Kikongo in 1624, and reedited in 1650. Printed copies or handwritten copies of worn-out printed texts provided the model of instruction.

Teaching was in the form of a dialogue, with the teacher asking questions and students repeating the answers in unison. Children of all statuses and classes would assemble before their master, who introduced the lesson by making the sign of the cross, which the students immediately imitated:

"Kuna nima a kisinsu kia Santa Cruz kutukangila e Nfumuêtu Zambi a Mpungu etu, kua ambeniêtu" (By the sign of the Holy Cross our Lord, our Zambi a Mpungu [Kikongo for God] saves us from our enemies). From here followed lessons on the basics of the faith:

"What is a Christian?"

"One who follows the law of Christ."

Non-Christians were "slaves of the Devil, exiles from Heaven" in this formulation. Then came an explanation of the Holy Cross, in which more specific instructions were given and examples followed on making the sign of the cross.

This was followed by memorization and a dialogue explication of the major prayers, the Lord's Prayer, Hail Mary, and Hail, Holy Queen (the Salve Regina). The catechism went on to cover the articles of the faith, the Ten Commandments, the nature of deadly sins and venal sins, the sacraments of the Church, and finally a lengthy section on proper Christian life.[16]

The teachers did a good, thorough job. Countless travelers in Kongo commented on the degree to which the basic elements of the faith were known in the country. Everyone could say the prayers, even in rural areas far from the centers of culture, even in sections of the country that had not seen an ordained priest in anyone's lifetime. Many European priests who visited and worked in Kongo thought of them as sinful, sometimes wondered about their penchant for such things as sacred stones and ancestors' graves, even thought them deep in the clutches of the Devil. But they never doubted that the Kongolese knew at least the outlines of the Faith.

Even in the islands and lands of far-off America, across the ocean, where the civil wars had condemned so many Kongolese to serve as slaves, priests who inquired discovered this fund of Christian knowledge. Even there, in such a distant exile, one still met Kongolese saying the prayers they had been taught as children.[17]

During the long periods between visits by teachers, the local

[16] The catechism was first printed in Lisbon, and the second edition, in Rome. A modern edition, with Portuguese, original Kikongo, modernized spelling of Kikongo, and French translation has been edited by François Bontinck and D. Ndembe Nsasi, *Le catéchisme kikongo de 1624: reédition critique* (Brussels, 1978) ch. 1, nos. 1 and 6. I have translated the Kikongo directly into English, since it differs somewhat from the original Portuguese.

[17] On Christian knowledge in Kongo and among Kongolese slaves in America, see John Thornton, "The Development of an African Catholic Church in the Kingdom of Kongo, 1491–1750," *Journal of African History* 25 (1984), and "On the Trail of Voodoo: African Christianity in Africa and the Americas," *The Americas* 44 (1988).

community would assemble on Saturdays and say the rosary, their principal regular religious observation. Typically these would be led by the local elite, such as Dona Beatriz' father. Aside from this, everyone took part in certain holidays. Christians all over the world observed Easter, of course, and it was not neglected in Kongo, nor was the larger season of Advent–Christmas–Epiphany, although it took place in the midst of the rainy season when travel was difficult.

But in Dona Beatriz' Kongo, the biggest and most important holidays were Halloween–All Saints' Day and the day dedicated to Saint James Major, 25 July. Both these days were respected because they had special meaning in Kongo rather than because they had such significance in the round of Christian observance.

Halloween and All Saints' Day together formed a special holiday in Kongo because they represented a merging of ancient Kongolese religious belief with Christianity. Long before Portuguese sailors had delivered the first Christian priests to Kongo in 1491, Kongolese believed that when people died they did not go to some distant underworld or to Heaven. Rather, they remained in spiritual form around the grave where they had been buried. There, they used the powers that residence in the Other World gave them to look out for their still-living descendants. People were attentive to the graves of their ancestors for these souls could help them in daily life, or they could punish them with ill luck and sickness if they were displeased.

These beliefs did not disappear with Christianity but continued despite an occasional priestly reminder that in Christian belief souls go to be judged fit for Heaven or damned to Hell, but do not linger on. Father Marcellino d'Atri, who visited Dona Beatriz' valley during this time, devoted a sermon to the concepts of Heaven and Hell because he knew that his parishioners thought either that "no one died" or that "upon their death, everyone went to another world much more pleasant that this one." This did not imply universal salvation but, rather, that the Other World was both immanent in and superior to This World.[18]

[18] D'Atri, "Giornate," p. 129.

Halloween and All Saints' Day provided Kongolese with a good opportunity to pay appropriate respect to their ancestors in a Christian tradition, and it was among the most important holidays in the whole country. On Halloween, all the families assembled and recited the rosary together, as they often did on Saturdays. Then, taking up candles, they formed a great procession, which fanned out to the cemeteries of the area, each family going to the place where its own ancestors were buried. In Kibangu, where the royal city was, the king made a special pilgrimage adorned by the ringing of bells to the graves of past rulers buried at the royal chapel. Sometimes a family's ancestors were buried in a church as it was hallowed ground, although in other instances other spots, such as the crosses erected by priests and blessed by them in the countryside, served as places of meeting and Christian worship. The families then placed the candles in a circle around the graves and again said the rosary. Throughout the rest of the night they alternated between processions and vigils at the graves. When night passed, and All Saints' Day dawned, the worshippers again said the rosary; if a priest was available, they would hear Mass.

All Saints' Day was also the occasion to make major offerings to the Church, although dedicated to the ancestors. The main street of Kibangu's town, for example, was thickly lined with worshippers who offered money gifts, as well as large quantities of food. An altar was erected in the public square decorated with an image of a skeleton with a sickle in one hand and an hourglass in the other. A huge mound of offerings in kind, including chickens, piglets, various legumes, and grains, as well as cloth and tobacco, was piled before it. Such offerings were taken by the staff of the Church or its local representatives as a part of Church income. Whatever misgivings priests may have had about the fate of the dead among their parishioners, they were enthusiastic about this day of worship.[19]

If Halloween was the primary religious holiday in Kongo, Saint

[19] This account is based on combined notes of practice in Soyo and Kibangu, in Giuseppe Monari da Modena, in Calogero Piazza (ed.), "La missione del Soyo (1713–16) nelle relazione inedita de Giuseppe da Mo-

A Christian burial in eighteenth-century Kongo. (From "Missione in
Practica" ca. 1750)

James' Day was a more secular and political holiday. Formally,
the day commemorated the patron saint of Spain and Portugal
and brought to Kongo by the Portuguese in the fifteenth century.
Known as "Matamoro" or "Killer of the Moors" in Iberia, Saint

dena OFM Cap," *L'Italia Francescana* 48 (1977): 209–92; 347–73, with pagination of original; and d'Atri, "Giornate," pp. 531–2 (1701). There are
present-day reminders of the cult of cemeteries and crosses found in
tradition and modern observation: see François Bontinck, "Les croix de
bois dans l'ancien royaume de Kongo," *Miscellanea Historiae Pontificiae*
50 (1983), pp. 199–213; and Jean Cuvelier, "Lusansu lua nsi a Kongo,"
pp. 69–70, which gives a list of a number of these burial grounds still
recognizable in the Zaire and Nkisi valleys. Excavations in 1938 by Georges Schellings in one "necropolis" of the early eighteenth century have
been carefully studied in J. van den Houte, "De Begraafplaats van
Ngongo-Mbata (Neder-Zaire), thesis, Hoger Instituut voor Kunstges-
chiedenis en Oudheidkunde, Gand, 1972–3. They contained gravestones
from the Order of Christ and grave goods, including images of saints
and crucifixes, dating from the early eighteenth century. A similar ex-
cavation was conducted at Pângala-velho in Soyo in 1980 by the Labro-
tório Nacional de Antropologia (Luanda); Abranches, *Sobre os Basolongo*,
p. 47.

James Major was a military saint, often seen in battle dress and on horseback leading the specifically Iberian version of the crusades.

In Kongo, however, the saint was associated most specifically with King Afonso I (ruled 1509–43), who had overthrown his pagan brother in the name of the Catholic Church with the aid of Saint James. In letters to Portugal shortly after the event, Afonso had described the miracle – challenged for the throne by his pagan brother, Afonso was left with only a handful of followers to resist the forces of his rival. Battle was joined, as the archers on both sides loosed arrows at their enemies.

"We were already covered with a great number of arrows," Afonso wrote, describing the first phase of the battle, "and now they wanted to advance upon us with sword and lance." The hand-to-hand phase, fought with sword and lance, would be the decisive one. Believing they were all but lost, Afonso and his men shouted "Santiago!" invoking Saint James Major. Much to their surprise, "miraculously we saw them turn their backs and run away in which ever way they could." The victory became a rout; "in the end, they lost a great number of men without us losing even one."

Bewildered, Afonso and his supporters "questioned those who had survived the fight, asking them why they had fled." They were told that "when we called upon the Apostle Santiago, they all saw a white cross in the sky and a great number of armored horsemen which so frightened them that they could think of nothing else but to flee."[20] Saint James' Day, then, became Kongo's national holiday, and the events of the battle were commemorated in Kongo's coat of arms, adopted in 1512 and still seen in Dona Beatriz' day on official documents, seals, the throne, and the royal regalia.

It was this miraculous event rather than the Iberian saint that Kongolese celebrated on 25 July, which might have been called "Afonso's Day" as far as they were concerned. Since Afonso was

[20] Afonso to His People, 1512, in António Brásio (ed.), *Monumenta Missionaria Africana*, 1st series, 15 vols. (Lisbon, 1952–88), 1:268 (this letter was prepared in Portugal from a now lost letter written by Afonso ca. 1509).

widely regarded as the founder of the Church in Kongo (even though, in fact, his father, João I Nzinga a Nkuwu, was the first king to be baptized), the day was also considered something of a birthday for the Church.

People often traveled for Saint James' Day, which was held in the middle of the dry season when traveling was easy. It was also an administrative day, for taxes were due then. Because of this, many went to the royal capital, in this case Kibangu, to celebrate the festivals, which went on for three days. The highlight was a military review since the call-up for taxes often involved the techniques of military mobilization and usually touched the same people. But this was unlike military call-ups, for whole families came, and Dona Beatriz undoubtedly accompanied her family all the way to Kibangu on occasion to witness the festival.

The *nsanga* or military review and dance that highlighted Saint James' Day was a great show of color and pageantry. Men came armed with "sword, scimitar, bows, spears, knobby clubs, battle axes." Some carried shields, a symbol of official rank though of considerably less use, as guns had become more prominent on the battlefield. Many, of course, carried guns, which were amply supplied with powder from the royal storehouses. Guns were often overloaded and constantly being discharged, so that the air was filled with their rattle, while billowing clouds of smoke covered the great public plaza.

Some people came attired in animal skins, wearing special caps decorated with lion's teeth, or with bird feathers in their hair. Others were painted in various colors, in order to seem more terrible.

The king himself then appeared, with a gold necklace around his neck set off with coral beads, silver bracelets, and red velvet slippers on his feet, proudly holding his own shield while being covered all the while by an umbrella. He was surrounded by a cavalcade of officials, musicians, hangers-on, and servants or other worthies. The band struck up martial music and his officials bore a great mass of *mpusu* cloth on the tips of their lances while turning in a circle.

A dozen young women dressed in spotless white linen, faces

proud and solemn, took up places on the sides of this mass, breaking through the cloud of gunsmoke that was set up by musketeers from among the soldiers.

Then, swiftly, the crowd formed into squadrons that faced each other for a half-acted, half-danced mock battle. Lieutenants bearing company colors took their places at the flanks. Muskets crackled, weapons were displayed – first one side advanced, than the other, while the musicians kept up a steady rhythm. Finally, the affair ended with a great banquet for all the soldiers at the king's expense, a sort of payment for the soldiers' services and a renewal of vows that the king retained their loyalty.[21]

Given her own training, the Christian emphasis of the spectacles, and the Christianization of much of the more ancient religion as well as the kind of religious instruction she received, Dona Beatriz naturally considered herself a good Christian, and expressed herself in Christian terms. This Christianity was a fundamental part of religion in Kongo, even if in many places it differed from that of Europe. It would be in Christian terms – but drawn from Kongo's own variety of this tradition – that Dona Beatriz would become a human home for Saint Anthony.

[21] This passage is based on d'Atri's (pp. 520–1) description of the festivities of 1701.

2

The Rival Kings

IN NOVEMBER 1695, when Dona Beatriz was eleven years old, Queen Ana Afonso de Leão, still living at Gando a Suka in Bonga, just a few miles from her town, announced that she was organizing a "Concert of Kongo" to attempt to resolve the disputes and win universal acceptance of one man as king. Politically active people, like those in Dona Beatriz' family, followed the events with interest, since contemplating another set of wars like those of 1690–3 was a gloomy prospect. To what degree would the royal candidates and their followers be prepared to put aside their personal ambitions for the common good?

Then, around Christmas of 1695, came the news that King Álvaro X, who had been Dona Beatriz' king virtually all her life, had died at Kibangu. He was promptly succeeded on the misty heights by his brother Pedro, now King Pedro IV. King Pedro was a young man of twenty-four when he came to the throne; he had been just a teenager when fighting alongside his brother in their overthrow of Manuel.

Pedro, too, was interested in the future of Kongo now that he was in a position to advance his family's claims. It was a good time – his long-standing rival Manuel was dead, he had recently defeated the armies of his other main rival, João, and Queen Ana, the self-announced peace mediator, was living within his territory and had once put her prestige behind his brother as king of all Kongo. His optimism was evident in his earliest letters, for he announced himself proudly as "Emperor," rather than king, of Kongo, a switch that reflected the difference in Kikongo between *ntinu*, the normal word for king, and *ntotela*, a term derived from the verb "to unite," implying a larger authority. His titles in the same letters gave some idea of the scope of his ambition, for he styled himself ruler not just of Kongo but also of Angola, Loango, Nzonzo, Ngoyo, Malemba, Ngobela, Makoko, and "the marvelous River Zaire."[1]

Most of these states had never been under Kongolese authority, although some had been in royal titles, reflecting largely honorary submissions in the sixteenth and seventeenth centuries. Pedro certainly had no hope of recovering even such symbolic authority, for it was enough to hold on to his lands at Kibangu and the Mbidizi valley and perhaps to extend his influence eastward into the Inkisi River basin.

As soon as the *Mvula a nene* (Great Rains), the second of Kongo's two rainy seasons, let up in March and April, the peace negotiations began. Queen Ana's ambassadors were busy inviting other players in the field to send their own representatives to her town at Gando a Suka. She even invited Pedro Kibenga and Alexio, her sworn enemies who now occupied her former lands, to send ambassadors. She interested the missionaries of the Capuchin order – whose base was at Nkusu in the Inkisi River basin east of Kibangu – in the plan on behalf of the Church. As neutral parties, they were prepared to support her in every way in her aim to reach a peaceful settlement to the disputes that were ruining the country.

Many Mwana Kongo nobles would acknowledge that Queen Ana had the right to convene a meeting to reunite the country. Peacemaker was an appropriate role for a elderly woman, especially since she made no claim to rule on her own. Moreover, she was the senior member and "mother" of the Kinlaza kanda, which she felt was the legitimate ruling line of Kongo.

Pedro, however, was quickly disappointed, for Queen Ana decided to throw her support behind the candidacy of João II of Bula, and the king in Kibangu was not invited to come except to pay homage to his rival. She could not forget that Álvaro had

---

[1] Da Caltanisetta, "Relatione," fols. 22–22v.

supported the plot of Alexio and Kibenga that killed Manuel and drove her from her home. She knew that Álvaro had even entertained the idea of having her killed, though he eventually balked at such treachery. Despite the king's eventual hospitality in allowing her to stay in Gando a Suka, she did not trust the Agua Rosada brothers, neither Álvaro nor his newly installed brother, Pedro, and had regretted her earlier recognition of their claim.

Queen Ana supported João's claim, though, not so much because she disliked the Agua Rosadas as because he was a member of the Kinlaza kanda. In her youth, over the issue of succession Kongo's ruling kanda had split into three: the Kinkanga a Mvika, the Kinlaza, and the Kimpanzu. This break was a crucial period in Kongo's history; even in the twentieth century people still remembered a proverb that said "Kinkanga, Kimpanzu, Kinlaza makukwa matatu malambila Akongo" (Kinkanga, Kimpanzu, and Kinlaza were three stones on which the Kongolese cooked [or operated]).[2]

The Kinkanga a Mvika took its name from the Kikongo name of its founder, Pedro II Afonso Nkanga a Mvika, crowned king in 1622. They ruled briefly under Pedro and his son Garcia I, and were driven from power by the Kimpanzu faction in 1631, though Kinkanga a Mvika nobles still held titles. The Kimpanzu faction was led by King Álvaro V Mpanzu a Nimi, and took its name from his own Kikongo given name. In Dona Beatriz' time Kimpanzu partisans claimed that the third branch, the Kinlaza, was descended from illegitimate offspring of the venerable sixteenth-century king Afonso I, while they, in turn, descended from the legitimate line – although, in fact, mid-seventeenth-century documents do not support them.

At the time of the split, the Kinlaza were led by two brothers, Álvaro and Garcia, who were brothers in turn to Queen Ana.

[2] Cuvelier, *Nkutama*, p. 73. The reference to three stones is widely used to describe items that come in threes. Cuvelier recorded it in reference to the clan history of the Nkanga at Nkondo, a village near Songolo, either orally or from local manuscripts, around 1927. One should not assume that this modern clan is somehow descended from the ancient Kinkanga, but, rather, that they have appropriated a widely used proverb to match their name.

Álvaro overthrew his Kimpanzu rival and became Álvaro VI in 1636; his brother succeeded him as Garcia II in 1641. In 1657, Garcia was able to smash the last remaining members of the Kinkanga a Mvika branch, so that in Queen Ana's day they were said to have been "put totally to the ground."[3] Although Garcia also sought to destroy or absorb his rivals from the Kimpanzu branch, they fled to the rebel province of Soyo, where the counts, who dared to take the ostentatious title of grand princes, allowed them refuge and support. Their strength, even in Dona Beatriz' day, sprang from the connection to Soyo.[4]

Queen Ana, the sister of Álvaro and Garcia, had now become the eldest and most important member of the Kinlaza, and therefore felt she had a right to mediate for her younger cousins and nephews, including João, to settle their disputes.

Of course, her concert never seriously considered potential Kimpanzu candidates. The Kimpanzu equivalent of Queen Ana was another former queen named Suzanna de Nóbrega, settled in on the Atlantic coast in Luvota, a province in southern Soyo, the traditional protector and patron of the Kimpanzu. Like Queen Ana, Queen Suzanna was an informal leader by virtue of her age and her relationship to former kings – she was sister of one, wife of another, and mother of three more. At one point, Kimpanzu hopes were pinned on Manuel, but after his death the leadership had passed to Pedro Constantinho da Silva Kibenga, now officially holding the title of Marquis of Wembo and ruling Nkondo as well. It was an uneasy leadership, however, since Kibenga was only a Kimpanzu on his mother's side, but was descended from the ruling kanda of Soyo, the da Silvas, on his father's side.

In Queen Ana's plan for restoration, Pedro Kibenga was now Queen Ana's deadliest enemy and, given his control of virtually the whole Mbidizi valley south of Kibangu's territories, also her most powerful one.

In Queen Ana's Kinlaza view of the world, the Agua Rosada

---

[3] APF:SOCG 476, fol. 331, Bernardo da Gallo, "Conto delle villacazione missionali."

[4] On the formation of these factions, Thornton, *Kingdom of Kongo*, pp. 50–53.

brothers were distinctly less legitimate than her favored followers, though not enemies like the Kimpanzu. The Agua Rosadas
had originated from fragments of the royal kanda on the mountain of Kibangu a generation later than the Kinlaza. Their mother
was a Kinlaza and thus connected to the queen, but their father,
Sebastião Mvemba a Lukeni, was a Kimpanzu, although one who
had gotten on the wrong side of the princes of Soyo and had been
killed by them.[5]

João's supporters in Bula responded favorably to the queen's
overtures, and in March the king led a group from Bula to São
Salvador to be officially crowned King of Kongo. Although João's
brother and predecessor, Pedro III, had been crowned in the old
capital before his own troops destroyed the city nearly twenty
years earlier, João himself had not been crowned there. His brief
occupation of the ruined city marked his official statement of his
intent to accept the crown from all Kongo.

To follow up on this initial step, the Church joined in Queen
Ana's project. Father Luca da Caltanisetta, representing the
Church's interest in the disputes, left Nkusu on 8 April to deliver
letters and handle negotiations with King João, accompanied by
ambassadors from the queen and her supporters.

The priest arrived in Lemba in time to celebrate Easter with the
king, who had since returned from his coronation visit to São
Salvador. João received him courteously in his apartments along
with his council. The priest met them as they stood around a
white sheet with a beautiful red cloth covering. They were anxious to know the details of the Concert of Kongo. Father Luca
greeted them by quoting Scripture: "In whatsoever house or city
you enter say first: peace be to this house,"[6] and then went on to
say, "I have followed this advice from the start of my mission in
Kongo, first at Soyo, then at Mbamba, Nkondo, Mbata, Mpangu,
Nsundi, Bula, Ngando, Bonga, and Nkusu," [and] "all the lords

---

[5] On the Concert of Kongo, d'Atri, "Giornate," pp. 127–8, Mendes, pp. 353
and 355; on Pedro's descent, APF:SOCG 576, fol. 355, da Gallo, "Conto
delle villacazione missionali . . ."
[6] Luke 10:10 (but translating from the Latin of the Vulgate as quoted in da
Caltanisetta, "Relatione," fol. 23v).

living in all these places want among all the rulers a holy universal peace, for the common repose of the body and soul." But then, to his surprise, the council interrupted him, saying such things were better discussed at another time.

In fact, it turned out that João's court was divided over the whole issue. Although there were few who did not want to see him accepted as king over all, they did not trust Queen Ana. Others were concerned about the snubbing of Pedro, and bore him some loyalty. Many were worried about João's own leadership qualities. He had been a minor when he succeeded his brother in 1683, and for more than five years had been dominated by his mother, Potencia. He even announced himself in letters as one "who tramples the lion [that is, stands on the lion skin that adorns the front of thrones] in the Kingdom of his mother." When Queen Potencia died, however, his strong-willed sister Elena took her place, since João's health was bad and his behavior erratic.

It was symptomatic of the problems at Bula that João (or Elena, acting through her brother) had required many of his nobles to sign an oath of absolute loyalty to him, declaring that if they were to become traitors, they would "be deprived of all aid of the Divinity and of Mary and the Saints, and all of their merits, and be totally given to the Devil, making him the master of their body and soul."[7] Other Worldly sanctions rarely held people to loyalty, especially in times like those.

While Father Luca was attempting to reconcile these interests and win acceptance of a general peace, Queen Ana was undermining it. In July, her nephew Daniel led an army across the Mbidizi and captured Mbanza Mpemba from Kibenga's supporters, killing the marquis, Afonso, and turning the office over to Daniel. Then her favorite cousin and closest supporter, Pedro Valle das Lagrimas, combined with Daniel's troops to launch a surprise night attack on Alexio, the Duke of Mbamba chosen by Manuel when he was king. Valle das Lagrimas' troops entered the mbanza on some bluffs south of the Mbidizi River near the coast, and cut down all resistance, killing Alexio in the process.

[7] Da Caltanisetta, "Relatione," fols. 23–25v, on the negotiations at Bula.

The larger body of Kongolese nobles and people who had followed the Concert of Kongo with hope and interest became disappointed by this turn of events. When Valle das Lagrimas captured Mbanza Mbamba, he burned the body of Alexio as revenge for the latter's treachery against Queen Ana. This dramatic humiliation of his opponent might well have won acceptance from those who thought him wronged, but the act was in fact viewed differently.

When news of the war filtered back to the Mbidizi valley, it came accompanied by elaborated rumor. In the more popular version of the events, Valle das Lagrimas had not just burned Alexio's body, he and his supporters had actually disinterred both Alexio and Afonso, removed the heart and liver, roasted them, and ate them.[8]

This type of action goes beyond simple revenge, for in Kongolese thinking such things as eating people, disinterring the dead, and the like are actions appropriate to people known as *ndokis*. The term might be translated as "witch," although ndokis are not entirely like witches of Western folklore. Rather, ndokis are selfish and greedy people who will stop at nothing to get what they want. They enlist Otherworldly power that has been garnered by like-minded people and "eat" their victims either literally or symbolically, through supernaturally caused disease or induced misfortune. A *loka*, or curse, is the origin of these types of diseases or misfortunes as, indeed, the word *ndoki* is formed from the root *loka*.

The power to carry out a curse was *kindoki*, related linguistically both to loka and ndoki. But using this power was not necessarily bad; indeed, it might be good. The power of kindoki was simply the gift of possessing the ability to operate with the assistance of the Other World, and if it was done for good aims, generously, it was a positive virtue indeed. Thus, the power to curse was conversely also a power to protect, and so there could be good

---

[8] On the facts of the campaign, d'Atri, "Giornate," pp. 138–9; da Caltanisetta, "Relatione," fol. 26v; on the elaborated rumors, Mendes, p. 353.

and bad kindoki, depending on what ends the power to curse was used.[9]

This logic was also applied to rulers on the earthly plane, as for them the power to kill (or, by extension, exercise any of the coercive power of state) was analogous to the power to curse. If the power was exercised unselfishly and in the interest of the community, then it was positive; if for selfish ends, it was negative in the same way that bad kindoki was. Francisco de Menezes Nkanka Makaya, son of King António I and nephew of the queen, put it very well once when he was asked why he, as a likely candidate for the crown, did not take up his office. He argued that the common people would never accept him. "Why should we have a king who lives so differently from how we do and our ancestors?" This diversity, he explained, was because he had lived a long time in Luanda after being captured by Portuguese forces at the battle of Mbwila, "This one," they would say, "wears a shirt, coat, shoes, sleeps under sheets and eats in the manner of the whites, and does as they do." More to the point, though, it was not just in the matter of clothes that he was different, but in outlook, for, he argued, he was like the Portuguese, accustomed "to *bingar* [go around and beg or demand things] and eat by himself. Therefore," the people might say, "how can we put up with laws that are so different from ours, as we are accustomed to eat everything we have in one day, without leaving anything for tomorrow." Dom Francisco contended, in fact, that a true king should use his power in the interests of the people and not selfishly to increase his wealth, as people perceived the Portuguese were doing in Angola.[10]

Ndokis who used the power to curse for selfish ends in private

[9] On the use of the term *kindoki*, see Bockie, *Death and the Invisible Powers*, pp. 43–57, using his own knowledge and citing a number of other ethnographies written by Kongolese. Most relate to the northern and eastern regions of the Kikongo-speaking zone and not to Kongo proper, but they seem appropriate in this area.

[10] D'Atri, "Giornate," p. 438; for a modern view, based on fieldwork, and twentieth-century Kongolese testimony connecting kindoki and royal power, see MacGaffey, *Religion and Society*, pp. 135–68.

life were bad enough, but when kindoki was combined with political power, and both were wedded to selfishness, the combination was particularly dangerous, as, indeed, was the implication of the rumors about Pedro Valle das Lagrimas. Although these rumors were not true, they reflected popular belief about the higher reaches of the nobility in Kongo, that their greed knew no limits and would ruin the country.

Yet another piece of news confirmed suspicions that unprincipled people were running the country. The queen decided not to occupy Mbanza Mbamba, and recalled Pedro Valle das Lagrimas back to her, over his protests. As a result, the duchy fell into the hands of an adventurer of the Kinlaza kanda named Pedro Mpanzu a Mvemba. After the overthrow of the queen's forces in the Mbidizi valley in 1692–3, Pedro had withdrawn to the south, to the Marquisate of Mbumbe, where he had occupied and fortified a flat-topped mountain. From this impregnable fortress, he raided far and wide, ostensibly in the name of continuing the queen's war against Manuel and Kibenga. But much of his raiding was against travelers who happened along the road to Luanda, which passed beneath his mountain. Throughout 1694 he had raided the caravans of slaves who had been taken when Manuel was attacked and were bound for Luanda, the main port of Portugal's colony of Angola, eventually to be exported to Brazil.

In one raid, Pedro had captured the carriers of a Capuchin priest, Father Marcellino d'Atri, and in the affair the priest had received a wound on his hand – a serious breach of the peace because priests were supposed to be neutral and their followers respected. Although Pedro restored the priest's goods, the idea that he was as much a bandit as a partisan of the queen stuck and was known in Kibangu.[11]

These developments convinced Pedro IV that he would have to make himself King of Kongo if he expected to make good on any claims. Therefore he decided to go to be crowned king in São Salvador, especially as João had done so earlier in the year. Like

[11] On Pedro Mpanzu a Mvemba in 1693, d'Atri, "Giornate," pp. 75–90, 104; da Caltanisetta, "Relatione," fol. 16v; on his brief installation as Duke of Mbamba, d'Atri, "Giornate," pp. 138–9.

João and his brother Álvaro X before him, Pedro had not been crowned in the capital, but only acclaimed on his mountaintop. Coronation at the capital was essential to a serious claim to rule the country. The city's ruins, choked with weeds and overgrown with trees, contained the royal palace, the cathedral – dedicated to Jesus the Holy Savior in 1548 – and a dozen lesser churches and chapels, including a small one built on the occasion of the baptism of João I, the first Christian king, in 1491.

Since a coronation needed a priest, Pedro browbeat Father Luis, his personal chaplain, to perform the ceremony. But Father Luis came under protest, maintaining that he did not even know the proper rite. His protests were ignored and he was ordered to accompany the royal train.

The people of the Mbidizi valley, including twelve-year-old Dona Beatriz, were particularly involved in the coronation. Pedro ordered that the way from Kibangu to São Salvador be cleared for his train to pass. A great multitude of people started out first, clearing and widening the road leading from Pedro's mountain fortress to the capital.

Half a century earlier, the city and the surrounding countryside had held nearly 100,000 people, virtually all of whom fled when the city was abandoned in 1678. But they had left a strange legacy for Pedro's reoccupation party: an abundance of fruit trees across the wilderness. In the months after the city was abandoned, great herds of elephants had been drawn there to feast upon its thousands of banana trees, and had trampled down the walls of the fairly flimsy housing of the ordinary people. Now citrus, banana, sapodilla, *lemba-lemba*, and other fruit trees, no longer carefully watched or cultivated, had gone wild and tangled the city and the surrounding hills, forming a strange reminder of the dense population that had once lived there. Nearly twenty years had allowed some tropical species full growth even in the once grand public squares and right through the walls of stone buildings of the palace and churches.

As one approached São Salvador from the east, it appeared an impressive site even in ruins. It sat perched on the edge of 200- to 300-feet-high cliffs that overlooked the Luezi River. All along

the edge of the cliffs were the remains of the great city wall –
some 20 feet high and composed of dressed hematite stone with
limestone mortar. One could still make out the curious round
tower in the wall nearest the east side, from which, legend said,
the kings had proclaimed law to the people. From a vantage point
on the hills across the river one could locate the cathedral, all its
walls standing, although its roof, formerly of thatch, was long
gone.

Climbing up the steep hillsides to the top brought one into the
city. Two great stone-walled enclosures, each a mile in circumference, encircled what had once been the royal compound; inside
were the remains of the palace as well as a separate district for
the Portuguese who once resided there. Between these two sets
of walls, first erected by King Afonso in the 1510s and repaired
by Garcia II in the 1640s, stood the great plaza and next to it, the
largest church and former cathedral.

Pedro's advance guard decided to clear this square as completely as they could. They felled trees, cleared undergrowth, and
cleaned the great squares and ruined buildings. Under the guid-
ance of those who were old enough to remember the geography
of the city before its destruction and abandonment, the ruined
churches were cleared and the tombs of the old kings revealed.
The Church of São Miguel, one of the oldest, held the remains of
the great Afonso and some of the kings who ruled after him.
Although grass was cleared away, the trees that had encroached
on the walls and the altar were not cut down. After a lot of time
spent discussing and arguing about the location of old familiar
sites, these were discovered and excavated.

The elderly guides, many of them proud Knights of the Kongolese Order of Christ, had not ventured the few miles westward
from the Mbidizi to see the old capital since its destruction, and
their rediscovery was painful, both because its former glory could
still be fathomed in the imagination, and because its present ruins
testified to how far the country had traveled since then. Many
cried bitter tears to see their beloved city in such a state, some
said "they would give money to have the city the way it once
was."

Once this sad archeology was completed enough to conduct a ceremony, the coronation began on 2 August. On the great plaza before the cathedral, where generations of Kings of Kongo had been crowned in the past, Pedro and his Vicar General participated in the ritual. Those same old nobles who remembered the geography of the city also reconstructed the rites of coronation for Father Luis, and walked him through it.

It started with the nsanga – in which titled nobles displayed their expertise with the sword and battleax, and the rank and file filled the air with musket smoke as a mock battle was waged by his soldiers. Dona Beatriz' kinsman Miguel de Castro, acting in his capacity as Secretary Major, then read out a formal statement of the history and laws of the country, a major feature of coronations or Saint James' Day festivities.

"*Muna ntete* – in the beginning, there was a noble lady named Ne Lukeni, who lived at Kwimba, north across the River Zaire," he began, referring to the distant ancient time, probably the late fourteenth century, when there was no Kongo and its future ruler lived in a small state across the Zaire River from João's present domains in Bula.

"She wished to cross the river at a ferry, and became impatient at having to wait for so long, and so she began to insist to the boatman that he take her first, ahead of others. She was pregnant and demanded attention," de Castro continued.

"Are you perhaps the queen, or the mother of the king, that you don't want to wait patiently?" the boatman responded. "Wait until the others have passed, and then you too can go."

Ne Lukeni was very angry by this reply and flew into a rage at the boatman, and she went to her son, named Ntinu Lukeni, and told him all that had happened. Ntinu Lukeni, seeing how his mother was so troubled and agitated, consoled her by replying, "Go my dear mother, do not worry yourself, we will fix everything. Have you been called queen or mother of a king? Very well. You can be at least mother of a king, if not a queen, and I will be king, but not without a kingdom."

"Ntinu Lukeni left his homeland," the Secretary Major continued, "taking Ne Lukeni with him and crossed the Zaire. Having reached the shore of Kongo, he began to fight with the people of the land. He went to the Mount Vunda, or São Salvador today, drained a lake which he found there, and built a royal house for him to live in. In this way he easily conquered the two kingdoms of Kongo and Angola. Then he sent his sister Ne Nkenge, to Angola and ruled Kongo himself, appointing governors to the provinces."

De Castro went on from this founding story to detail the laws of the country, implicitly linking them with the history of the founders of the state. The tale, in some variants, had been a part of coronation stories for more than half a century, and was a history that emphasized royal power and authority.

The arbitrary nature of the conquest, the violent seizure of power, the appointment of provincial rulers – all these were the hallmarks of the highly centralized Kingdom of Kongo of days past. At this stage, the story was intended to justify these matters to King Pedro's subjects, and to reinforce the point that in his own lands, at least, Pedro could still be the court of last resort, that he could appoint and dismiss his officials, demand taxes and military service, without entertaining any discussion. But as everyone present knew, such power was exercised only as the ruler of Kibangu among his much more limited group of subjects, and not more widely as the King of Kongo.

Guided by his senior councillor, the Marquis of Vunda, Pedro went to the Vicar General and received his crown, a cap something like a Turkish fez, called *mpu* in Kikongo. The royal crown was very skillfully made and decorated with Kongo's coat of arms – five mailed arms, each bearing a sword, arranged on a silver background. The coat of arms dated to 1512 and reflected Kongo's earliest political miracle, when King Afonso I had defeated his brother in a civil war through the aid of a blinding vision of Saint James that was celebrated every Saint James Day.

Pedro IV then sat upon his throne before the whole people, who instantly fell to their knees bowing in deep reverence. So great was their respect for the throne itself, that the people were bowing to it as much as to its occupant. Pedro sat for some time, drinking in the feeling of power and majesty that the earlier kings had enjoyed.

But the glory of the moment was short-lived. The very next day nervous messengers brought word that João II had heard of Pedro's daring occupation of the city, and was preparing an army to attack him. The king did not feel up to the showdown, and quickly ordered the city abandoned. The common people, who had labored to clear the city and provided his audience, were sent home; the retainers and the king moved off the next morning to abandon the city, and two days later were back at Kibangu.[12]

If the reoccupation of São Salvador had given King Pedro some feelings of royal splendor, these had been lost on Queen Ana, who was busy advancing the Kinlaza agenda. On 3 September, her armies led by António de Leão Mpanzu Kivangi – son of the late King Álvaro VIII of Kongo – Garcia Makunga, and a nephew, Dom Álvaro, hammered into Nkondo and besieged Pedro Kibenga. Thanks to a "stratagem of war" Kibenga avoided the fate of his other allies, Alexio and Afonso, who had been killed. He managed to flee after pillaging the church in Nkondo of some thirty-four trunks and many boxes of goods, and with this train managed to make his way north to Bula, where he sought asylum with King João.

But the powers in Bula were unable to deal with Kibenga any more than they could deal with Queen Ana's overtures, and he was sent away. Eventually he made his way to Kibangu and

---

[12] On the occupation, d'Atri, "Giornate," pp. 139–42. The geography of the city is reconstructed from Pigafetta's account of the 1580, and several nineteenth-century descriptions of the ruins; cf. Filippo Pigafetta, *Relatione del Reamé di Congo et delle circonvincine contrade, tratta dalli scritti e ragionamenti di Odoardo Lopez, Portoghese* (Rome, 1591, facsimile ed. Rosa Capelens with Portuguese translation, Lisbon, 1949–51), p. 40. Modern edition *Relazione del Reame di Congo* (ed. Giogio Raimondo Cardona, Milano, 1978), with original pagination marked, also marked in the French translation of Willy Bal, *Description du Royaume de Congo et des Contrées Environnantes par Filippo Pigafetta et Duarte Lopes* (Louvain, 1963); Adolph Bastian, *Ein Besuch in San Salvador der Hauptstadt der Königreichs Congo* (Bremen, 1859), pp. 122–3; W. Holman Bentley, *Pioneering on the Congo* (London, 1914), pp. 139–41. The coronation story is slightly reworded from the version recorded by Bernardo da Gallo and written down in 1710. The original Italian is published in Calogero Piazza, "Alcuni traditione orale nel Regno de Congo," *Annali Lateranensi* 34 (1973): 237–59.

threw himself at the mercy of King Pedro. Pedro, who had no reason to be happy with Queen Ana, accepted Kibenga as a refugee and began heaping honors on him. He proclaimed him Captain General of Kongo, and allowed him and many of his kinsmen to build a separate camp some three miles outside King Pedro's city on Kibangu.

Since Queen Ana reoccupied her old capital of Nkondo, making the commander Garcia Makunga Marquis of Wembo, she was no longer to be counted in Pedro's stretch of the Mbidizi valley, and her opinion could be ignored. But Queen Ana was definitely angry that Pedro had thwarted her revenge on Kibenga, and placed a blockade on the roads leading to Kibangu. Although it was a largely symbolic gesture to indicate her displeasure, the queen was now in an excellent position, for once again she controlled the great Mbidizi provinces of Mbamba, Mpemba, and Wembo.

The queen pressed her advantages further, and early in 1697 her forces had advanced into Wandu, southward along the Lukunga River from her capital in Nkondo. Although the mbanza, or capital, fell to her hands and was granted to Dom Clemente, the old count who had been appointed by Kibenga refused to surrender and withdrew southward, fortifying himself in the steep mountains along the gorges of the river.

At the same time she was utilizing her army to extend her power, Queen Ana continued to speak of peace. In November she began a systematic campaign to placate Soyo. Her followers reviewed the survivors of Valle das Lagrimas' attack on Mbamba and located those connected to Soyo. Alexio had married a wife from Soyo's elite, and his daughter was returned to her maternal relatives. Other highborn Soyolese were located and many promises made, in the hopes of moving the princes to be more supportive of the Kinlaza.

António III Baretto da Silva de Castro, Prince of Soyo, had seized power earlier that year. When electors called a meeting to resolve disputes over the sucession, António brought a pistol with him and coolly shot his rival in the midst of the gathering. He was not particularly moved by the display of friendship from Queen Ana – being as thoroughly cynical as she was – although he did accept the returned prisoners. He did not, however, withdraw his support from the remaining Kimpanzu led by Queen Suzanna in his domains at Luvota.[13]

The situation on the Mbidizi and at São Salvador had come to a standstill, and Pedro now turned his attention eastward, where the rivalries of kingship were less. East of Kibangu the highlands were deeply cut by the valley of the Lefunde River, one of the Mbidizi's cousins, and beyond this deep valley was a broad, high tableland coursed by the Inkisi River and its many tributaries.

The Inkisi flowed northward into the Zaire River and this highly populated region was a critical part of Kongo. Long before, much of the region had been under the fabled "Seven Kingdoms of Kongo dia Nlaza," an ancient state whose territories had been absorbed into Kongo in the sixteenth century.

It was famous now, as it had been for generations, as a region where huge quantities of cloth were made, something on the order of one hundred thousand yards a year solely for export. Iron deposits also abounded, so that the area was a manufacturing heartland for Kongo. The people were reputed to be industrious, hardworking, and deeply divided politically. Pedro's interest in maximizing his control in this wealthy area would certainly bolster his position against the queen and João.

Three Kongolese provinces dominated the valley. In the north, there was the Duchy of Nsundi, once the appanage of the heir apparent to the Kongo throne. The great King Afonso I had governed the province when he was first baptized, and for that reason Nsundians sometimes claimed their province was the real birthplace of the Kongolese Church. In 1668, the Kimpanzu king Álvaro VII had placed a member of his kanda in the ducal seat, and in the confusing civil war that followed those days, no one had successfully recalled him and he remained in hereditary control. As a result, a Kimpanzu line of dukes controlled Nsundi – nominally loyal to the Kingdom of Kongo but not to any of the

---

[13] On the peace entreaties, da Caltanisetta, "Relatione," fols. 28v–29; on Antonio III Baretto's succession, Antonio Gradisia da Zucchelli, *Relatione del Viaggio e Missione di Congo* (Venice, 1712), 225; da Lucca, pp. 228–9.

kings who had tried to rule since then. By this time Nsundi was a regional power and was expanding southward in a period vaguely remembered later as being dominated by a founder figure called Ne Kiangala.[14]

South of Nsundi was the smaller Marquisate of Mpangu. Like Nsundi, it had fallen under the control of a line of marquises who recognized the Kingdom of Kongo but not its kings. In the 1690s, though, this line was divided into rival kandas, and Nsundi had intervened in the struggle to extend its influence southward.

Pedro's interests in the Inkisi basin were not focused on those northern states, whose fates he could not control and whose loyalty was strictly nominal. Rather, he hoped for more influence in the Duchy of Mbata, whose lands lay directly east of Kibangu. Mbata was an ancient province, an independent kingdom even before the rise of Kongo. In those days of the fourteenth century, Mbata had joined Kongo voluntarily, and the dukes had the nominal right to assist in choosing Kongolese kings. Rule of Mbata had always been hereditary, the kings of Kongo exercising no direct appointment powers, and had been held since ancient times by the Nsaku Lau kanda. Under Kongo's auspices, in the sixteenth century Mbata had conquered huge territories to its east, including the famous Seven Kingdoms.

When Kongo's civil war broke out, the rulers of Mbata were not as directly affected as other provinces, since they had always been under the control of the Nsaku Lau. But in the 1690s, the open succession promoted by the absence of a royal influence had led to a split. In March 1696, while Queen Ana was organizing the Concert of Kongo, the split had led to a war between Miguel

---

[14] The tradition of Ne Kiangala was recalled in the early twentieth century by the Kiangala Masumpu kanda. The version printed by Cuvelier in *Nkutama*, p. 5, recalls that Ne Kiangala fought a war with Mpangu and Mbata around 1700, and then goes on with some statements about Ne Kiangala and his thirteen crowns while locating modern kandas in their villages. The use of a date is remarkable in traditions, and may have come from the original text, or perhaps from the editorial hand of Cuvelier, who was, after all, knowledgeable about the documentary sources used here.

Kilau and Miguel Ngoma Mpasi. The two dukes fought indecisively for most of the dry season, and in the end managed to split the duchy in half, with Miguel Kilau taking the western districts and Miguel Ngoma Mpasi taking the eastern ones.

Pedro put his support behind Miguel Kilau and the eastern section, although not committing his army wholly to the effort. The interests in the east now became of greater import in Kibangu, for Pedro found there a more satisfying theater of operations, if for no other reason than it took him from the larger and more threatening situation to his west.

The long string of events in 1696 had radically changed the prospects for peace, to the extent that Father Lucada Caltanisetta, who had sought to use the opportunity to help bring peace to Kongo, decided in October that the peace plan was thoroughly dead, and sadly returned to the Capuchin hospice in Nkusu. The priest was convinced now that while everyone wanted to restore Kongo, everyone also only wanted a restored kingdom of their own liking.[15]

A twelve-year-old girl living in the Mbidizi valley might well have drawn strong impressions from all this – the restoration of the capital, the grandeur of the old city and its present ruin, the sadness in the old men's voices and their faces, and the fear of attack that caused its abandonment had its impact. So, too, did the increasing belief that true restoration could not take place while evil and selfish people, people possibly dealing in the deadly trade of the ndokis, were making the decisions. Dona Beatriz was not alone in starting to think that it would require more than simply business as usual to make their world whole again.

As Dona Beatriz grew older her interest and abilities in the spiritual side of life and its social consequences increased. It became obvious that she was specially gifted and could be an *nganga*, a medium to the Other World. Nganga derives from a Kikongo root that means "knowledge" or "skill," but specifically the kind of

---

[15] Da Caltanisetta, "Relatione," fol. 29.

skill that applies to religious matters. Catholic priests were called ngangas, as were many people who claimed they could access knowledge and seek assistance from the Other World. Although a Catholic priest received his title through study and training, others normally had to show some demonstrable ability to contact the Other World to be acknowledged as a nganga.

Ngangas were possessors of kindoki, which gave them many means of contacting the Other World – they could be diviners who read the patterns made by throwing stones or tossed-up strings, or they could interpret dreams that they or other people had. They might see visions or hear voices, all of which were means the Other World used to communicate with This World. Ngangas could also be possessed by beings from the Other World. A possessed nganga, such as *nganga ngombo*, would go into a trance, either through taking special drugs or, more commonly, through various forms of hypnosis induced by drumming, dancing, or simply rhythmic chanting and hand clapping. Once this state was achieved, some being from the Other World would enter the nganga's head, and then use his or her vocal cords to speak. In this way, ordinary people without special gifts could hear the words of those in the Other World. They could ask questions of the spirit and receive answers. They could be advised of the cause of sickness or misfortune, and of appropriate steps necessary to address the problems.

Dona Beatriz began her initiation as an nganga when still quite young. She entered a particular category of this office called *nganga marinda*, whose special tasks were to address social problems as much as individual ones. Because it was socially oriented and served the common good, this office was much respected, whereas those offices that dealt more with personal problems were inclined to be suspect. Individualism was likely to be accompanied by greed, the prime ingredient in motivating ndokis.

The nganga's work typically involved helping people with problems that could have origins in the Other World, often on a fee-for-service basis. People who had problems with sickness, bad luck, or economic misfortune went to a nganga, such as a nganga ngombo, and asked spiritual entities from the Other World to identify the cause of the problem. Sometimes the Otherworldly entities would suggest that the client had offended some ancestor or broken some taboo established by a nkita, a guardian deity of the land, which might be identified with an ancient spirit, a Christian saint, or Guardian Angel. Often, too, they would name another person or people who were working bad kindoki, in the form of lokas, or curses on them because of jealousy, greed, or anger. This might be done intentionally by ndokis, or unintentionally by people who harbored negative feelings. Once the source of cursing was identified, the ngangas could guide their clients in taking steps to address the problem, perhaps bringing the ndoki to trial, or rectifying the cause of strife or tension between people or families.

Dona Beatriz may have done some of this sort of work, but she was much more strongly drawn to the social aspects of the same set of beliefs, perhaps because her upper-class background gave her a higher awareness of politics and of social problems. Social mediation was similar to the individual mediation that ngangas practiced on behalf of their clients. The health, luck, or economic success or failure of a community were investigated in the same way as those of an individual, and often the same sorts of problems were identified – collective violation of a taboo, offending some common ancestor or perhaps a nkita like Lusunzi, guardian of Kibangu and its neighborhood. Alternatively, a nganga might use his or her own kindoki to identify sources of hostile kindoki, often coming from within the community itself.

One remedy for this sort of social kindoki was a ceremony called *mbumba kindonga*. After consulting with the Other World, an nganga might determine that bickering, social strife, or intercommunal jealousy had created a generalized distress for the community. Guided by the nganga and advice from the Other World, the community would have a cathartic meeting in which old jealousies were aired and unspoken anger released, culminating in a decision literally to bury these dissensions and start anew. As a symbol of renewed harmony, each household would take some personal item from among its possessions, and bury it along with items from all the others in a sort of grave, the mbumba kindonga.

Dona Beatriz, as a nganga marinda, was involved with another social remedy called the Kimpasi society. The word *kimpasi* means "suffering" in Kikongo, and an important motive for forming one was a feeling that a community was suffering. There were chapters of the Kimpasi society throughout Kongo, but there was no central direction to it, so that each chapter was independent. For all the local independence, though, there was a certain feeling of solidarity between all initiates into the society. A community or group of communities suffering from calamities and problems would call on some ngangas, perhaps an nganga ngombo, perhaps an nganga marinda, to organize the society for their community.

The founders built a large enclosure in an uninhabited area, often in woods or in a wild area – for such places were on the edge of the Other World and far from the troubles or comforts of This World. A large mound was constructed in the middle of a palisade of trees or logs, called the "Walls of the King of Kongo," around the enclosure, circled by a ditch. Special medicinal plants were planted along the inner walls of the enclosure along with thorns and other quick-growing hedges, both to provide some security and to supply special needs of the group.

Then an altar was erected on the top of the mound, with steps leading up to it. In the middle of the altar the builders placed a cross, which was simultaneously an invocation of Christianity and a marker symbolizing the junction of This World and the Other World common to the whole Kikongo-speaking world, both Christian and non-Christian. To stress the Christian connection, Kongolese Kimpasi chapters also placed such specifically ecclesiastical goods as censers and aspirators on the altar. Two *kitekes* – statues in human form that had been invested with the power to "see" wrongdoers, ndokis, the jealous, the greedy, or the cruel – flanked the cross. The kitekes were surrounded by other empowering items, such as claws of predators to catch wrongdoers symbolically, horns of black (for This World) and red (for the boundary between worlds), and animal tails, like the *msesa*, or buffalo tail, that symbolized power.

Initiates were then chosen from the community, often young people just entering adolescence, as Dona Beatriz was when she was first initiated. They came to the gate of the enclosure, and were then tied up with a thin string by the nganga and the nganga's assistants. As the bonds were tied on and redoubled over the initiates' bodies, they gradually lost consciousness, and eventually fell into a deep trance – a catatonic state that people believed was death. Now apparently dead, the initiates were carried inside the enclosure for their initiation.

Once inside, the dead were revived through careful treatment. But as they revived they were aware that they were no longer the same people. Their bodies had been possessed by a nkita which worked through them. This possession was not exactly identical to that of the ngangas, which was total but transitory because initiates retained much of their own personality. Nkita possession was for the rest of their lives. Nkitas both calmed the sources of kindoki, the troubling power that disturbed the community, and enabled the initiates to repel that type of force.

The initiates remained in the Kimpasi enclosure for some time – houses were built for them in the rear of the compound, and they received secret instructions in occult knowledge. They were taught a new language, like Kikongo, but with subtle changes in grammar and vocabulary which made it sound strange and not always intelligible. They were also required to swear a solemn oath of secrecy – that they would not reveal their occult knowledge, or the location of the Kimpasi enclosure to anyone, and that they would defend the enclosure from all intruders. The rest of the community was warned not to approach the Kimpasi on pain of death.

The rebirth gave them a new identity; as an indication of this new identity, the initiates were said to be exempt from the taboos against incest because their old relatives were in effect no longer their own. At the end of the process they were given a beaded belt to wear around either their wrist or their waist, then sent home. Although they were no longer physically at the Kimpasi, they remained important in their communities, above the law and sometimes feared by their neighbors by virtue of the knowledge they had gained in the Kimpasi society.[16] Dona Beatriz came to share in their vision and their lore.

[16] In reconstructing Beatriz' involvement as a nganga, one starts with her own story in da Gallo, "Ultime," fol. 304. Contemporary accounts of the Kimpasi are found in d'Atri, "Giornate," pp. 408–12, 442; da Caltanisetta, "Relatione," fols. 69v–70v, 71 for physical layouts. For the religious explanation of the event, the only contemporary sources are in da Gallo, "Ultime." Useful material from somewhat earlier (1650–60), probably applicable for this period, is found in Girolamo da Montesarchio, "Viaggio al Gongo," in Calogero Piazza (ed.), La Prefettura Apostolica del Congo alla metà del XVII secolo, fols. 61v–62, and Giovanni Antonio Cavazzi da Montecuccolo, Istorica Descrizione de' tre regni Congo, Matamba ed Angola (Bologna, 1687), ¶85–6. This interpretation, including an expanded interpretation of the seventeenth-century sources, is buttressed by some modern works, using sources first of the early twentieth century, and then more recent fieldwork from the 1960s; see MacGaffey, Religion and Society in Central Africa, pp. 74–8.

3

Priests and Witches in Catholic Kongo

WHILE DONA BEATRIZ was undergoing inititation into the Kimpasi society, the Italian Capuchins established a hospice in Kibangu. They had a hospice at the village of Mbambalelo in the Marquisate of Nkusu, some forty miles east of Kibangu across the deep canyon of the Lefunde River, and only occasionally visited the Kibangu region.

It was politics and not religious devotion that brought the Capuchins to Kibangu. At the start of 1698, King Pedro received a letter from Garcia Makunga – who held the title of Marquis of Wembo for Queen Ana – that they would like to recommence the Concert of Kongo. The queen had decided not to support João any longer and was now proposing the coronation of another of her Kinlaza relatives, António de Leão Mpanzu Kivangi, who, as a son of King Álvaro VIII (who ruled briefly in 1668) was eligible for the office.

King Pedro was greatly disturbed by this development, which would put another barrier in his way to full acceptance, and decided he needed to take direct action of his own. He calculated that whatever hopes he might have would probably rest on getting Capuchin support, since he had been a witness to the effectiveness of Father Luca da Caltanisetta in the last Concert.

Therefore, King Pedro sent a big army under his new Captain General, Pedro Constantinho da Silva Kibenga, eastward into Nkusu, attacked the Capuchin hospice, and seized its goods and people, carrying them back to Kibangu. At the time, all the priests were out on mission and were therefore absent when the army arrived. They would have to come to Pedro if they wished to recover their goods.

Pedro's hopes of gaining wider recognition as king were bolstered by news that reached Kibangu in late May that King João, his rival in Bula, had died and had been succeeded by his sister Elena. It seemed likely that she could not hold formal power, and the tensions between her supporters and those leaning more toward King Pedro were likely to tear Bula apart. Moreover, the Duke of Nsundi, Álvaro Afonso de Santa Maria Maior, had taken the opportunity to attack Bula, perhaps hoping to extend his own virtually independent province's power westward along the Zaire River.

On 9 July Father Marcellino d'Atri arrived at Kibangu to negotiate the return of the goods from Nkusu and to deal with the king. King Pedro was elated that the priest had come to his mountain, but he soon learned that the Capuchins would have their own irksome demands to make, to the detriment of his prestige.

Father Marcellino wasted no time in asserting what he felt were the Church's prerequisites. Finding the quarters offered him by the king's representative who received him inadequate, Father Marcellino pointedly stayed with a secular priest from Portuguese Angola named Father Gaspar Ferreira. Father Gaspar and his assistant, Manuel Rodrigues, were in Kibangu on a commercial venture, and Father Marcellino knew him personally from a visit the Capuchin had made to Angola earlier. That evening, the two priests conferred, and Father Marcellino was particularly anxious to know how Pedro treated the clergy in his court. He asked Father Gaspar how the king had received him on his first arrival.

"I was introduced into the private audience chamber," Father Gaspar related, "and found him seated on his royal throne with a carpet underneath his feet, wearing a cloak of black Baietta, beneath an umbrella held by a nobleman. He approached me with his arms outstretched," he continued, "but never offered me a seat, and I remained standing." Secular priests received relatively little special respect at court, for as Father Luis de Mendonça, who had served at Kibangu for a number of years, would later relate, they were treated by the kings as "slaves and servants" made to stand in the royal presence and then ignored.

Father Marcellino was not pleased to hear this. "With me, he will have to do differently, if he wishes to see me tomorrow."

Pedro kept the priests waiting for a long time, finally sending them a messenger around noon to tell them he would see them "at dawn." This dawn, Father Marcellino learned, was the special dawn of misty Kibangu, defined to be whatever time of day the sun finally broke through the clouds. At last, a lesser nobleman from the court came and conducted him to the first courtyard of the palace.

Pedro's palace, like all respectable palaces in Kongo, was not a single large building but a complex of buildings arranged within three concentric circular walls, the outer one of which might be as long as two or three miles in circumference. A courtyard bounded by the residences and buildings of various royal officials and servants lay just within the entrance to each of the walls. The courtyards were aligned with the main entrance, so that one had to pass three such courtyards to reach the king's private residence and his private audience chamber housed in a separate building. One's status on the palace staff depended on where one resided, the lowest officials being in the outside circle, and the highest in the interior.

Once Father Marcellino arrived at the outer courtyard, he told his guide, "Go and tell the king that I am in the first courtyard, and will receive him here."

"This cannot be," the guide replied, recognizing that for the king to come to the priest in his outer courtyard would place the priest in a higher position than if he were received in the inner enclosure. "It is not customary."

Here Father Marcellino decided to cite history. "How is it not customary to do so!" he exclaimed. "The first time our Fathers arrived in the country, the kings customarily came out to meet the missionaries on the road." Such an action, of course, had the effect of giving the missionaries higher status than the kings themselves.

"Not only has this not been done, but he will not even come out to meet me in his own palace, after having given me a house so shabby and dirty that I had to stay with Dom Gaspar."

The Capuchins had been able to claim this high prestige for more than half a century thanks to the politics that had brought them to Kongo in the first place. These politics represented a complicated compromise between Kongo, Portugal, and the Vatican over control of the clergy in Kongo. In the days of King Afonso in the sixteenth century the king of Portugal had tried to use the Church in Kongo as a means to gain political leverage. Although in 1521 Afonso had gotten Rome to elevate his son Henrique as bishop, it had not given Kongo an independent church. Again, in 1596, when King Álvaro II had won Vatican approval for Kongo to have its own bishop at a cathedral in São Salvador, the crown of Portugal had managed to squeeze the right to nominate the bishops of the See of Congo and Angola from the Vatican.

Interminable struggles over the appointment of clergy and control of the bishops in the early seventeenth century finally led to a compromise. While Kongo would not have the right to choose the bishops who now resided in Portuguese Angola and were very reluctant to ordain any Kongolese priests, the Vatican sent missionaries to Kongo to perform the sacraments. These missionaries were to be Capuchins from Italy, a "neutral" European country that would not damage either Kongo's or Portugal's place in international relations. Since Kongo already had a parish organization, the Capuchins established separate hospices and were not allowed to perform the sacraments within five leagues of any practicing secular parish priest without the secular's permission.[1]

Father Marcellino's short invocation of this history had its effect; the guide left the priests and went inside for further instruc-

---

[1] For a survey of the background of the Church in Kongo, see John Thornton, "The Development of an African Catholic Church in the Kingdom of Kongo," *Journal of African History* 25 (1984).

tions. He returned a short time later and repeated, "It is not customary for His Majesty to come out of his palace to receive anyone," he said, "this is not the style of any king of Kongo."

"This is true enough, when speaking of his vassals or other noblemen of the kingdom," Father Marcellino replied, "but false when speaking of Religious Missionaries." In the eyes of Capuchins, and indeed the Vatican itself, *regular* clergy, monks living in apostolic style, were the highest order of humanity and should be treated with special respect even by kings. They should be treated better than secular priests, who did not always share their noble birth and vow of poverty.

"When King Dom Garcia II received us," Father Marcellino continued, reminding them of the first arrival of the Capuchins in 1645, at the height of the reign of Kongo's most powerful monarch, "he came in person to visit the Fathers in their residence, to invite them courteously to come the next day to an audience. Therefore, if King Pedro wants to see me, he would do well to do the same."

The royal ministers politely accepted this argument, but countered by saying, "The king might have received you outside his palace if you had been recently sent by Rome directly to him. But as you are a missionary who has already been in these regions for many years" (Father Marcellino had been in Kongo seven years, in fact), "knowledgeable in the practices and customs of Kongo, it is not necessary to do such a ceremony."

"I am new to you here," Father Marcellino shot back, "and the fact that I am an old missionary is hardly a reason to lose the respect and decorum I am due." To conclude the argument, the priest asserted, "To receive me in this manner is an affront, not to me personally, but to the Holy Congregation for the Propagation of the Faith, of which I am a minister."

After negotiations and more bluffing, the two reached a compromise. Father Marcellino entered the third, and inner, courtyard, where the private audience chamber was located, and Pedro met and warmly embraced him at the door.

If the king had let up on his royal dignity, however, it was because he very badly wanted to have the Capuchins on his side for rounding off the Concert of Kongo and its claims to place one of Queen Ana's loyal kinsmen on the throne. Still, he maintained dignity, for he kept his royal cap, the mpu, on his head.

He spoke briefly with the priest, inquiring about the Capuchins' recent mission to the king of Ngobela, which was beyond Kongo's eastern border near the modern city of Kinshasa, and his success in bringing that country into the fold of Christendom. The king ensured, too, that both he and the priest were seated, an important courtesy in a country where rulers sat on chairs and subjects stood, sat on carpets, or even lay facedown on the floor. The meeting concluded and Father Marcellino returned to his residence.

The next day, Pedro sent his royal secretary, Miguel de Castro, Dona Beatriz' kinsmen, to tell the priest that he would arrange to have his residence built directly in the palace in the inner enclosure, an important honor. When de Castro showed the priest his new quarters, Father Marcellino invited the king to hear Mass.

Mass was the occasion for another showdown of precedence and status. Pedro delayed attending Mass, and sent word to the priest to wait until he appeared. Finally, after a long wait, Father Marcellino felt his dignity was again abused, and threatened to leave Mass to one of the secular priests. Only then, when a crisis was reached, did Pedro arrive.

Following an old tradition, the king entered in high style. His personal guard armed and firing off muskets preceded him, followed by his musicians. A special praise-singer strolled among the musicians, extolling Pedro's greatness, liberality, and prudence, directly followed by two heralds bearing the double clapperless bells that were universally regarded as royal symbols in central Africa. Knights of the Order of Christ, wearing their special white tunics emblazoned with the red Templars' cross pierced by an arrow that symbolized the order, accompanied their sovereign. The king himself was carried on a litter with fringed sides and a seat and back cushion of crimson velvet, their fringed poles covered in snakeskin. Another official walked with him carrying a wide silk umbrella.

Leaving his litter and carriers at the door, the king entered the church, preceded by four pages, one carrying his leopard skin shield and a jeweled scimitar. A second page carried a staff covered in red velvet with a silver head adored by small bells; a third carried a silver bow with two or three golden arrows; and the fourth carried a white linen over his shoulder. The king himself was flanked by two nobles who fanned him constantly, and was prominently wearing his mpu under the open umbrella of his favorite noble right into the church.

The king advanced across the newly carpeted floor to the two chairs, the only seats in the church, that had been placed for the king and his most favored courtesan. One was of red velvet, the other blue, each with a velvet cushion for him to kneel on before it.

The priest, not outdone by this pomp, sent his interpreter, Bernardo, to tell the king that he should remove his cap upon entering the church and keep it off until he left. Furthermore, Father Marcellino was well aware of claims that the king would make, also of hoary tradition, to participate in the service. Father Marcellino knew that Kongolese kings had long-standing customs which included wearing the mpu in the service, participating in the Mass through kissing the bread plate, holding the priest's hand during the purification of the communion wine, and having their royal umbrellas open during the service. All these, which tended to place the rulers on an equal footing in ecclesiastical matters, were precisely the kind of thing that Father Marcellino hoped to eliminate.

Pedro, however, immediately sent an answer back by Dom Bernardo. "What you ask cannot be, for this is the style and custom of my ancestors."

Father Marcellino continued the service, passing the reading of the Epistle, and saw that the king still wore his mpu as he bowed. He would let pass the open umbrella and the general nature of the king's pomp, but he was going to stick on the issue of the covered head. "Tell His Majesty to take off his mpu," the priest whispered to one of the royal officials who held the Bible, but the official, not moving, replied that he could not do this. Miguel de Castro, who was nearby, joined him in explaining that this was not the custom in Kongo. Finally, Father Marcellino, losing his temper, said that if the king did not remove his mpu, he could not continue the Mass.

Still, no one would go to the king. One made a threatening gesture to his sword saying, "This is a crown sent to him by the Holy Pontiff, and therefore, he can not take it off."

Father Marcellino was not put off by this. The kings of Kongo had once received a crown from the pope, which was conferred ceremoniously on Garcia II in 1652. But that crown had been lost at Kongo's disastrous defeat by Portuguese armies at the battle of Mbwila in 1665.

"This is a cap and not a crown," he said, "if he does not take it off, he will be a heretic, a Jew, and not a Catholic Christian if he does not submit and disobeys by keeping his head covered." As to the threatening gestures he had seen, Father Marcellino noted that he was prepared to give his life for ecclesiastical liberty. Finally, his friend Father Gaspar came to the priest on his knees, begging him to continue the Mass. Father Marcellino was adamant; at last, when the secular priest went on his knees to appeal to the king, the monarch took off his mpu.

After the Mass, King Pedro commended de Castro and his other officials for standing up for him against the priest. It would be an effort to maintain relations with the Capuchins, but Pedro needed to salvage as much of his royal prestige as he could.

Father Marcellino was running a risk, even knowing that he was needed by the king. The Capuchins had virtually no worldly power in Kongo. They could not count on any effective support from the secular world. After being defeated by Soyo in 1670, even the Portuguese of Angola were uninterested in taking on Kongo again.

The Capuchins owned no land and had only a handful of slaves (technically freedmen known as nlekes, or "children") around their hospices who grew them some food, cared for them, and helped transport their goods for them when they traveled. In this situation Pedro could display his superior temporal power to Father Marcellino subtly over the next few days by sending him little food – of poor quality – and infrequently reminding him of an ancient Kongolese custom of pressuring the Church, known as "local excommunication." As a foil to ecclesiastical excommunication, kings used their power to ensure that priests would receive no wood, water, or food from royal subjects until they resolved their disputes, and disputes of precedence between church and state were long-standing in Kongo.

Pedro had not forced the missionaries to come to Kibangu to argue about precedent, but to assist his larger schemes. In an audience on 15 July, Pedro paid the priest great respect, seating him on the right hand of this throne before all his officials and counselors, a stark and significant contrast to the way Father Luis, the secular, was routinely treated. Then, dismissing all but a handful of his closest advisors, he told the priest forthrightly that he was anxious to have Capuchins at Kibangu permanently. He quoted Jesus' words on the cross repeatedly: "My Father, why have you forsaken me?" Finally, he threw himself at the priest's feet, begging him not to abandon him. If Kibangu seemed remote to the priest, Pedro told him he would soon be transferring his capital to São Salvador. In fact, he noted, he had not ordered the walls of his palace rebuilt the past Holy Saturday, when by custom every year a great host of slaves and workers rebuilt them in a single night. Soon they would fall down, since he fully intended to abandon his palace for São Salvador.

Royal palaces in Kongo were built primarily of wood, thatch, and tough grasses, which deteriorated quickly in the tropical climate, especially in Kibangu's local climate with its misty season that promoted all sorts of growth. To meet the health and hygiene challenges of maintaining wood and grass structures in such a climate, Kongolese simply abandoned or rebuilt their structures often. It meant that houses, palaces, and even whole villages or towns were impermanent and could be abandoned often. Wealth was displayed through furnishings rather than through buildings.

While impressed with King Pedro's desires, the priest said nothing definite, for he was not in a position to make decisions himself about the location of a hospice or where he should or could go.

On 25 July, Saint James' Day, Pedro made a concrete step toward his promise of being king in São Salvador. At the annual festival, he announced with great pomp that he planned to reoccupy the capital permanently, to follow up his coronation of 1696 and make good his claim to be king of all Kongo. Now that João's forces were likely to be in disarray if the rumors of his death were borne out, the occupation could proceed. He ordered people living in the valley of the Mufulenge River, which flowed northward from Kibangu toward Bula and Nsundi, to choose colonists and displace themselves toward São Salvador. The move was like a military expedition and created by the same legal apparatus. Occupation of the capital was not likely to go unchallenged from the north, and only by having a well-emplaced and powerful army already at the city could Pedro hope to make São Salvador his real capital.

At the same time, he sent an army under Pedro Constantinho da Silva Kibenga northward to receive the vassalage of some seven or eight nobles from Bula who had taken this opportunity to pay homage to Pedro as their new king. Kibenga had his own very large quarter in Kibangu, with relatives and an army that was personally loyal to him. His presence on the mountain was problematic, although King Pedro hoped to use his forces and his services as much as possible.

Father Marcellino had additional audiences with Pedro, making further demands: first, on his own dignity; second, that the king pay certain Luanda merchants who had lent him money or goods on credit and had been waiting five or six years for repayment; and finally, that Pedro allow the head of Manuel I, which had decorated the main square of Kibangu for some five years, to be given a proper Christian burial.

In exchange, Pedro demanded firmly that the Capuchins remain with him, and that his decision to seize the hospice in Nkusu had been prompted by the fact that he, as king, had a legal right to demand they reside at his court. To buttress his case, Pedro had Miguel de Castro pull an important document from his royal archives. This was a papal bull, *Celsorum Decorum*, from Innocent XI addressed to King Garcia III, dated 3 January

1677.[2] Garcia III was the real founder of the settlement of Kibangu, having moved there during the confused period of civil war that followed the death of King António I at the battle of Mbwila in 1665. Several kings presented themselves during that period, and several had been put down. In 1668, Garcia, thwarted at São Salvador, withdrew to the security of Mount Kibangu and relative obscurity while others battled furiously over the city for the next ten years. But the Church recognized Garcia and sought strongly to have him recognized by the other pretenders.[3] The bull of 1677 was part of the strongest case Pedro had for papal recognition of him and his line as the rulers of Kongo. As it also contained language ordering the Capuchins remain with the king, it was a strong precedent for his forcing them to come to him.

Father Marcellino countered by arguing that the constant wars of the period had forced the Capuchins to abandon the capital and seek safety and security wherever they could. It was for this reason, he argued, that they had moved to Nkusu, which was also on a mountain and secure. But the force of Pedro's argument and the strength of the papal bull was such that Father Marcellino had to admit the king's claim. He promised to write about it to the prefect of the Capuchin mission, Father Francesco da Pavia, in Luanda.

Over the next few days, more mundane business was settled. Father Marcellino absolved Pedro's brother, Álvaro X, of an excommunication that had been placed on him earlier and technically could have required the priest to disinter the former king from holy ground. He also arranged to bury, at last, that symbol of betrayal, the severed head of Manuel I. The priest absolved Pedro Kibenga of an earlier excommunication as a preliminary to discussing the goods and people from the hospice of Nkusu. Ne-

---

[2] Printed in Paiva Manso, *História*, p. 263.

[3] António de Oliveira de Cadornega, *História Geral das guerras angolanas (1680–81)*, ed. José Matias Delgado and Mathias da Cunha, 3 vols. (Lisbon, 1940 [reprinted 1972]), 2:416–20; Garcia was also the recipient of an earlier bull, *Magno quamnis*, 11 March 1673, printed in Brásio, *Monumenta*, 13:215–16.

gotiations finally led to a complicated restoration of the property, and on 22 August, Father Marcellino left, bound for Nkusu.

As the priest left, King Pedro summed up the exchange by first commending his own life and that of his people to the Church. Then, he said, "God and Father Saint Francis require me to be the means by which the cathedral of São Salvador is restored, since I am disposed to do so. Since God has given me the good fortune to undertake this enterprise, I ask you to return quickly to encourage my people and implore Divine help in bringing about such a task in His service with confessions, processions, and penances."[4]

News of the Capuchin arrival, and the intricate deliberations of the king and the priest, soon found its way throughout all of King Pedro's domains. Dona Beatriz undoubtedly had a good account because her kinsman Miguel de Castro was in the king's inner circle and had been present at all the deliberations. But Dona Beatriz was much more attuned to the religious than the political consequences of their visit.

For Dona Beatriz the arrival of Capuchins in Kibangu had other implications than it had for King Pedro. Because she was working as an nganga, the priests represented a serious challenge to her and all other ngangas who were not themselves ordained priests. In his discussions with King Pedro concerning the removal of excommunications from the late King Álvaro so he could be buried in hallowed ground, Father Marcellino had proposed that "witches and priests of idols" had been responsible for misfortunes including these deaths. He proposed that the king announce this, and expose these wrongdoers on the public plaza to receive "the fury of the people" and the penalty of death.

His language could scarcely be lost on the ngangas against whom it was directed, including Dona Beatriz. It represented the theological side of the political negotiations between priest and king. In fact, the Capuchins simply charged that all ngangas,

---

[4] On d'Atri's disputes with Pedro and the politics of the time, see d'Atri, "Giornate," pp. 351–86. A description of his arrival in church and older customs of the kings is found at pp. 515–18, but it relates to another incident in 1701.

whatever their practice, if not ordained by the Church, were ndokis, those who worked evil by supernatural means. They called them *fattucieri* in Italian, that is, "witches," and in so doing charged that all their work was selfish and greedy and hence the bad sort of kindoki.

Their arguments on this point were rooted in European and not Kongolese theology, and for this reason were never wholly accepted by most Kongolese. In the Kongolese view, various people might possess kindoki and use it for either good or evil purposes. It was the purposes and intentions of those using the power that counted, not the simple possession of the power or the nature of the beings in the Other World who were consulted and carried out the work of kindoki.

But priests argued otherwise. They contended that alth ough God, Jesus, or the Saints could help those who appealed to them, they would only do so for those who made their appeal through methods approved by the Church and conducted by ordained priests. All other attempts to elicit information and support from the Other World, even if done for the best of reasons, and addressed to Jesus, the saints, or the Virgin, would not be heard by those Christian entities, but instead would be intercepted by the Devil. The Devil might allow the work to be carried out, even if it were beneficial, but for his glory. This, Capuchins argued, was witchcraft, and it could be carried out unwittingly, even if one did not invoke the Devil. Intentions were of no significance. Only the procedure counted.

Since their first arrival in 1645, the Capuchins had made the suppression of what they considered witchcraft their special duty, and they pursued it with a zeal that other religious groups did not. Jesuits, who had been in Kongo since 1619, devoted little attention to witchcraft, although they did not tolerate it and in theory shared the views of the Capuchins. The secular priests were even less inclined to seek out witches, although they might become involved in the workings of kindoki in their daily lives. Dona Beatriz knew that these theoretical arguments would soon come to action, and she would not be wrong.

Toward the end of 1698, news reached Nkusu that the prefect

A Capuchin destroys a "Witchcraft House." (From "Missione in Practica" ca. 1750)

had authorized Capuchins to stay with the king, and by the start of 1699, Fathers Marcellino and Salvatore da Lago Negro came to Kibangu to open a hospice. While their initial program called for clarifying with King Pedro their status and their relations with the monarchy, they also wasted no time in attacking what they considered local witchcraft.

On 24 March 1699, some students in the school at Kibangu told Father Marcellino about a Kimpasi society initiation lodge located a few miles from the new hospice, and the priest went along with them to investigate. Taking with him some students and Dom Miguel, the local authority, Father Marcellino snuck up on the enclosure, sending two small boys first to spy the place out. They reported that the area seemed empty, but that some of the younger initiates were playing outside the walls.

The priest stormed into the enclosure and seized the various "instruments" of their worship, then ordered the buildings set on fire. Standing amid the flames, and grasping his crucifix, Father

Marcellino quoted Psalm 68: "God shall arise; His enemies shall be scattered; those that hate him shall flee before his face."

The smoke and flames attracted the initiates who were away from the camp, and they returned, armed, to defend it. The society leader came rushing at the priest, both hands grasping a sword high in the air. Dom Miguel, at the head of his people, rescued the priest, parrying the blow with his own staff of office. Then he ordered the people to disperse, and they obeyed. The priest returned to the hospice bearing the spoils of his work. He entered the chapel and there gave thanks for being delivered from the Devil, for that is precisely how he viewed the Kimpasi and its initiates – devils incarnate, in the most literal way.

The very next day he located a second Kimpasi camp, and found that everyone but the nganga-in-charge, an elderly woman, had fled. Again he seized the goods of the Kimpasi camp, including their cross and kitekes and various other ingredients, had the trees uprooted, and burned all the houses. All the goods were placed together in the chapel for safekeeping, for Father Marcellino decided that he would wait until another companion, Father Luca da Caltanisetta, returned from a mission trip to destroy them.

The next Sunday, the priest preached a fiery sermon on the subject. Declaring that the people had ceased to worship the True God, he turned the crucifix and the images of the two principal saints venerated in Kongo, Saint Anthony of Padua and Saint Francis, on the sides of the altar backward. He then declared all the initiates of the Kimpasi society excommunicated, and especially the leader.

In Kikongo, the word for excommunication was *kumloko*, a word meaning a powerful curse derived from *loka*, the same root that kindoki and ndoki were. Its use told Kongolese that Capuchins possessed kindoki themselves and could locate others who also had it, or use their contact with the Other World to curse and harm others. The Capuchins claimed, in other words, to have the power to name and locate ndokis, and to use that power to curse them effectively.

As it happened, the Kimpasi leader was blinded, "deprived of his corporal vision," Father Marcellino wrote later, "as he had already been deprived of the spiritual vision."[5] Although this type of preaching was a long-standing part of the Capuchin program in Kongo, it was new to Kibangu itself at this point. The question of kindoki was immediately raised for all by the attack on the Kimpasi society, and the Capuchins were putting forth the idea that the Kimpasi society was in fact an organization of ndokis.

Such a view, while a radical one, could be accepted in Kongo, though not by everyone. Certainly those who had been initiated knew that they had not been working kindoki for selfish or greedy ends, and a good many others must have agreed that the priest was simply wrong to imagine that this, or perhaps any other Kimpasi society, was only a means of concentrating selfish kindoki for their own evil purposes. But the possibility existed, and, as all knew, banditry, war, and betrayal had made these evil times.

In any case, it was not long after the Capuchins arrived in Kibangu that Dona Beatriz decided to stop her practice as nganga marinda. She concluded that the practice was too close to evil kindoki, and decided to devote herself more fully to private life, perhaps taking their teaching and her own experience to heart.[6] It was not a rejection of the concepts of kindoki that she turned from, for that remained central to her life and teaching. Rather, she rejected the local and immediate practices of the ngangas of her area, which she believed must have become corrupted.

If Capuchin preaching had influenced Dona Beatriz to renounce the Kimpasi society and her own calling as nganga marinda, however, she harbored suspicions about the priests as well as about other ngangas. Her doubts were heightened by Capuchin behavior in the political and personal realm. Their widely accepted claim to be able to discern and combat ndokis through their own powers of kindoki could be valid, but like all such claims,

---

[5] D'Atri, "Giornate," pp. 408–12.
[6] Da Lucca, "Relatione Annua del 1706," fol. 267.

Kongolese believed it had to be tested against motivation. If the claim for respect was perceived simply as a claim for self-aggrandizement, then there were grounds for suspicion that the priests were misusing their power for their own goals.

That the priests were accused of being ndokis already by some people suggested that they were failing the test. Father Luca da Caltanisetta, who joined the group in Kibangu in 1699, was himself accused that same April of poisoning, through kindoki, the ruler of Songi dia Zombo, a district in the Duchy of Mbata, and was driven away by the people who scorned him.

For King Pedro, however, the religious side of his situation was less important than the political strength the missionaries gave him. With Capuchin priests in his territory, he was in a good position to outmaneuver Queen Ana and her kinsmen. Indeed, his arguments had been sufficiently impressive that he had won Capuchin opinion over to his side.

Father Luca, in particular, had been greatly disappointed with Queen Ana's behavior during the 1696 Concert, and was now leaning toward Pedro as a better candidate for king. In January 1699, Marquis Miguel of Nkusu brought him news that Queen Ana's favorite cousin, Pedro Valle das Lagimas, had stormed the city of Mbanza Mbamba and killed Pedro Mpanzu a Mvemba, who had held the duchy in the queen's name but was never very loyal. This time Valle das Lagrimas triumphantly carried the former duke's head to Nkondo, and was installed himself as duke by the queen. On hearing this news, Father Luca remarked sadly to Marquis Miguel, "This is the miserable and deplorable condition of the lords of Kongo, that they all die violently!" To which Miguel replied, "Death is the same for everyone, whether in bed or by the sword." This resignation to the state of constant violence troubled the priest greatly, for he doubted that peace could come from such sentiments.

Encouraged by the support of the Capuchins, King Pedro moved to strengthen his position with the major contenders, beginning with Pedro Kibenga, whose followers were serving in his army. He declared Kibenga to be prince, a possible successor to him.

This action infuriated Queen Ana, particularly since Kibenga's troops raided her lands just across the Mbidizi so often that there was a virtual state of siege of the villages in the region. Father Marcellino, passing through the region with a group of his nlekes, the freed slaves who carried his goods, on his way from Nkusu to Nkondo to visit the queen in November 1699, came upon one of her villages just at sunset. Surprised by the unexpected arrival of a large number of men, the villagers fled in great haste, leaping walls to get out of the village fast. They reassembled, following a preconceived plan, in the fields outside, bearing arms and prepared to fight. The priest shouted out to them that his was a priest's entourage and not the soldiers of Kibenga. After the district leader had sent an emissary to determine the truth of the assertion, the people returned.[7]

While Queen Ana's border subjects were suffering under this insecurity, the queen herself, although still officially angry with King Pedro, was more inclined to compromise. Having found few takers, the queen quietly abandoned her plan to have Álvaro accepted as king.

The main negotiator in the new peace initiative was to be the Capuchin prefect, Father Francesco da Pavia, who arrived in Kibangu on 29 March 1700. He had already had discussions with the Prince of Soyo in hopes that he would recognize Pedro IV. He made official the movement of the Capuchin hospice from Nkusu to Kibangu, despite the strong objections and reservations of Father Luca, who was suspicious of reconciliations of this sort. "I tried to dissuade him from this undertaking," Father Luca wrote in his diary, "as this was not a propitious occasion, but he, confiding in God, wanted to press on, not judging that the black lords, while discussing peace were organizing their war machines for abominable treachery."[8]

On 5 June, Father Francesco went to the separate encampment of Pedro Kibenga below the mountain near the border between Kibangu's territory and those belonging to the queen, in order to begin the process of reconciliation with Queen Ana. Again he met

---

[7] D'Atri, "Giornate," p. 441.   [8] Da Caltanisetta, "Relazione," fol. 90v.

with success, for the queen and Kibenga agreed to forget their differences.

So it came to be that Queen Ana, Pedro Kibenga, and King Pedro IV came together in mid-June at Lusunzi's sacred stone of Kibangu to swear an oath of nonaggression and peace among themselves, and to recognize Pedro IV as their king. Queen Ana, for her part, swore on behalf of herself. Duke Pedro Valle das Lagrimas who held Mbamba for her, Álvaro who held Mpemba on her behalf and had once been her candidate for king, and António, her Marquis of Wembo, as well as others of her followers and relatives whose residences were too far away to be brought to Kibangu, swore through ambassadors.

The sacred stone was a good place to make such a reconciliation: all their lands lay in territory drained by the Mbidizi River, which originated at the stone, and Lusunzi, like all such deities in Kongo, was essentially devoted to harmony and peace. Before the crowd the prefect made a speech devoted to peace and reconciliation. On behalf of the king, Miguel de Castro made a historical speech appropriate to the occasion.

Historical speeches on Saint James' Day in Kibangu, as elsewhere, focused on the all powerful rights of kings over their subjects: the story of Ne Lukeni and her son Ntinu Lukeni stressed these rights. But Pedro IV's newly restored Kongo was not such a state – obedience was strictly nominal, and the king entertained no fond thoughts of controlling appointments of officials to lands held by Queen Ana. Consequently, de Castro's speech focused on a different sort of founder.

"The Kingdom of Kongo," he began, "was founded long ago by a wise and skillful blacksmith who settled differences among the people." By focusing on the original nature of Kongo as a community of consenting powers, ruled through a great mediator, the speech could allow Pedro to play a role like that of this mythical founder. Throughout central Africa, mythical blacksmiths were regarded as representing a principle of peace and reconciliation, and even as representing "feminine" characteristics of government, possibly because the act of creating steel from earth was likened to childbearing.

In continuing the speech, de Castro evoked the memory of the great sixteenth-century monarch widely regarded as the founder of the Church in Kongo, Afonso I. As de Castro told it, Afonso had two children, the respective founders of the Kimpanzu and Kinlaza kandas, and these two had contended over the throne – a position which was not precisely historically correct, but which nicely simplified the affairs for the present occasion. With the battle of Mbwila, he continued, the latent conflict had broken out into open warfare, which was now being laid to rest.[9]

King Pedro's spokesman was careful to avoid placing any order in precedence to the Kimpanzu and Kinlaza, and since the Agua Rosadas were descended from both great kandas, he could pose as the ideal mediator between the factions. Certainly Father Francesco was more than willing to accept this compromise, and, to further the cause of peace and the refoundation of the country, proposed that he persuade the pope to bless a new crown for Pedro.

Kongo's old papal crown, presented in 1652 to Garcia II, had been lost at Mbwila when Kongo's king António's head, crown attached, had been carried to Luanda for display and then sent on to Lisbon. Efforts to retrieve it had failed, and at this juncture a new crown, given in the spirit of reconciliation rather than the raw power that Garcia exercised, seemed singularly appropriate.

From this high point, the prefect then set out for Bula to make the final gesture and win the recognition of whoever ruled there. Alas, the situation in Bula turned out to be a disappointment. King João, although rumored to be dead for nearly a year, turned out to be alive. He had suffered a serious illness, perhaps a stroke, which had kept him out of sight and fed rumors, even in his own court, that he had died. His sister Elena had run the country as

[9] On Francesco da Pavia's mission, see d'Atri, "Giornate," pp. 463–4; da Caltanisetta, "Relatione," fols. 90v–91. The speech is recorded as a historical summary in Francesco da Pavia's report to the Propaganda Fide, undated, but filed after his return to Luanda, Archivio "De Propaganda Fide," Scritture riferite nelli Congressi, Congo, vol. 1, fols. 141–42, though the sources do not directly identify de Castro as the speaker, he seems a likely choice.

a regent on behalf of her brother, but she had not been accepted and there was major dissention among the nobles of the country.

Father Francesco found that while Elena could bring her brother out in public to demonstrate that he was alive, he was paralyzed and completely unable to speak. The prospect of recognizing Pedro as king did not appeal at all to Elena or her supporters, who politely but firmly rejected the idea. Their opponents, on the other hand, who had been openly negotiating with Pedro for nearly a year, were well prepared to accept King Pedro's claim and abandon their own ineffective ruler.

The prefect quickly realized both that Bula was not going to recognize Pedro as king and that they were not in a good position to resist him either. It was perhaps still a good time for peace, so he pressed Elena to make peace with Soyo, as Father Giuseppe Merolla had tried to do a decade earlier. Perhaps, since Soyo was favorably disposed to the Concert of Kongo, he could bring in Bula through its reconciliation with Soyo.

The differences between the two went back to 1683, when João's elder bother, Pedro III, had been treacherously killed with Soyo's complicity. Soyo had offered to broker a peace between the Kinlaza King Pedro and his Kimpanzu rival Manuel de Nóbrega, whose brother King Daniel I had been killed by Pedro when he sacked São Salvador in 1678. De Nóbrega had taken refuge in Soyo's southern province of Luvota and was intent on revenge. The Prince of Soyo, a long-standing Kimpanzu partisan, negotiated a truce which was to be sealed by a wedding exchange. But when Pedro came with his wedding train to a pre-arranged meeting place, he found the train from Soyo contained de Nóbrega dressed as a woman pretending to be his new bride. The disguised bride produced a pistol and shot Pedro to death.

João's first official act as prince under the regency of his mother, Potencia, was to attack Soyo and annex its province of Kiova kia Nza, which lay south of the Zaire River along their common border. João had refused to return the province, which was rich in iron ore and a major source of the best steel in the country, to Soyo in the proposed reconciliation of 1688, as he also refused when Father Luca approached him about it in 1696. The prefect, for all his goodwill, could not achieve any of his goals and, reluctantly leaving this end untied, set out for the Inkisi valley.

Unfortunately, the situation in the Inkisi turned out to be just as intractable. There was an ongoing war between Nsundi and Mpangu, as the great northern province of Nsundi pushed its claims southward, a war still remembered in tradition in the twentieth century.[10] When Father Francesco sought to visit the Marquis of Mpangu, he was refused solely on the grounds that he had first visited Nsundi, whose duke supported a rival candidate for Marquis of Mpangu. Likewise, Mbata was still torn between two rival dukes, and since one of them was a partisan of King Pedro, he could not proceed any further on that front.

Although Father Francesco had not brought about a real peace and the recognition of Pedro IV, he had at least reconciled Queen Ana, Pedro IV, and Pedro Kibenga, an achievement in itself – at least if Father Luca's deep reservations about the reality of any such negotiated peace were false.[11]

Before the prefect left on his diplomatic mission, he instructed Fathers Luca and Marcellino to establish the Capuchin hospice at Kibangu. Father Luca visited with King Pedro to establish the guidelines, while Father Marcellino left to go to Prince Pedro Kibenga's fortified camp to keep him involved in the process. The prince put on a good show for the priest – he came to greet him outside of his camp, accompanied by a group of boys singing the "Hail Mary" and "Salve Regina" in Kikongo. He embraced the priest and accompanied him into his camp. The next day, dressed stunningly in a spring overcoat with laced crimson boots, he performed a nsanga for the priest, bearing a crucifix in his left hand and a saber in his right. His subjects filled the air with gunpowder smoke, while a dozen young girls fanned the smoke away from the priest with white linen fans. That evening, fine points of the

---

[10] Cuvelier, Nkutama, pp. 5–6, attributes the war to a duke of Nsundi known as Kiangala. Contemporary documents cite only the duke's Christian name, Álvaro Afonso de Santa Maria Maior.

[11] Da Caltanisetta, "Relatione," fol. 103.

peace agreements were worked out, and the priest returned to the king's town.

On 15 July, the Capuchins presented King Pedro with a lengthy document of eighteen points, outlining the rights and procedures for maintaining a permanent establishment of Capuchins at Kibangu. It specified clearly that the Capuchins were to be protected, as were their servants, and never to be harassed for any reason. They were free from all taxation, and could travel anywhere without interference.

The dignity of the Church was to be maintained by specified rules governing the king's behavior in church. He was to appear at a seemly hour for Mass, not midday, and was to remove his cap in the church and make no special show upon his arrival. The king was allowed to kiss the Bible in the lesson, and at the same time, thanks to possession of the title "Defender of the Faith" (a title conferred on Afonso I in the sixteenth century), he could stand during the reading with a drawn sword in his right hand and a lighted candle in the left.

The king was also enjoined to "search out the magicians, to punish all those who have recourse to them, seek to capture and sell them" as slaves, giving the proceeds of the sale to the Church. Thus, the Capuchins were to receive material and physical support from the king in their project to suppress all the ngangas of the kingdom save those ordained by the Church.

Finally, the king was to preserve the peace. He was to do all in his power to keep the roads safe from thieves and bandits, and, moreover, he was to submit every military project to the priests. They, in turn, were to determine that his ventures were "just wars" and only then could he prosecute them.[12] That being done, the Capuchins moved to Kibangu, confident that they would soon be in control of all religious affairs. But the optimism was ill-founded, as they were soon to discover.

[12] D'Atri, "Giornate," pp. 464–8.

4

The Crisis in Faith and Force

_____

WHILE THE GREAT POWERS of Kongo were seeking reconciliation, Dona Beatriz was getting married. Women in Kongo married young, probably almost as soon as they were likely to bear children. Since Dona Beatriz had ceased her life as a nganga, at least for the time being, her relatives wanted to have her married. Like aristocrats everywhere, Dona Beatriz would have little control over her marriage, which was a matter for the senior men of her kanda to decide for her. It did not mean that she was completely unable to influence the events, if she had ideas of her own, but girls of her age rarely had made any choices.

She had grown tall and was physically attractive, and for this reason, along with her station in life, her elders were soon beset with suggested suitors. Eventually a likely young man appeared, bearing gifts and asking for her hand. The men clustered together, bargaining hotly over the _mbongo za longo_, the "bride wealth." Depending on how one looks at it, bride wealth was either a compensation to her family for losing her services, or it was a means to create a financial reason for her family to support her marriage. In any case, bride wealth was paid by the kanda of the husband to that of the wife. Should the marriage fail, the bride wealth would have to be returned. This was nicely expressed in the Kikongo word for marriage, _sompa_, which also means "to borrow" and reflects the idea that the man was only borrowing the woman from her family.

Bride wealth was typically paid in money, although the amount

An elite Christian marriage. (From "Missione in Practica" ca. 1750)

could be considerably augmented by other gifts and expenses that
were not strictly a part of the bride wealth. For someone of Dona
Beatriz' station, her family might expect 500 to 600 *libongos* (cloth
pieces that served as money), which might buy several slaves at
current prices, and which was many times the bride wealth of a
commoner. Once the negotiations were complete, Dona Beatriz
was then prepared for marriage.

Dona Beatriz had to go for a time into a small house only for
her, where she was instructed in the duties of a married woman
by elder women, and underwent a number of exercises. Her body
was dyed red with *takula*, a red-dye wood imported from the
forests of the north, across the Zaire River. Red was the color of
transition from one state to another, and so takula was liberally
used in all sorts of symbolic ways to indicate this.

She was required to have a fire lighted in the house at all times
and never to throw anything out, including all the food wastes,
which remained there with her for the whole period. During this
period she left only occasionally to visit her home and see her
father or uncle. They would embrace her and bounce her on their

knees like a little child as if saying goodbye and missing her child-hood.

Finally, her husband-to-be sent her some roasted chicken, some takula, and a needle, all symbols of women and women's duties, to indicate that her time of confinement was over. At the same time, another male relative, preferably a brother, sent her some more takula and a piece of cloth, which she would wrap around her loins in order to be strong and have many children. Then she emerged to a large and joyous wedding feast, attended by many friends and relatives. In the course of the festivities, she gave some of her takula to her husband and parents to rub on their bodies, and took the remainder and left it at an intersection of two roads, another symbol of transition.

At this point, Dona Beatriz was officially married. But the marriage could be easily broken if the two people, formerly more or less strangers to each other, found that they could not live peace-fully together. Should they find that they could maintain a tran-quil household after a few years, they would go to a priest and take on a Christian marriage, which was viewed as a final seal of the relatively long process of marriage. Because of this complex-ity, the number of Christian marriages in Kongo performed each year were fewer than they would be in Europe, since Christian marriages were unbreakable.[1]

Dona Beatriz was not able to adjust to married life. Her time as an nganga had made her accustomed to freedom of action and independence. As a married woman she had to pay a deference to her husband that was difficult for someone with the spiritual gifts that she possessed. Her first marriage ended quickly, to be followed by a second one that also did not survive the initial

---

[1] On marriage, I have followed da Lucca, "Lettera Annua," pp. 182–5; and Biblioteca Nacional de Madrid, MS 3165, da Pavia, "Viaggio," fols. 83–83v. These two descriptions, though very detailed, actually apply to Soyo at this time. For a more "eastern" perspective, but for modern times and ideals, I have used João Makondekwa (with editorial remarks and English translation by Hazel Carter), "Ntsaasuka yenndongoka zamwisi-koongo" (Raising and Upbringing of a Kongolese), African Studies Program, Madison, Wis., 1968 (written by a native of Quibocolo in the former Marquisate of Nkusu), pp. 187–219.

phase of living together. In each case, she was returned to her parents for a refund of the bride wealth, and remained at home.

Dona Beatriz had decided she could not remain as a traditional nganga, but neither could she adjust to the life of a married woman and merge back to normal society. Although she needed a spiritual future, she was not sure exactly what it might be. Meanwhile, events around her gradually forced her to accept a new social and spiritual role.

While Dona Beatriz was grappling with marriage, King Pedro was seeking to consolidate the gains that he had from the Concert of Kongo of June 1700. Since the Concert had brought him peace on the south, and at least a neutralization of João on the north, he continued his moderate expansion eastward. There Pedro wanted to bring the Duchy of Mbata under his authority, and was thus supporting Miguel Ngoma Mpasi against his rival, Miguel Kilau. In September, King Pedro dispatched his *mwene lumbu* or majordomo, the head of his administration, Manuel da Cruz Barbosa, to provide additional military support to Ngoma Mpasi. Kibangu's candidate for duke decided to relocate the capital to a place nearer his supporters in the small district of Kiova, formerly a wilderness. By cutting down trees in the midst of a forest and then creating a living stockade, he established a much more secure mbanza, or capital, than the previous one, which he had burned to keep it from the hands of his rivals.

Peace between Pedro Kibenga and Queen Ana, or recognition of King Pedro, then, did not bring peace, even to the environs of Kibangu. But while Dona Beatriz may have been aware of the problems coming from the eastern war, it was on the spiritual front that matters were more immediately alarming. Father Marcellino, who had been permanently stationed in Kibangu for the Capuchins, was carrying his war on witchcraft to new and startling extremes, when he declared in December that the sacred stone of Lusunzi was an object of witchcraft.

On 15 December, Father Marcellino listened carefully to reports concerning local worship at the sacred stone, the giving of offerings, and the caretaker role of religious leaders not recognized by the Church. Concluding that the reverence people had for the stone was a form of idolatry, and hence witchcraft, he resolved to seize it and destroy it.

The stone was not something readily identified with evil kindoki by most Kongolese, and many people were concerned about the priest's obvious interest and increasingly transparent intentions with regard to it. They were particularly puzzled by his emerging views because, only a few months earlier, the prefect, Father Francesco himself, had convened the solemnization of the Concert of Kongo at the stone, and had had the participants swear an oath to keep the peace there. Lusunzi as the guardian of Kibangu was a deity of peace and harmony, highly appropriate for a peace treaty, scarcely one associated with the selfish and greedy side of kindoki.

The Church, moreover, had its own history with sacred stones, which was well known and even celebrated going back to its very foundations. In 1491, when João I Nzinga a Nkuwu, Kongo's first Christian king, was initially baptized, one of his nobles had found, miraculously it seemed, a perfectly formed cross-shaped stone on the banks of a river near the capital. When the stone was displayed to the king and the Portuguese missionaries who accompanied him, it was declared a "sign and revelation" by the priests and, indeed, was one of the most important revelations that confirmed for King João the validity of Christianity. A church was built to house the stone, where it became a central relic for centuries afterward. Although that stone had been lost when São Salvador was destroyed, it was clearly in the same category of sacred objects as Lusunzi's stone.

Father Marcellino, however, did not see the symmetry of the two stones, and viewed this one as simply a trick of the Devil, since its power and symbolism lay outside church approval. He finally persuaded some of his personal servants to take him to the stone. When they arrived, the two servants parted the thick covering of grass that obscured it, but showed great reluctance to touch it "as it if were some poisonous thing." The priest rebuked them. "Do you believe in this stone like the others?" They reached down and picked it up, but then announced that it was not the stone they were looking for.

The priest was not fooled for long, and on 16 December returned and seized the stone. But its seizure was not easy. Many people heard of it and demanded the stone's return. "The country will be ruined," they said, fearing the wrath of the ancient guardian of the land, "and the king will be very upset." But Father Marcellino would not be threatened or cowed: "Neither you nor the king will make me return the stone." He took it and placed it in the hospice, waiting for an opportune occasion to denounce it formally.

Indeed, the kitome who was in charge of ministering the religious ceremonies around the stone went promptly to King Pedro, complaining that the country would be ruined if deprived of Lusunzi's protection.

The next day, Dom Bernardo, the king's principal judge, came to demand the return of the stone. It had been taken, he said, out of territory that was assigned to Dona Isabella, the king's sister, for her income, and was thus under royal protection. When the priest refused to accept this legal argument, Dom Bernardo began to demand the stone stridently, finally almost pleading for it. The king, he said, "has punished me for not guarding the stone properly by taking all my people and selling them, and is also even threatening my life." In fact, his life was spared, but he was fined a slave and a hundred lengths of cloth.

Undeterred, the priests found an opportunity to deal with the stone on Epiphany 1701. Father Luca and the secular Father Luis took blacksmiths' hammers and beat on the stone, three strokes in honor of the Holy Trinity, proclaiming that the sparks that flew from it were symbols of the fires of Hell that the stone symbolized. Placing the stone at the church door, Father Luca then ordered everyone, of whatever status or condition, to kick it as they passed. They obeyed, but with evident anger and concern.

The uproar created by the seizure of Lusunzi's stone had barely subsided when Father Marcellino created another one, this time on the issue of precedence. Any nganga's claim to be working kindoki against ndokis and for the good of the country was tested against his or her ambition and personal conduct. The Capuchins were able to maintain their claims to exercise positive spiritual power and accuse other ngangas of being ndokis largely because they lived lives of personal poverty and lack of concern for the material world. This personal disregard of the power of the world lent credence to their claim to respect for the Church, but it also placed them under constant scrutiny to see if the respect and power were used for personal aggrandizement.

While the debate over the stone went on, Father Marcellino received an Aragonese named Juan de Rosa, who came to Kibangu from Mbwela, a state that was south of Kongo and partially in the orbit of Portuguese Angola. De Rosa had been close to the Capuchins in Mbwela and had served the Church in a variety of capacities as a layperson. Father Marcellino decided to take him into Capuchin service and introduce him at court. But the priest considered court etiquette degrading not just for priests but for Europeans, and told de Rosa as they entered the royal audience chamber that "in no way should you follow, as is their usual custom, the practice of covering your face and eyes with dust, as you are white and not black, and moreover are in my company."

Then, when the two entered King Pedro's throne room, he told the king that de Rosa would enter doing the "ceremonies that are customary among the whites of similar ranks," and specifically that he would admit no placing of dirt on the face and eyes, claiming for all whites the same privileges of special greetings that the priests had.

Pedro would have none of it. "This cannot be," he fired back, "if he is to remain in my kingdom, he must follow its customs." A two-hour debate followed, in which Father Marcellino threatened to leave the country without a priest if he did not get his way. Pedro was furious but would not back down, even though he did not want to lose his priest. A two-day standoff ensued.

Inevitably, the matter of precedent took on a connection to the issue of kindoki. Stories soon began to circulate that de Rosa was "a refined witch and had killed his mother by magic" and had fled Europe for Angola. Even in Angola, the rumors went, he had killed the ruler of Mbwela, Dona Ines, and her daughter through his kindoki, most definitely of the bad kind, and had finally fled to Kibangu to seek Father Marcellino's protection. Father Marcellino wrote to his superior, Father Luca, to inquire about the incident, but Father Luca felt that he had blown the incident out of proportion, and decided that he would send de Rosa to their mission in Nkusu, far from court, to calm the situation.[2]

Word of both incidents reached the whole of Kibangu's territory, and in the aristocratic milieu of which Dona Beatriz was a part, it was discussed angrily. Dona Beatriz shared in a strong, even stubborn pride that Kongolese, especially nobles, shared. It was so much a part of Kongolese character as the Portuguese of Angola saw it, that *orgulhoso*, or "proud," became the usual epithet for the Kongolese, the two words so frequently used together that they became almost inseparable. The people of Pedro's court lived up to this reputation. Father Marcellino himself noted a widespread belief that in "all the world there is no nobility, greatness or lordship which surpasses Kongo, and that there was no part of the world more delicious, agreeable and fertile than it." In fact, "God assigned the Angels and His other ministers with the care of the rest of the world, in order to place the chaos in order at the beginning of the world." He went on to add, "He reserved for Himself alone the formation, according to his inclination and spirit, of the lands of Africa, and especially the Kingdoms of Kongo."

The incidents were therefore a serious blow to the status of the Capuchins at Kibangu. Their insistence on respect, galling enough in light of long-established customs at court, when coupled with their extreme claims with regards to kindoki (though certainly taken seriously) had already led some to suggest that they might be exercising their claims to the power for their own benefit and not the general good. If such were the case, they might be considered ndokis themselves, and there were already those who were reaching this conclusion, for accusations against them had always been phrased in terms of kindoki before.

Later, yet another incident reflected on the larger issues of

[2] D'Atri, "Giornate," pp. 499–500; da Caltanisetta, "Relatione," fol. 101.

peace and kindoki. On the night of 10 February 1701, Manuel da Cruz Barbosa, the majordomo, attacked a village on the border between Kibangu and Mbata with a small force. The king had heard rumors that the *nkuluntu*, or head, of the village had secretly entered into negotiations with Miguel Kilau to undermine Ngoma Mpasi's authority, and hence the king's influence, in the district.

The operation was a success, and fifty-eight people were brought back to Kibangu as slaves. A Capuchin, this time the much more popular Father Luca, interviewed the unfortunate captives and discovered that many were not residents of the village at all. They had come from elsewhere, some from areas firmly under Pedro's control, to conduct business or visit friends. Surely they were innocent of the crime of treason that the nukuluntu had committed.

Father Luca did not protest the fact that rebels and disloyal people might be enslaved – indeed, he felt it was a just punishment which the Church itself had specified as appropriate for hardened ndokis. It was obvious to him, however, that Pedro and da Cruz Barbosa saw this operation as a means of profit: "with these captives they buy hats and other merchandise, making no distinction between the innocent and the guilty," as Father Luca indignantly wrote in his diary.[3] Father Luca remembered an incident several years earlier that had imprinted itself on his mind and shaped his views toward small wars and the consequences in terms of the export slave trade.

The incident took place on 14 July 1695, in the Marquisate of Ndamba in the Inkisi valley, and concerned a *pombeiro*, or a merchant's agent, working for the Portuguese trader Francisco Pereira Bravo – a merchant with connections in Luanda and at Kibangu who lived in the small state of Mbwela. The pombeiro was in Ndamba to buy slaves for his master to send to Brazil. He was negotiating over the price of a female slave, who was present at the transaction with a small baby, still nursing. When she realized from what she overheard in her master's conversation that

[3] Da Caltanisetta, "Relatione," fol. 99v.

she and the child were to be sold overseas, she went into a terrible rage, and "she took up her son and furiously threw him against a stone, and then she grabbed some arrows from the hands of a man and angrily pierced her breast," thus killing both herself and her child.[4]

Knowing that overseas export, with all the resulting misery, was likely for the captives, Father Luca reminded Pedro that one of the conditions the Church had placed on him when they agreed to build a church in Kibangu was that the king would wage no "unjust wars." Clearly this was an example of injustice, tainted with greed. The priest refused to hear Pedro's confession until he made restitution to the innocent people who had been wrongly enslaved.[5]

The role of the Capuchins as peacemakers was again enhanced when, in May 1701, the prefect returned from his long tour of Kongo's provinces trying to make the Concert good. Upon meeting with King Pedro, he decided that the next logical step would be for Pedro to reoccupy São Salvador permanently. It was pointless to claim to be king of all Kongo and not live in the capital. In any case, he would be safe doing so at this time.

Pedro made the proclamation on Saint James' Day that year amid the usual great festival and military review. None were to rebuild their homes (which was typically done regularly), or even to plant fields again, until they had advanced toward the new capital. The task of leading a force to move toward the capital fell to Pedro Kibenga and his army, which was closer to the capital than Kibangu was and, moreover, had already been deployed on other operations. King Pedro had already tightened his connection to Kibenga by marrying the Captain General's twenty-year-old niece, Maria Hippólita (known simply as Hippólita), daughter of Kibenga's sister Petronilla, on 13 June 1701, blessed by the prefect, Father Francisco.

In spite of the general good spirits of Pedro's announcement at the Saint James' Day celebration of 1701 that he would reoccupy

---

[4] Da Caltanisetta, "Relatione," fol. 20v.
[5] Da Caltanisetta, "Relatione," fols. 99v–100.

the capital permanently, the festivities were marked by a significant tragedy. The son of Dom Bernardo, the Justice Major, was gravely injured when sparks from a musket ignited some stored gunpowder on the ground. He tried to put out the fire and was burned on the face, hands, arms, chest, and stomach. People could not help but notice that it was the same Dom Bernardo who had borne the blame for the seizure of Lusunzi's stone earlier that year.[6]

Over the next few months, colonists began advancing on the capital again. The northern group, from the Mufulengi valley, had been in place for over a year protecting the advance from the forces of Bula. Now two other groups were sent forward into the Mbidizi valley and the hills beyond. On the north a group under the majordomo, Manuel da Cruz Barbosa, occupied positions in Mbuli, while on the south Pedro Kibenga's army and colonists advanced across to Manga. They kept to the hills, and in this relatively virgin territory they established villages and fortified positions to create secure areas from which the final advance to the capital could be made.

This large movement of people was possible because the Kongolese commoners who were liable to military service lived simple lives and possessed little in the way of material encumbrances; thus they were capable of literally moving whole villages fairly easily, and by moving soldiers one also moved the people who supported them. Most lived in relatively small villages, the *vatas*, which had something on the order of two hundred people each. For the nobility, these villagers were baseborn people, beneath contempt, and calling someone a *muvata* (village dweller) was an insult.

Village houses varied from region to region, as did the form of the villages. In the coastal regions, houses were round with thatched roofs, but in the inland areas they were rectangular and

---

[6] The act of marriage, which was later recalled from the Kongolese archives, has survived in APF: SOCG, vol. 651, fol. 340. For a full review of this marriage and the problems of dating it and fixing proper relationships, see Carlo Toso's annotation on the modern edition of d'Atri, "Giornate," p. 269, n. 529.

somewhat larger. This was perhaps because the people in the highland interior faced more cold weather than the coastal people did, and so needed somewhat larger houses because they spent more time in them.

Houses were of very simple construction and renewed every year as tropical conditions caused deterioration and infestation by various insects, snakes, and other vermin. While they might often be reconstructed on-site, they could also be moved when they were scheduled to be rebuilt. Thus the Kongolese peasants had a certain advantage in moving frequently from one place to another, not being tied down by investments in houses.

Pedro IV's peasant subjects were also unencumbered by ownership of land. Unlike Kongolese villages of the nineteenth century or the present day, a seventeenth-century vata's land was held in common, undivided by family group. It was worked in common, and its product was shared by families "according to the number of people in each." Anyone who cared to clear land could do so, as long as the land was not being worked by another person, or was not fallow land soon to be worked.[7]

Household equipment was simple. Most peasants had just three tools: a hoe, a large knife for cutting bush and trees, and an ax to be used in war as well as for cutting. They also had a few gourds which were used to store dried foods. Most households had beds, low-built frames with a latticework middle, called nzalos, on which they placed one or two mats and a wooden headrest. At night they were often covered by the same cloth they had worn as clothes during the day. Their cooking utensils consisted of two or three plates of wood, two or three gourds to serve beverages, a large pot for cooking, and a wooden spit for roasting meat.[8]

The common use of land and the agricultural practice also contributed to the potential mobility of commoners. Without being tied legally to ownership of one or another plot of land, and without having invested much in agricultural improvements, they

[7] For a picture of the rural village from seventeenth-century sources, see Thornton, *Kingdom of Kongo*, pp. 28–37.

[8] D'Atri, "Giornate," pp. 502–3.

were freer to move than peasants in parts of the world where private property in land, or investments in irrigation or fertilization, made particular pieces of land too valuable to leave.

The mobility of the peasantry had served kings well, as, indeed, it was serving Pedro's plan for colonizing São Salvador, for it meant that with proper direction and orders, large numbers of people, along with their productive and military capacities, could be moved where rulers wanted them to go. Thus, thousands of people, many soldiers and their families, moved from Kibangu and its immediate environs into the Mbidizi valley. There was great enthusiasm among the colonists; for many, it was the closest they had come in their lifetime to a real reestablishment of Kongo.

Dona Beatriz' home was directly in this line of advance, and the whole of the valley was seized with enthusiasm. Peace was coming, they felt, the wars would end, and the capital would be restored. But there were still reservations. King Pedro was not among the colonists, and despite his resolutions not even to rebuild the walls of his palace until he had moved to São Salvador, he remained secure on the mountain.

Pedro was holding back because he was concerned about developments in the south among vassals of Queen Ana and her rivals. On 8 April 1702, Palm Sunday, Manuel de Nóbrega Vuzi a Nkenge, based in Queen Suzanna's territory in Luvota, attacked Pedro Valle das Lagrimas' capital in Mbamba in an unsuccessful night foray. As a result of the attack, Valle das Lagrimas decided that his former capital was untenable and opted to rebuild it in a forest that lay on a high mountain in an area Europeans dubbed "the Alps of Mbamba." De Nóbrega, for his part, decided to proclaim himself Duke of Mbamba in spite of his inability to defeat Valle das Lagrimas, and constructed his own new capital, in an equally inaccessible place called Kindezi.

It was a major and violent blow to the Concert of Kongo. Although the prefect's mission had patched up relations between the queen, Kibenga, and King Pedro, he had not attended to the demands of the Kimpanzu faction in southern Soyo. His talks with Soyo had ensured its adherence to the peace agreement, but did not necessarily apply to Soyo's protected Kimpanzu friends of the de Nóbrega group in Luvota. With their attack, they made their claim for power. The claim was also troublesome because it could possibly involve Pedro Constantinho da Silva Kibenga, half Kimpanzu and half da Silva (from Soyo), who could have important sympathies with the new rebels.

The opening attack of the de Nóbrega group did not end the war. Valle das Lagrimas sent a letter to Queen Ana asking for help, and in a short time she had organized an army under her nephew Daniel, the Marquis of Mpemba, and enlisted the aid of the Prince of Soyo, António III Baretto da Silva de Castro in defense of the Concert and Pedro IV. Between them, alliance members raised an army of 20,000 soldiers to take on de Nóbrega.

At the same time, the queen was anxious to reassure King Pedro. In late April she wrote directly to him, urging him not to distrust her as a result of the war and her mobilization. She was anxious to let him know as well that relatives of Pedro Kibenga were involved, as a means of reminding him that the peace depended on the relations between her and Pedro's heir apparent and Captain General.

Soldiers were mobilized for this war from one end of the Mbidizi (at Luvota and in Mbamba) to the other (in Mpemba and Nkondo). Queen Ana sent an embassy to Mbamba and Soyo on 29 April headed by Father Marcellino, whose tour of duty in Kongo was over and who was to return to Luanda and then to Italy after being relieved by newly arrived Father Bernardo da Gallo. Father Marcellino's clerical neutrality would guarantee safe conduct in the tense regions of Mbamba he would have to cross as they followed the Mbidizi to its mouth in Nseto. The signs of war were evident all along the route. Virtually all the villages were empty, having been destroyed either in de Nóbrega's attack or in the desultory fighting between the two that followed, or abandoned by the people who sought safer refuge in mountains and forests. Where people were seen, they were armed and in military units. Even outside the actual zone of operations there were implications, for there, mobilization for the army had stripped the villages of their able-bodied population. This is what happened in Nseto, one of the secure core areas of the de Nóbrega

group's region. The embassy found the villages were populated
only by the elderly, women, and children. All the men and many
of the young women had been called up to serve in de Nóbrega's
army.

Even when no major battles were fought, a large-scale war like
this one had important and damaging effects on the ordinary people. Although not everyone actually responded to a military mobilization, a sizable enough proportion of the population
complied to give travelers the impression that the whole male
population was gone, since it was prudent for males who were
avoiding military service to go off into hills and woods to hide.

The twenty thousand soldiers mobilized for the war from the
lands of the queen and Soyo represented a powerful military
force. The Prince of Soyo had several thousand musketeers at his
capital in 1702, probably the largest such force in Kongo, as well
as dozens of cannon, including a number of mobile field pieces.
Although Queen Ana's troops were not quite so well equipped,
they had fought frequently over the period of war with Kibenga,
and had seen service in Mbamba as well.

In the end, however, this powerful army did not bring de Nóbrega's forces into action. They moved toward Luvota, but as
supplies ran low and soldiers became disorderly, the command-
ers decided to abandon the operation. By the time the rains began
in October they had returned to their home bases.

Even though the last phase of the war did not involve any
major action, this did not mean it was without cost, however. Not
all those mobilized were called to fight: many were required to
serve as porters, carrying food and supplies – in fact, there were
probably half again as many porters as combatants. In this way,
there might have been as many as 50,000 people actually mobilized to produce the 20,000 soldiers that Queen Ana and the
Prince of Soyo brought to help Valle das Lagrimas in Mbamba.
The noncombatants included thousands of women, who served
in the baggage train and as cooks, nurses, and field companions
of their husbands or male relatives in the army. Every time there
was a war, then, thousands of people served, which meant that

the war had already affected and disrupted them before a single shot was fired.

As the army began to move toward its objective, disruption continued. Those who had not been called up but whose homes lay on or near the line of march quickly evacuated the region. Armies might have carried two weeks' rations, but everyone knew that campaigns were quite likely to last longer, and any food that might be found along the way was commandeered. Fields and granaries were likely to be quite full from the last major harvest of the rainy season, when campaigns began. De Nóbrega's mobilization, for example, had clearly begun in late March, and operations extended until long into the dry season.

Armies moved slowly and news of their advance preceded them much faster. But the peasants of the villages where they passed, with males often mobilized and away from home, could not save the crops and houses, which were seized or destroyed. No matter who won the war, there was likely to be hunger, if not starvation, long before the dry season ended and a new crop could be planted; and then three months needed would have to go by until the harvest.

To counteract this, in areas like the Mbidizi valley, where armies had marched so frequently, villages had moved from the level areas around rivers into the many flat-topped hills, called *tadis*, and the densely wooded regions known as *mfindas*. Often houses could be constructed on the tops of the ntadis and crops could even be grown, although usually the lowlands at the foot of the hills still had to be cultivated. The central portions of the woods could be cleared for farming, although often it was not the best agricultural land and wild animals in the uncleared places posed real hazards to the people.

Village movement had already begun in the Mbidizi valley and the lands around it, so that armies had even more trouble resupplying than in earlier years. In the end, it was the absence of pillaged supplies and the inadequacy of rations supplied in advance that brought campaigns to a halt, although usually not before the soldiers had suffered real privation themselves. It was true in 1702, for the powerful army that Queen Ana and the Prince of Soyo had to withdraw from the field before obtaining its revenge on de Nóbrega. It had run out of supplies and food and could not find enough by foraging to keep in the field.

The cost of warfare went way beyond battlefield deaths, hunger, loss of houses and possessions, and disruption. Wars always resulted in the capture of people as slaves. Anyone, combatant or not, could be enslaved, and it was as much the fear of being enslaved that caused the countryside to empty out as it was the fear of advancing armies foraging for food and supplies. Naturally, on the battlefield, too, opponents were liable to be enslaved, especially the numerous porters who were inadequately armed and whose numbers included many women and even children. Victory in war usually meant the capture and enslavement of thousands of people.[9]

Dona Beatriz had witnessed five great wars in her time, but the great wars were in some ways only the most dramatic manifestation of the violence of the world she lived in. Although wars were critical moments, mobilizing thousands and disrupting, robbing, and enslaving thousands more as well as leaving whole provinces on the brink of starvation, there was not complete peace between the wars. Indeed, one might say that wars were not more frequent only because they left the contestants temporarily exhausted even if there were no major battles. Civil war was also conducted on a smaller scale.

When war ended and the armies returned home, a number of people remained mobilized and carried on wars on behalf of their leaders. All the major powers possessed permanent armies, usually equipped with muskets and often the elite of their forces, deployed to guard palaces and protect the leaders. They were also used to conduct small-scale raids against their opponents. After the war of 1702 both de Nóbrega and Valle das Lagrimas continued hostilities, sending smaller forces that required fewer supplies and less public mobilization on raids against each other's

[9] On the war, the peace mission, and the costs of war, see d'Atri, "Giornate," pp. 545–54; Zucchelli, *Relazioni*, pp. 337–8; da Lucca, pp. 63, 261.

territory. The function of these wars was to weaken the enemy, seize people and goods, harass each other's resources so that perhaps in the next major confrontation events would turn out differently.

Villagers who had withdrawn to hills or forests might be taken by surprise in such operations, for their well-defended locations could not support their population and crops in the field could not be protected. Travelers were particularly vulnerable to these smaller forces, which preyed on anyone passing through enemy territory, sometimes even on their own. Any disappointed duke or marquis driven from his capital in a major conflict might keep up this sort of war. At the time there were several such low-level confrontations. To the south of Dona Beatriz' home, in Wandu – a province split by the Lukunga, a tributary of the Mbidizi – there was a squabbling rivalry between Clemente, appointed Grand Duke Clemente by Queen Ana, and a rival who had been appointed during the earlier rule of Pedro Constantinho da Silva. Travelers on the valley road were often robbed, and all the settlements were located in the many mountains of the region rather than on the plain.

In Mbata, lying in the Inkisi valley behind Kibangu, there was another long-simmering rivalry between two claimants of the ducal throne. Miguel Kilau controlled one part of the duchy, while Miguel Ngoma Mpasi controlled the other with the support of Pedro IV, who occasionally sent his armed bands to support him.

Whether captured in major wars or the raids and harassing attacks of the period in between, people were always being enslaved. Slaves were valuable in Kongo, for they could provide additional workers on the lands of their owners and potentially allow the fielding of larger armies, or the population of larger areas.

People who were enslaved in the course of military operations of whatever scale were securely bound, often with a *lubambu*, a chain placed around the slave's neck, sometimes binding two people together. They were assembled in the public plaza on the return of the army or raiding force, and according to law four out of every five people who were captured became the property of the state; the remaining one become the property of the captor. Since people were usually captured in groups by groups, rarely by individuals on their own accord, presumably the remaining 20 percent were divided among soldiers of a unit, or perhaps were retained by the commander.

Some of these captives remained in Kongo, now integrated into the families and villages of the rulers of their opponents, but the majority were exported. During the period between 1700 and 1709, somewhere around 70,000 people were exported from Kongo – on average, nearly 7,000 per year from a population of something around 600,000.

Exports were important in the context of the wars because slaves could be exchanged for munitions. As muskets and powder became more prevalent as weapons, having a large stock of them on hand was important for anyone who wished to hold power. Because these items were not produced in Kongo, they had to be purchased from Europeans or from those with access to European markets at the coast. The need to acquire these items had to figure into many military decisions made in Kongo, although the decision to make war typically was rooted in the politics of civil war rather than the economics of the export trade. Nevertheless, especially in the raiding intended to weaken and harass rivals in periods between major military episodes, the prospect of an economic motive bordering on outright banditry – where people were more or less stolen for sale – undoubtedly figured in such operations as well.

Prisoners designated for export left by one of several routes. They could be sold to merchants or their agents from the Portuguese colony of Angola, such as Francisco Pereira Bravo. People enslaved through operations conducted by King Pedro in his eastern war in the Inkisi valley, or by Queen Ana in her wars in Wandu, were taken through Wandu from Nkondo, or up the Inkisi valley to the Portuguese posts at Cahenda or Mbwela, where they were subsequently transferred to Luanda for export. Others might also go across Mbamba directly to Luanda, or to Nsulu, where they were then taken by ship to Luanda. People whom Valle das Lagrimas' or de Nóbrega's armies captured in their contest over Mbamba were likely to be transported out of the country by these latter routes. Such old routes reflected the long presence of the Portuguese in Angola and, in the end, led to Brazil, almost the only place Portuguese merchants dealt with by the end of the seventeenth century. During the first decade of the eighteenth century, Angola exported about 70,000 people, although probably fewer than half came from Kongo.

A second set of routes, equally old, led to the north rather than the south, and delivered captives to the lands around the mouth of the Zaire River. Mpinda in Kongo's province of Soyo had been an Atlantic port since 1483 when the first Portuguese ships called there. Within half a century other ports north of the Zaire River – Kabinda in the small state of Ngoyo and Malemba in its northern neighbor, Kakongo – were also exporting slaves for the Americas, and shortly afterward the ports of the larger kingdom of Loango joined. Although these states considered Kongo their spiritual home and nominal overlord, and their inhabitants spoke dialects of Kikongo, they were, and always had been, effectively independent of their southern neighbor.

Portuguese ships had called at all these ports since the sixteenth century, and continued to do so regularly in the eighteenth century, delivering cargoes of slaves, local cloth, ivory, redwood, and copper to Luanda for subsequent re-export. But the northern ports, including Soyo, had also been the central African ports of call for Dutch, English, and French merchants. The Portuguese had kept them out of Luanda, even though a Dutch expedition of 1641 had seized Angola for seven years. The princes of Soyo and the rulers of Ngoyo, Kakongo, and Loango were more than willing to welcome the northern European traders to their ports, especially since they had a reputation for delivering quality merchandize at competitive prices. Unlike the Portuguese, who might have to fight African powers and were thus reluctant to deal in weapons, the northern Europeans were more than willing to sell guns and powder in quantity.

Thanks to these commercial advantages, merchants from the northern ports were able to draw slaves from far in the interior to their coasts. These merchants, who spoke Kikongo but were not subjects of the Kingdom of Kongo, were known collectively in Kongo as the Vilis, and already by the middle of the seventeenth century had settlements throughout Kongo and even into the hinterland of Portuguese Angola. Vilis were therefore also in a position to deal with slaves captured by forces loyal to Pedro IV or Queen Ana and the prisoners in the struggle for the control of Mbata, competing with Angola-based merchants even in Mbamba and Wandu.

The Vilis' trade network was managed through their religious devotion to the Lemba society, which, like the Kimpasi society, was an initiation cult that regulated human affairs and provided a flexible legal framework for their collective interests. As merchants who dealt in human beings and accumulated wealth through competitive trade relating to kindoki, they needed a spiritual means to heal the evil released by their activities.[10] Vilis were usually not Christians, although converts were certainly not unknown, and from the Church's point of view they were heathens to be expelled.

Indeed, the Church had made religion a crucial element in the competition over the export of slaves. The bishops of Angola had determined in the 1680s that it was wrong to export slaves to those powers or places that were in the hands of the "heretics," as they called Protestants, or "heathens," as they called the Vilis. This policy thus favored export through Soyo rather than the more northerly states, although efforts had been actively under way since the 1660s to convert the northern rulers to Christianity. More important, it favored Portuguese Catholic merchants, even in the north, over either Vilis or their northern European trading partners. France had seen fit to dispatch an ambassador to Soyo in 1702; he was received with great pomp and was greatly impressed with the country, undoubtedly because as Catholics they were a logical alternative to Portuguese merchants.[11] But France

---

[10] On Lemba from a historical perspective (but especially in the nineteenth century, when it underwent major growth), see John Janzen, *Lemba, 1650–1930: A Drum of Affliction in Africa and the New World* (New York, 1982).

[11] On the reception of this ambassador in Soyo, see da Lucca, "Lettera Annua," p. 83.

did not yet play a big role in the slave trade of Kongo, for between 1700 and 1709 French ships carried only about 2,600 people away.

Of the Protestant "heretics" engaged in the slave trade, the Dutch were favored by the Church because they took slaves to the Spanish Indies, where at least they would become or could remain Catholics. English merchants, who exported the lion's share (over 33,000 people) of the Protestant exports in the first decade of the century, suffered a disadvantage in this religious program, since their cargoes were directed to the Protestant English colonies of the Caribbean and from there to their developing North American holdings. They sought to build up their trade with Kabinda, accepting slaves smuggled there from Soyo and by Vili merchants operating farther east. The kings of Ngoyo took advantage of this by charging English shippers the highest prices on the coast, and in 1687 the lords of the Royal African Company wrote him a sharp letter denouncing his pricing and taxation policies.[12] Moreover, the English suffered from Soyo's own meddling in Ngoyo's affairs, for when a Soyo army invaded Ngoyo in 1689 they sought to repel the attack of this difficult Catholic prince, landing marines and artillery from their ships. But it was to no avail. The Soyo army stormed the bulwarks and captured the artillery and the battle flags of the British marines. Fortunately for the British, Soyo did not annex Ngoyo or expel their merchants.[13]

English merchants adapted to the situation by maintaining that they would be willing to export slaves only to "the Spanish Indies," where they could be Catholics, even claiming that they represented Catholic interests in England. The Church allowed this argument, and priests were called upon to issue licenses to such merchants should they present convincing evidence that they were indeed serving Catholic and not Protestant destinations. When the merchant James Barbot came to Soyo in 1700 to buy slaves to carry to the English West Indies – Protestant country to be sure – he was asked pointedly by Prince António III

---

[12] Public Records Office, London, T/70, vol. 50, fol. 56v, Royal African Company to King of Cacongo, 16 February 1687.
[13] Biblioteca Nacional de Madrid, MS 3165, da Pavia, "Viaggio," fols. 95–95v; Zucchelli, *Relazioni*, p. 198.

Baretto da Silva de Castro if he intended to ensure that the slaves were sent to Christian, and he meant Catholic, countries as was required. In the end an unnamed priest, who Barbot thought wrongly to be Portuguese, did not allow him to buy slaves, and although he did some illegal trading, he took on most of his cargo north of the river.[14]

The Princes of Soyo were not pleased with the Church's position on the trade with "heretics and heathens," and resented the interference in their commercial life. They viewed the bishop as being pro-Portuguese, and Portugal was regarded with suspicion in Soyo, even after a treaty signed in 1690 ended the twenty-year-long technical state of war between the two. The issue of the trade in slaves greatly divided the princes from the Capuchin priests; several episodes in what was a fairly stormy relationship went back to the issue of freedom of trade.[15] Prince António III finally took the matter in hand in 1701, and wrote to Rome directly. In his letter he requested a dispensation from the restrictions that the bishop of Angola had imposed on his right to sell slaves freely to whoever would buy them. His argument was that he needed the munitions he received from the Protestants to protect his state, and that the Catholic Portuguese were unwilling to supply him with these.[16]

The war of 1702 and its aftermath caused great concern among the colonists in the Mbidizi valley. After the enthusiasm that the reoccupation of São Salvador began, the return to war, even when not in the valley itself, led to a feeling of disillusion and doubt among many of the Kongolese who were not in a position to make decisions. Would wars and enslavement finally end, or would yet another round of violence and loss ensue?

---

[14] James Barbot, "Abstract of a Voyage to the Kongo River and Kabinda in 1700," in Thomas Astley (ed.), *A New and General Collection of Voyages and Travels Comprehending Everything Remarkable of its Kind in Europe, Asia, Africa, and America*, 5 vols. (London, 1746), 3:203, 204.

[15] Da Lucca, "Lettera Annua," pp. 228–9; Girolamo Merolla da Sorrento, *Breve e succinta relatione del viaggio nel Congo* (Naples, 1692), pp. 202–17.

[16] APF:SRC Congo, vol. 3, fols. 288–288v, António Baretto da Silva to Propaganda Fide, 4 October 1701.

5

Saint Anthony Arrives

EARLY IN 1703 DONA BEATRIZ, like her neighbors in the Mbidizi valley – both residents and the new colonists destined for restoring São Salvador – was in a state of expectation and concern. She was naturally most interested in the spiritual fervor which was developing in the valley. But big news was brewing. Soon the report circulated that a peasant woman from among the colonists in Pedro Kibenga's column had seen a vision of the Virgin Mary. In this vision, the Virgin told her that Jesus was angry with the Kongolese and that they must ask his mercy. To do this, it was necessary to say the Hail Mary three times, following it with three calls for mercy. Soon the movement caught on and thousands were following her ritual.

The idea of restoring Kongo and winning peace in the face of renewed large-scale war and continued smaller operations with their demands on the common people was now taking on religious dimensions. King Pedro had encouraged this before, with his vows about restoration connected with Saint James' Day and the involvement of the Capuchins in the peace process as mediators. Since the Concert of 1700 had been more directly under the influence of the Capuchin prefect and was aiming for the restoration of Kongo under Pedro IV, expectations were raised among the people about the king and religious elements.

King Pedro himself, however, was still reluctant to come down from Kibangu and throw himself personally into the effort, and this was increasingly viewed with suspicion by the commoners, whose own lives were at stake should reoccupation lead to large-scale war. But Pedro had genuine concern since the outbreak of the war in 1702. He had entrusted a great deal to Pedro Kibenga, and the claims that Manuel de Nóbrega was making on behalf of the Kimpanzu were directly relevant to the Captain General's loyalty. Pedro's trusted majordomo, Manuel da Cruz Barbosa, had been sending him reports that suggested that Kibenga was planning some sort of treachery. One did not have to look too far into Kibenga's checkered past to see that he was not someone to be trusted. So the king decided to bide his time and see how Kibenga responded to the situation.

He decided when the "Great Rains" let up in April, to encourage the new Capuchin priest, Father Bernardo da Gallo, to make his annual mission round first among the colonists. He wanted the priest, who would be seen as a neutral party to whatever political problems might be brewing, to make a report.

Father Bernardo went first to the camp of da Cruz Barbosa, who told him in no uncertain terms that he was quite sure that Kibenga was indeed planning revolt. He would, the majordomo believed, be the first to reoccupy São Salvador, given the position of his army, and would use the opportunity to revolt on behalf of the Kimpanzu. If he could win Soyo's support, a de Nóbrega might end up being proclaimed king. Da Cruz Barbosa thought that the king should begin the restoration of the city immediately, and proposed that Father Bernardo lead a procession to São Salvador, bearing a cross. The Capuchins, he said, had been traditionally viewed as the last people to leave the great city when it was abandoned, and it would be fitting that a Capuchin should be the first to reoccupy it. Giving his spiritual blessing to the enterprise might deter other rivals. Reports of strongly spiritual stirrings in Kibenga's camp led da Cruz Barbosa to believe, moreover, that the priest's explicit blessing of the king's authority might undermine Kibenga's claim. Father Bernardo, however, deemed this too dangerous and declined the offer.

But when Father Bernardo then went on to visit Kibenga's colonists, he rapidly began to appreciate why the majordomo had been so insistent on a spiritual presence in the royal reoccupation.

There was a mood of religious fervor in Kibenga's camp that needed diversion if the royal reoccupation were to succeed. He came face-to-face with the spiritual revival, and heard the daily recitations of the Hail Mary and the cries for mercy. He thought it a laudable novelty of the devout, and he asked Kibenga about it. Kibenga related to him an account of the peasant woman's vision of the Virgin.

Curious, Father Bernardo asked Kibenga for permission to interview the prophet who taught this new mode of prayer. He was suspicious of the movement as he learned details, for it was obvious that its source was spontaneous and not the action of one of the local church leaders. Always anxious that the official church lead all religious life, he wanted to make sure it could be controlled. "She is an unknown woman," Kibenga replied blithely, "and even I do not know her, or know where she is to be found." Father Bernardo decided not to pursue the matter, although he would soon regret the decision.

Having heard Kibenga make light of the movement, Father Bernardo suspected that the Captain General was manipulating religious sentiment to draw the king away from Kibangu prematurely and into a situation where he could be usurped. He returned to Kibangu to deliver his disturbing report of incipient revolt to the king. Pedro felt that the reports had done nothing to convince him to take charge of the reoccupation of São Salvador.

If the initial spiritual movement had begun among Kibenga's colonists, it soon spread into the Mbidizi valley as a whole. A man began preaching on the basis of his revelationary dreams of a small child telling him that God was going to punish the Kongolese if they did not occupy São Salvador as quickly as possible. Just like the small children who played with Dona Beatriz in her own youthful dreams, this child was a spirit from the Other World, and the message must be taken seriously.

The movement was taking on more political overtones as well as strictly religious ones. God's anger was directed specifically at those who, by delaying the reoccupation, were also delaying peace. In late 1703 or early 1704, yet another prophet, Apollonia Mafuta, appeared, pulling several of these messages together and adding a bit more.

Mafuta was an old woman, and like the peasant in Kibenga's camp, had a vision of the Virgin. The Virgin told Mafuta that she had thrown herself prostrate at the feet of her son, begging him to be merciful with the Kongolese. Jesus told her that he was particularly angry with the people of Kibangu for their wickedness, and for not coming down from the mountain to restore the city. Finally, Mafuta discovered a curiously shaped stone near the Mbidizi, a sure message from the Other World. This stone, which had the shape of a deformed man's head, she believed was the head of Jesus wounded by the hoes of those impious women who had worked on Sundays and holy days, or by the knives of wicked men. Like Lusunzi's stone or the ancient stone in the shape of the cross, it was an Otherworldly token that could not be ignored.

Jesus' anger, Mafuta learned from her apparitions and dreams, was directed especially at King Pedro, the principal cause of the slowed pace of resettlement. If he did not come down very soon, the mountain would be burned and then thrown down. In August, Mafuta met Father Bernardo while he was making his rounds around the base of the mountain of Kibangu. She showed him the stone and described her visions, but he was not impressed, later writing that he regarded her as insane though not dangerous.

But priestly scorn did not slow Mafuta's ministry. A large crowd of people followed her around, and she began denunciations of various people as ndokis. Following the pattern that priests had long established, she denounced as witchcraft all *nkisis*, which she believed to be polluted with negative kindoki. Since the term nkisi was used for objects of Christian devotion (a church was *nzo a nkisi*; the Bible, *nkanda nkisi*), as well as for various charms used to embody spirits that were not approved by the Church, she included crosses and religious medals in her bonfires. As far as Mafuta was concerned, any nkisi could be an object used in witchcraft if its access to kindoki was dedicated to selfish or evil ends, and her campaign stressed the generalized war against such evil.

Seen in this light, her actions were not anti-Christian, but represented a purification of Christianity of the involvement that people had with negative kindoki as a result of greed, jealously, civil war, and treachery. Mafuta confirmed the essentially Christian message, for she cured a woman of a snakebite simply by making the sign of the cross and reciting the name of the Holy Trinity. For Mafuta, and for her followers in the Mbidizi valley, the religious movement was profoundly Christian, although it relied on Kongolese concepts of kindoki and not the witchcraft lore of the priests.

Mafuta carried her message to Kibangu itself before the end of August. Crowds listened to her there, including one of her most careful listeners, King Pedro's wife Hippólita. From very early on, the followers of the new religious fervor were from all classes and stations, although their interest in the movement varied widely.

King Pedro was unsure how to handle this novel player in the political game of Kongo. Father Bernardo pressed the king to arrest Mafuta and deliver her to him to examine more fully. Then perhaps he could correct any doctrinal error she was preaching, and thus confirm the supremacy of the Church in all matters pertaining to the spiritual realm. The priest was also fearful that she was somehow connected to Kibenga's potential treason, especially given the tenor of her message.

The king did not want to leave this matter entirely in ecclesiastical hands, however, and so he called Mafuta to appear before him, questioned her, but did not arrest her. He, like the priest, was concerned about the possible connection to Kibenga, especially given the influence that Mafuta was having on his wife, Kibenga's niece – but her advocacy was the same message he had received from many quarters, including the majordomo da Cruz Barbosa, his most trusted aide. Consequently, he released her and did not turn her over to the Church.

King Pedro's decision was not well received by Father Bernardo. Furious that he had been thwarted, he closed the church and refused to engage in any ecclesiastical functions, though he did not excommunicate anyone.

As Mafuta's ministry continued, Dona Beatriz fell ill with the supernatural sickness that would lead to her death and rebirth as Saint Anthony, in August 1704. No sooner had Saint Anthony entered her head and revived her dying body, than she rose from her sickbed and informed her relatives of the events that had taken place. She told them she had received a divine commandment to go and preach, and she had no choice. She must go to preach to the king in Kibangu. Following the example of the Capuchin missionaries she immediately began to distribute her small store of personal property, freeing herself of the encumbrances and the potential for greed implied by possessions. Thus liberated, she set off directly for Kibangu.

Dona Beatriz' sickness, death, and resurrection as Saint Anthony returned her to life as an nganga, albeit one with a much more elaborate mission than most ngangas, or even the initiates of the Kimpasi society, from which many elements of her teaching were drawn. Unlike other initiations into the society, hers was induced from the Other World and for a much higher mission than that of a local Kimpasi society.

Like Mafuta before her, Dona Beatriz waged a war against all forms of greed and jealousy and its most obvious manifestation, misuse of kindoki. She climbed the slope of Kibangu to the city on the sacred mountain, and carried her message to the king. One of her first actions was to go to the large wooden cross that stood in the plaza outside the church, where it served as a focus for outdoor services when the church could not accommodate everyone. She began to push and pull on it, trying to tear it down. Royal guards, hearing the commotion, rushed over to stop her.

They took her to the palace, where her preaching rapidly drew attention, and like Mafuta before her, she was carried before the king. She entered the throne room gracefully, walking on the tips of her toes so that she almost seemed to float. Smiling broadly as if filled with great joy, she circled the king.

Then, using the authority that her possession gave her, she rebuked him for not immediately occupying São Salvador and bringing the wars to a close. She also denounced Father Bernardo, accusing him of being a jealous and envious person, both important characteristics of ndokis, and adding to this a new accusation, that he did not want there to be black saints in Kongo. It was for this reason, Dona Beatriz maintained, that he had demanded to have Mafuta handed over to him, so that he could punish her.

Principally, however, she argued that both the king and his Capuchin priest lacked the will and determination to restore the kingdom. Dona Beatriz, however, asserted that she could restore the kingdom, and since the present rulers lacked the necessary will and strength, she would do it herself. Pedro accepted this remarkable discourse without doing anything. Perhaps he recognized the popular sentiment and the respect that her possession had won her, and understood the feelings behind her popularity. It would be unwise to do anything that might alter such sentiments and turn them even further against him. It was hard to balance his need for security and the wisdom of staying put in Kibangu a bit longer against the rising popular expectations.

Shortly after Dona Beatriz' arrival at the palace, an excited young man, a servant at the Capuchin hospice of Kibangu, rushed in to see Father Bernardo, bringing him news as he sat brooding in the closed chapel. Saint Anthony, he told the priest, had come to preach in Kibangu. Father Bernardo wanted nothing to do with it.

"Oh, go away," he replied to his earnest visitor, "go away and leave me alone!" He was sure that all Kongolese people were just looking for another way to vex him.

But his visitor was not so easily turned away. "In fact," he said, "the news is certain, and they say that it is a young woman and not an old one" – referring to Apolonia Mafuta – "who works miracles." Wherever she passed when climbing up the steep mountain paths to Mount Kibangu, "all the twisted and fallen trees straightened themselves out! She is now in the palace of the king confirming against you all that the old woman said," Father Bernardo's visitor continued.

Father Bernardo decided not to do anything, feeling lost and abandoned with the situation out of his control and hands. As a result, he neither reopened the church nor went to the king, but instead let Dona Beatriz go unchallenged at court. After a few days, having said her piece in Kibangu, Dona Beatriz returned to spread her message to the increasingly excited people of the Mbidizi valley who were her principal congregation.

While in the valley, Dona Beatriz gradually developed the message that was first revealed during her possession and that she had preached at Kibangu before the king and the interested common people of the mountain. She continued this teaching through a number of sermons.[1]

These sermons focused on several issues: first, that Saint Anthony was the most important saint. It was not difficult to convince people of this, for Saint Anthony, as patron of Portugal, was regarded as being a patron (along with Saint James Major) of Kongo as well. Dona Beatriz compared him with Saint Alexis, who left his wife and family to preach and live a solitary life. Her sermons took the form of dialogues between Saint Anthony and Saint Alexis, but were constructed in such a way that Saint Anthony was the most important. To emphasize the primacy of Saint Anthony, she demanded that the people pray only to him.

Second, she confirmed the general tenor of Mafuta's earlier teaching, placing emphasis on Jesus' anger and the impending punishment. She urged prayer and the calling for mercy that had been announced by the first woman to see the vision of the Virgin.

Third, however, she urged the Kongolese to be happy. Good things were to be delivered to Saint Anthony's devotees. She told them that her arrival meant that the Kongolese could have saints of their own just as Europeans did.[2]

This last point led her to the final element in her sermons. Ever since the Capuchins had reestablished themselves on Kibangu in 1698 there had been debates over precedent. The Capuchins had insisted, using their powers of kindoki if necessary, that they had to be strictly respected, even by the king and the nobility. This was a break from the practice of the secular priests, who had

[1] Da Gallo, "Ultime," fols. 291–294v.
[2] Da Gallo, "Ultime," fols. 304–304v.

never insisted on such respect. Even though the Capuchins had always been sticklers for their dignity through their noble origins and the privileges their order had won in Kongo, the people of Kibangu and the Mbidizi had not experienced this in most of their lifetimes.

The Kongolese were prepared to accept many of the Capuchins' claims, as long as they were backed by virtue and clear selflessness. Generally the priests won high marks on this score, for they were a serious mendicant order and practiced strict celibacy and poverty that was admirable and respected. But some of this had been eroded by the incident with Juan de Rosa, and since then the possibility that they might make claims to superiority of a racial sort had to be weighed in on the scale, a scale that no Kongolese accepted. The Capuchins' insistence that the Church had originated outside Kongo, that its earlier leaders were Europeans, and particularly that the saints most venerated in Kongo, Saint Francis and Saint Anthony of Padua, were both Italians like themselves, increased their authority and gave weight to their implicit claim that there were no Kongolese saints.

Thus, when Dona Beatriz began pointing out that the images of the saints that adorned the altar in Kibangu, Saint Francis and Saint Anthony, were Europeans, people might question why these priests, who were not above demanding special privileges for nonclerical Europeans solely on skin color, might be deceiving the people on the issue of the saints. Dona Beatriz countered by throwing her own prestige and visible kindoki into a radical reinterpretation of the history of the Church and the role of Africans and Kongolese in it. Her challenge to Father Bernardo – that he did not want the Kongolese to have black saints – was followed up by a defense of the Kongolese origin of the Church and its saints.

God revealed another and truer version of church history to her. The Capuchins were not telling the Nativity story correctly, and the Kongolese needed to know the truth. Jesus had been born in the royal city of São Salvador, and when the catechism mentioned Bethlehem, it was this city that was meant. He had been baptized in Nazareth, but this was really a disguise for his real place of baptism, which was the northern province of Nsundi. Jesus and Mary were actually Kongolese; Mary's mother was a slave of the Marquis Nzimba Mpangi when Mary gave Jesus birth.

Dona Beatriz' history of Christianity was also a parallel reworking of the history of Kongo which Kongolese historians of the late seventeenth century had done. King Afonso was given credit for the founding of the Church as well as being the father of the various royal lines; to make history fit this new version, they denied that Afonso's father had been baptized before his son, as contemporary documents affirm, and indeed as histories written in Kongo in the mid-seventeenth century attest. Instead, for one reason or another according to the new version, the priests had gone to Nsundi, where Afonso was governor, and had baptized him first.[3] The parallels between São Salvador and Nsundi that were in Dona Beatriz' Nativity story worked on the same symbolism, though on a larger plane.

In Dona Beatriz' revised Christian history, Saint Francis – to whose cult the Capuchins as a Franciscan order were devoted – was also Kongolese, coming from the same *kanda* as the Marquis of Vunda. The Marquis of Vunda was widely reputed to be descended from the original settlers of São Salvador. The marquis crowned the king and sometimes related the history of the country in the formal ceremonies of investiture. Saint Anthony, of course, was now present in Kongo, inside her own head.

Since Dona Beatriz was now conveying a revised history of the Church, she was also charged with reforming it. From the beginning of the preaching she introduced new, truer versions of the prayers found in the catechism. She changed the words of both the Ave Maria (Hail Mary) and Salve Regina (Hail, Holy Queen), claiming that she was recovering their original content.

She was particularly drawn to the prayer Salve Regina, addressed to the Virgin Mary. As Kongolese knew the prayer at the time, printed in the catechism, it went:

[3] This story was recorded in Biblioteca Nacional de Madrid, MS 3165, da Pavia, "Viaggio," fol. 92.

Salve [Save] the Queen, mother of mercy, sweetness of life, our hope.
Deus [God] save you; we cry out for you, we the exiled children of
Eve; we sigh for you, kneeling and weeping in this valley of tears.
Therefore, you, our advocate, cast your merciful eyes on us and after
that exile show us Jesus, the fruit of your womb; Ehe, you the merciful,
Ehe benevolent one! E sweet one! the perpetual Virgin Mary. Pray for
us, *Santa* [Holy] Mother of Nzambi a Mpungu, so that we may be
worthy of the promises of Christ.[4]

In Kikongo, this prayer had several untranslated words in Portuguese in it, including *salve* (save), *Deus* (God), and *Santa* (holy),
although in other places in the text, these same words are given
in Kikongo; hence, *kanga* appears for "save" in the line "*Deus* save
you" while God appears here in its Portuguese form; but later,
in "Mother of God," the word "God" is given in its Kikongo
form, as *Nzambi a Mpungu*.

The Salve Antoniana, as Dona Beatriz' new prayer was called,
was more like a commentary on the original prayer than a mod-
ification of it. Father Bernardo, who recorded the prayer, unfortunately only in his own Italian translation, felt unable to
comment on it. He thought it was "unworthy, disordered and
without any connection." It contained "so many outrageous statements that I do not know if I should call them diabolical craziness
or truly desecrating blasphemy." He was quite certain that the
prayer did not originate from some Catholic heretic theologian,
such as Miguel Molinos, whose work was popular in Iberian

---

[4] The original text of Salve Regina in Kikongo is found in Mateus Cardoso
(ed.), *Doutrina Christãa*, (Lisbon, 1624), ch. 5, no. 1. I believe the term
Eheüauuequigunda as printed is a mistake for "Eheüauuequingunda"
[*Eye, wavwa kigunda*], which was used to translate the Portuguese "Ó
piadosa!" making it "Eye benevolent one." Note that I have translated
directly from the Kikongo version of the prayer into English, skipping
the Portuguese version contained in the catechism, its Latin original form,
and authorized or standardized English translations such as those found
in modern catechisms and prayer books: "Hail, Holy Queen, Mother of
Mercy, our life, our sweetness, and our hope! To thee do we cry, poor
banished children of Eve; to thee do we send up our sighs, mourning
and weeping in this valley of tears! Turn then, most gracious advocate,
thine eyes of mercy towards us; and after this, our exile show unto us
the blessed fruit of thy womb, Jesus. Oh clement, Oh loving, Oh sweet
virgin Mary!"

countries. He considered a possible Protestant origin, introduced by Calvinist Dutch merchants who frequented the Atlantic coast of Kongo, drawn by the endless numbers of slaves captured during the civil wars, but rejected this idea. Instead, Father Bernardo finally decided that the origins of the heresy must have come from within Kongo itself, from its own peculiar form of Christianity.

Examining the Salve Antoniana as a product of Kongolese Christianity, one can divide it into three parts, the first of which seems to place the new prayer in the context of the old one, and the next two of which form commentaries on it.

It begins by asserting that the average Kongolese said the Salve Regina without really understanding it, perhaps because the untranslated Portuguese word *salve* robbed it of meaning:

Salve you say, and you do not know the reason you say it. You receive *Salve* and you do not know why. You beat *Salve* and you do not know why.

After this introduction, though, the Salve Antoniana moves on to a commentary of the passage "*Deus* (God) save you" that allows an explication of salvation. In fact, this section sounds very much like a Protestant rather than a Catholic prayer, and may well reflect the theological essence of Saint Anthony's new teaching. It denies the power of the sacraments, and instead maintains that the intention of the believer is more important than the performance of sacraments:

God wants an intention, it is the intention that God grasps. Baptism serves nothing, it is the intention that God takes. Confession serves no purpose, it is the intention that God wants. Good works serve no purpose; intention is what God wants.

The stress on intention rather than sacraments was crucial to the prayer. In Kongo, of course, intention is critical to determining whether the use of kindoki is positive or negative, and hence to be considered helpful or evil, so that these lines transport the concept of kindoki firmly into the prayer. In the end, God is going to judge people according to their intentions seen in this light, and not by their formal performance of the sacraments. In this way, Dona Beatriz had arrived at conclusions similar to Protestant thought by an entirely different route.

In the final portion of the prayer, the Salve Antoniana shifts from denying the validity of the sacraments to reasserting the concept of advocacy of the Virigin and the saints before God which characterizes the original prayer and, indeed, Catholic theology. But with one exception. The new prayer takes the virtues of Mary from the Salve Regina and substitutes Saint Anthony, progressively increasing his power and significance until he becomes a figure equal to God Himself, starting with the popular images of Mary holding the baby Jesus:

The Mother with the Son on her knees. If there had not been Saint Anthony what would they have done? Saint Anthony is the merciful one. Saint Anthony is our remedy. Saint Anthony is the restorer of the Kingdom of Kongo. Saint Anthony is the comforter of the Kingdom of Heaven. Saint Anthony is the door to Heaven. Saint Anthony holds the keys to Heaven. Saint Anthony is above the Angels and the Virgin Mary. Saint Anthony is the second God . . .

At this point, the idea of the protective power of the nkitas like Lusunzi, or the nkitas that possess the initiates in the Kimpasi society, is evoked. Of course, in the Kongolese view, the saints and the Virgin Mary were also powerful nkitas, they lived long ago but were the ancestors of no one in particular. They were free from the petty concerns and willingness to do evil on behalf of their descendants, which was true of the recently dead ancestors. They were positive, even stern, moral figures who were nevertheless nonpartisan and protecting.

The prayer did not end with this – when recited by her followers it became a long, indeed unending, harangue, which gradually rose to a crescendo as more and more attributes of Saint Anthony were added to the list. Saint Anthony would pray, while her followers replied with the lines "*Tari, Tari*," or "Mercy, Mercy,"[5] as

---

[5] In Kikongo, both today and in the seventeenth century, the word for mercy was *kiyadi* (*quiari* in earlier orthographies reflecting the "r" that was replaced in the eighteenth century with "d"). *Tari* or *Sari* might

they had been taught to do by the earlier visionaries, and no doubt in response to the original prayer's mention of Mary's "merciful eyes" and its own calls for mercy. This call-and-response pattern led to higher and higher intensity as the prayer reached its climax.[6]

About two weeks after Dona Beatriz left Kibangu to go back to the Mbidizi valley, perhaps late in September, Father Bernardo and King Pedro made up their differences. Now, when the priest heard that Dona Beatriz was preaching freely, and when King Pedro appealed to him for a decision on how best to deal with this new challenge to church and royal authority, he decided he should put aside his quarrel, and reopened the church.

Dona Beatriz, hearing of this, took the opportunity to return to Kibangu to see the king. King Pedro was uncertain about her, but decided that he would send her to Father Bernardo to get his opinion of her preaching. In order to ensure her cooperation, however, Pedro assured her that the priest would not be allowed to harm her and that she was under royal protection. To make certain that his wishes were respected, the king sent several councilors, headed by his Secretary Major and Dona Beatriz' kinsman, Miguel de Castro, to visit Father Bernardo.

They came to the priest on a Sunday, while he was preparing to say Mass. He was still irritated with the king for what he considered an overtolerant attitude to Dona Beatriz and all the other prophets.

"Ah, you are already filled up and convinced by the superstitions and diabolic lies of your black Saint Anthony?" he testily greeted the little party. "I thank the King, my son, for the good work he has done," he added sarcastically, convinced that if the king had allowed him to discipline the movement from the time that Mafuta began teaching, it would not have gone so far.

---

simply be mistakes of the priests who recorded it, though the likelihood of this is reduced by considering that da Gallo could speak Kikongo and undoubtedly knew the catechism. Rather, it is more likely that the form was deliberately altered, as was often the case with kimpasi language, to make it seem archaic or esoteric.

[6] Da Gallo, "Ultime," fols. 304v–305.

To assert his status, however, the priest decided to keep the king waiting. He reminded them that it was Sunday and he had to say Mass. They should return first thing on Monday.

Thus rebuked, the party left and returned to the king. Dona Beatriz greeted this news with excitment, believing she might be able to convince the priest that she had indeed been endowed with great spiritual power and he might back her up. The next day, therefore, she accompanied the king's advisors to the chapel and waited outside while they entered first as a means of introducing her in what was likely to be a difficult meeting for her, although crucial for her mission.

The advisors approached Father Bernardo and explained that Dona Beatriz had come to see him, and then ensured that he understood she was under royal protection for the moment and he could not seize her or harm her in any other way should the interview not go well. Having thus cleared the air, the advisors called for Dona Beatriz to enter.

Dona Beatriz moved through the door and, without hesitating, walked across the room to the statue of the Virgin Mary, which, along with the other religious images in the chapel, was covered with a cloth. Kneeling on the floor, she bent over and struck her forehead forcefully three times on the ground. She then paused for a short time, praying, and stood up.

A radiant smile crossed her face as she turned to Father Bernardo, and slowly she walked around him in a circle. Surprised, the priest asked the royal advisors what this all meant. They said it was a sign of joy; she had done the same thing whenever she saw the king. De Castro added, as a further explanation, "If she appears a bit confused it is because she has recently died and has been revived from the dead."

Dona Beatriz, a strikingly attractive woman, taller than average with her hair cut very short and even on all sides, like most Kongolese women of her time, did have an unusual bearing. She was "walking on the tips of her toes, with the rest of her feet not touching the ground, and she swayed her body from side to side just the way a snake moves." As she moved about, "she held her neck stiff as if possessed; she had bulging eyes, her speaking was frenetic and delirious," while her language, probably the special language reserved for the Kimpasi society, was often incomprehensible, and her movements were clumsy and unpredictable.

De Castro considered her behavior and demeanor appropriate for a possessed person, and was curious if the priest considered this possession to be a revelation of Saint Anthony. For Kongolese, after all, earthly death and resurrection as a possessed person were fairly commonplace, especially for someone, like Dona Beatriz, who had been a member of the Kimpasi society. It was widely enough accepted that in 1665, King António I had proclaimed himself not only Lord over Kongo but even over the "matombolo or the resurrected dead."[7]

Dona Beatriz' hopes that he might accept her mission were set back, however, by the priest's reply to de Castro's explanation: "Fine, you are right, considering that you do not know what you are talking about."

Father Bernardo then began to question her, partly to satisfy the royal councillors that he had made a good-faith effort to determine her status, and partly to answer his own curiosity. Speaking in Kikongo, he asked her if she knew who it was that she had been worshipping when she knelt before the statue of the Virgin.

"It was the Madonna," she replied, and then continued by pointing out two other statues, which, like the one of the Virgin, were covered with cloth. One was of Saint Francis, and the other of Saint Anthony; each, she went on, could easily be distinguished from the others.

The royal councillors were stunned at this answer, and stood in amazed silence, convinced she had known this by some supernatural power. For them, it was a miracle, and something to be taken seriously. Father Bernardo appeared less impressed and continued his questioning.

"Who are you?" he asked her.

She replied gravely, as if every word were a serious matter, and slowly, as if carefully considering each remark, "I am Saint Anthony, come from Heaven."

---

[7] Declaration of War, October 1665, in Brásio, *Monumenta*, 11:549–50.

"Fine," Father Bernardo answered sarcastically, "and what news do you bring from up there? Tell me, in Heaven are there blacks from Kongo, and if there are, do they still have their black color in Heaven?"

It was a revealing question in light of the de Rosa affair and Dona Beatriz' teaching about the Capuchins. "There are black Kongolese up in Heaven," she replied without hesitation, "little ones who have been baptized, and adults who had observed the laws of God on earth. But," she continued, "they are not black in color nor white, because in Heaven no one has any color."

The last statement was too much for Father Bernardo, whose temper was short anyway, and he launched into a tirade. "So in Heaven there are Kongolese children who have been baptized and adults who have observed the laws of God?

"Therefore, I and the other missionaries, preaching the Faith of Christ, the Divine law and the observance of the Ten Commandments, things that are necessary for eternal welfare do not preach lies, but the truth?

"Therefore," he went on, "administering the Holy Sacraments of the Church, principally Baptism, penance and matrimony, we are not betraying the people?" Becoming more angry, he continued, "Therefore, the Holy Father is not a liar, seducer, and does not send us here to betray and stir up the people as you say, but sends us here to teach, instruct and place them on the road to eternal well-being."

Facing this tirade, Dona Beatriz was taken aback. She had expected that Father Bernardo would support her, or at least that her statements would not anger him. Cowering away, she began to cry.

"I am sorry, Father," she answered him, "but I did not say anything against you or the Pope. What you have heard about this is all lies. In fact," she continued, "I have spoken on your behalf before the people and on behalf of the Holy Father, telling everyone that the Holy Pope is the Vicar of Christ on earth, and that you, a priest, had been sent to Kongo to be our spiritual Father. For this reason you deserve every honor and reverence."

Indeed, whatever denunciations might be made against Capuchin priests would not be a group condemnation, but against individuals, for the role of priest as a positive person was not in doubt, only the status of individuals. Though testy and as anxious about status as any Capuchin before him, Father Bernardo had not favored his personal or racial views over the general good.

At this point, de Castro came forward and held Dona Beatriz, comforting her and trying to calm her down. "Do not worry, daughter," he said to her. "You can speak freely, Father Bernardo cannot harm you, since you are under our protection."

Father Bernardo was even more upset when he saw de Castro defending her. He was already upset that de Castro apparently believed that she might indeed be possessed by Saint Anthony, and that she was in fact resurrected from the dead. De Castro was a nobleman, the king's interpreter, a Master of the Church, and an educated man. He, a good Christian, ought to be unhesitatingly on the side of a priest, and yet he was willing to accept Dona Beatriz' account, and even to defend her.

"Ingrate," the priest shouted at de Castro. "Are you not ashamed to be treating a nganga marinda as a daughter, and defending this black woman who is sewing seeds of dissension among the poor Christians here? You are obviously in danger of losing your Holy Faith. Are you not called Master of the Church? Therefore should you not always be on my side?"

When Father Bernardo confronted de Castro over his defense of Dona Beatriz, then, he was expecting obedience because Masters were supposed to obey the priests. But at the same time, the Master spoke his own part freely and did not hesitate to contradict the priest. Priests were well treated or poorly treated depending on their recognition of their real powers to demand obedience and not on their formal ability to demand it. In any case, de Castro was far more than simply a Church Master, for he was also Secretary Major and an important lay official of state.

Confronted with Father Bernardo's attack on him for comforting Dona Beatriz, de Castro replied, "I cannot deny that she is my daughter, for she comes from my kanda."

"But I had never heard her say such words," he added shortly, himself a bit irritated that the priest was making what might have been wild accusations, based on rumors. She had not been the firebrand of denunciation when she visited the king in person that she had been, or was reported to have been, while preaching in the Mbidizi valley.

"In the Mbidizi valley," Father Bernardo shot back, "did she not burn crosses along with objects of witchcraft? Did she not try to get rid of the cross in the royal square, if the king had allowed it?" he went on. "Deny this!"

Dona Beatriz answered before de Castro could. She had taken heart from his defense of her, and now wanted to speak up for herself. "Yes," she said, "it is true. But the crosses of the valley also had superstitions attached to them."

Father Bernardo had now recovered his composure, although he was still angry, and decided to continue questioning her. He was upset that de Castro had not taken up his position, but he wanted to finish the interview.

Turning to Dona Beatriz, he asked, "If you are a woman, how then could you say you are Saint Anthony?"

Now she had the chance to explain herself, and Dona Beatriz took it, explaining how her possession had come to pass, how Saint Anthony had sought to come to Kongo, first in Nseto, then Soyo and Bula. "Finally," she concluded, "Saint Anthony came into my head to be able to preach in Kibangu, and has been well received with applause and happiness. This is why I have been teaching the Word of God and instructing the people, hurrying to go to court and confirming what the old woman said."

Father Bernardo now decided that he had had enough of what he had now come to believe was "frivolity and nonsense." He had interviewed her fully and no one could accuse him of simply dismissing her out of hand. He was convinced beyond a doubt that she was possessed by the Devil and that he must do something to stop her. He signaled to her that the interview was over and that she could go.

While Dona Beatriz was meeting with Father Bernardo, a crowd of people gathered outside the chapel, waiting and listening anxiously to whatever they could hear. Many people had learned that she was being seen by the priest, and they had come by to hear what they could and to witness the outcome. They could not help but hear Father Bernardo's shouting, mostly at Miguel de Castro, and now they were sure that the priest would speak against her. They were sure their saint would be delivered into his hands or, rather, that the king would now be persuaded to take action against her.

After the interview Father Bernardo decided what would be the official reaction of the Church to Dona Beatriz and her teaching. He had concluded that she was not explicitly pretending. He was sure that she was possessed. Indeed, the gap that had developed between his interpretation of Dona Beatriz and that of de Castro was not over the reality of what they were seeing, it was simply over who was in possession of Dona Beatriz – Saint Anthony or the Devil. For Father Bernardo there was no question who was possessing her – it was one of the demons or the Devil himself.

Although Kongolese regarded possession as a normal and acceptable form of revelation, European Catholic priests like Father Bernardo were reluctant to accept that any possession could be anything but diabolic. Catholic priests were often willing to seek revelations through a variety of divination practices, just as their counterparts the Kongolese ngangas did. They read the stars (though not as astrologers), searched for signs, paid attention to their dreams, matched events with the feast days of saints. They might be quite willing to accept the apparition of the Virgin Mary to a Kongolese as being a genuine revelation. The first priests to come to Kongo, after all, had accepted a variety of revelations, from the dreams to the mysterious stone, as being just that, and vouchsafed by miracles.

But European traditions did not accept the idea that divine revelations came in the form of possession. This was probably because possession by saints was uncommon and suspect in Europe; more often possession was by the Devil. The Church had a whole rite of exorcism designed to end these uncontrolled and evil possessions. Even when possession favored missionary work, they were unlikely to see it in a positive light.

With this background, Father Bernardo never considered the

possibility that Dona Beatriz was actually possessed by Saint Anthony; at best it was a minor demon. Still, the king had asked him to make a determination on the validity of her message. As de Castro's remarks indicated, Kongolese did not share the European priest's ideas about possession and were quite willing to admit the possibility that she was indeed possessed by Saint Anthony. If that were so, she must be carefully attended to.

Father Bernardo wasted no time in making his report. That very evening he went to the king, who received him with his attendants in waiting. The priest certified that he was convinced that Dona Beatriz was not Saint Anthony, as some people believed.

Rather, he argued strongly that Dona Beatriz was a witch, possessed by the Devil. God had permitted this to take place, he suggested, because Pedro had been too hard on the people, and had not been sufficiently responsive to their will.

Father Bernardo, like many others, thought that Pedro's policy of reconciliation was not decisive enough. In the priest's view of the matter, he needed to restore the kingdom and put an end to the civil wars. Failing to do that, even at some personal risk, would only prolong them, and the people's suffering along with it.

"You should remain happy, however," the priest continued, "and not fear anything, because all is remediable with the help of God." Furthermore, he said, "you should remain constant in the Holy Faith." Father Bernardo added as a suggestion that Pedro take vigorous measures against Dona Beatriz, Mafuta, and the others. "You should help me with the 'temporal arm' in all that might be necessary." As much as Father Bernardo might have wanted to seize Dona Beatriz and bring her to the kind of justice the Church reserved for anyone who trafficked with the Devil, he was acutely aware that he had no ability to enforce his will. Only the king, and the king's cooperation, could bring her to justice and defend the Church against what might well be public outrage were Dona Beatriz brought to justice.

King Pedro listened gravely and attentively to this speech. Obviously, there was no hope that the Church would support any sort of alliance between his vision of Kongo and that of Dona

Beatriz. He decided that the time had come to act decisively on this point, at least. He had worked hard to get the Church to come to Kibangu, whereas Dona Beatriz was a person of uncertain origins, and not either predictable or controllable.

He snatched the silver embroidered cap that served as royal crown from his head and flung it straight into the chest of the *mwene banzi*, one of his officials. Then, beckoning to his other councillors to join him, the king knelt before the priest, placing his hands on Father Bernardo's chest as if to hug him as a sign of devotion.

"My Spiritual Father," he said emotionally, "I never would have believed that a woman, after having lived a bad life, restless, the concubine of two men, and a witch, would become a saint so quickly without having done penance for her sins. Nor did I believe what she said, because how can it be possible that the Holy Pope, Vicar of Christ on Earth, could be false? A deceiver, a seducer of the people?

"How is it possible," he continued, "that the same Holy Father would send ministers to seduce the people, and to become the absolute head of all the world; other than to be the Father of all?" Pedro made it clear that he was willing to accept the priest's interpretation of the events without reservation. He at least would support the Church and had faith in its mission.

Looking up at the priest, he said, "And is it possible that you, my Spiritual Father, are deceiving me along with the people, and under the name of Spiritual Father, that you are my enemy?" Recalling the assertions of the Salve Antoniana, he went on, rhetorically, "Therefore, prayer is worthless, the sacraments are all in vain, and all the sacred ceremonies are fallacious? Baptism is futile, the same for Marriage; and confession serves nothing but to inform the confessor of everyone's secrets? Therefore, in order to serve God, is the intention all that is necessary, without outward good works?" Certainly, he understood both Dona Beatriz' and the Catholic Church's theology on the key issues here.

"Therefore must the cross which is symbol of the Christian be undone?" he asked the priest, "Must the Holy Faith be denied, a faith which my ancestors received with so much love and without shedding a drop of blood?" Both the Church and the Kongolese were proud that the Christian faith had come to Kongo not through conquest and forced conversion, but through the voluntary conversion of João I.

Now caught up in the passion of his speech, Pedro went on, "Oh, not this my Spiritual Father, I cannot believe it, nor do I want to believe it, nor will I permit it to be believed on any count!" The support of the Church was too important for him to throw it away, and he had to be careful to keep Father Bernardo on his side in all things. He was, however, not at all sure that he was ready to try to crush the movement, and he needed time.

His voice lowered as his tone became more analytical. "But, poor me, what a large population I carry on my shoulders! Poor people! I have more than just a few problems: I am surrounded by enemies, many of whom wish me evil, others are stirred up and still others are attempting to have my head. Poor me! I do not know what will happen to me, and am driven to anxiety by all sides."

King Pedro was afraid that Dona Beatriz could easily become the pawn of one of his rivals, and he had even entertained the thought that the movement might be a skillfully engineered political ploy. Unequivocal support from the Church might well prevent the ploy from working. "I appeal to you, my Spiritual Father," he said to the priest, "that you might pray to God for me and for my people and recommend me to our Father Saint Francis, my special advocate and protector. You are my friend, my father, my grandfather, my shield and all my hope. For the love of God, instruct me, educate me, and support me in these calamitous circumstances. I promise you that I will not depart one bit from your counsel and deeds."

Much as Pedro was thinking in both religious and political terms, so was Father Bernardo. He was touched by the speech, but he was afraid that it was just fine words spoken in the heat of the moment. He knew the political situation quite well, and realized that much of the king's fervor was motivated by a desire to rid himself of potential enemies. He was suspicious of the king's sincerity.

Still, he did not want Dona Beatriz to continue teaching, and Pedro's help was essential if this goal was to be accomplished. "Have no fear," he told the king as he helped him from the floor where he had been kneeling before the priest. "All things are possible with God's favor," he continued as he guided the king back to his seat. He would give the Church's support to King Pedro.

"Within the next few days," he told the king, "if you are present when I say Mass, I will preach a sermon publicly refuting the falsity and diabolically inspired insanity of the false Saint Anthony."

The audience over, each returned to his place, Father Bernardo to the church, the king to his advisors. But Father Bernardo did not make the public announcement as he had planned. When Pedro and his advisors came to church to hear Mass, the priest deemed that the crowd was too small and his message would not have the kind of general impact he hoped for. "My chest closed up on me," he would write later, "and I could not speak."

King Pedro was not at all sure that the time was right for refutation. Dona Beatriz had indicated that she wished to leave the palace, and he was unsure if it was wise to restrain her. He sent word to Father Bernardo that preaching against her publicly might simply cause her to flee, and that he should do as he saw fit, either by preaching or not.

Father Bernardo wanted her to be restrained if possible and asked the king to hold her, at least until Sunday Mass, which was sure to be well attended. However, their plans were in vain, because Dona Beatriz had a feeling of foreboding. Fearing that she might be harmed if she stayed on to Sunday, she left on Saturday, this time not following the Mbidizi down its valley, but going north and east, into areas where she had not preached before.

6

The Saint and the Kings

_____

WITH SAINT ANTHONY'S INCARNATION safely out
of the way for the time being, King Pedro breathed a bit
more easily. He decided not to go to Mass that Sunday, although
many people from the palace, the town, and the surrounding area
did appear.

Father Bernardo decided it was time to put the weight of the
Church against Saint Anthony. He preached a long sermon explaining that Saint Anthony had not appeared in the body of
Dona Beatriz. He related his audience with her, his assessment of
the answers she had given him, and his belief that the being who
spoke through her was not Saint Anthony but the Devil himself,
or at least one of his demons.

Then, having explained himself, he berated the audience. He
knew that Dona Beatriz had won many supporters, and even
those who did not openly support her were still not completely
convinced that she was not speaking the truth. He wanted to take
a strong offensive against those, like Miguel de Castro, who were
still undecided.

It was their weakness in faith that had allowed this to happen,
Father Bernardo told the crowd. Too many people had accepted
her as a saint without proof or the Church's approval. He, like
all the Capuchins, was anxious that the Church always be respected, and that people know unequivocally that it and its
priests alone were qualified to make decisions about matters such
as this. Only their king, he told them, had remained steadfast in
his faith. He praised the king highly for his constancy, even

Beatriz' travels, 1704-6.

though Father Bernardo had doubts about how steadfast the king really was. In doing this he had blocked any chance Pedro had of appearing equivocal on the question of Dona Beatriz' teaching and using this to keep her supporters in his camp.

Finally, the priest issued a call to return to São Salvador and restore the kingdom. While he knew very well how difficult this was, and why King Pedro was reluctant to attempt it, he also knew that the idea was popular with the people. Dona Beatriz had accused him, and the Church by implication, of not wanting the restoration of the kingdom, and he wanted to make sure he was above reproach on that score.

Dona Beatriz' departure from Kibangu therefore strengthened the king's resolve to move on without her support. While she was at court many people listened to her. She was charismatic and one could not help feeling that she was someone very special. It was dangerous to go against her in public, for she had the remarkable capacity to elicit sympathy even from people who doubted her claims to be Saint Anthony. Any appearance of forcing her could lead to riot or rebellion, and yet Pedro felt that the Church would not back him if he did not support it. Increasingly, it would be Pedro and Father Bernardo in alliance against the Antonians.

When she was in Kibangu, Dona Beatriz had announced that God was going to level Mount Kibangu and destroy everyone there. It was the same proclamation that Apollonia Mafuta had made, but this time Dona Beatriz had named a date. Everyone, even those who did not believe her, was apprehensive as the date approached. Would the mountain be leveled?

The day came and passed without even a rumble. No fire had come from the sky, no great earthquake had shaken the mountain. King Pedro and his closest advisors decided they should go to Mass and celebrate both the fact that the mountain was intact, and that events had disproved one of Dona Beatriz's claims.

As something of a symbol of victory, King Pedro and his followers all wore small crosses on chains around their heads, so that the crosses dangled on their foreheads. The wealthier of the assembly had metal crosses, made from crucifixes, which many

Kongolese wore as rosaries or simply around their necks. Those with fewer resources wore wooden crosses, some converted from rosaries, others made up for the occasion.

When the priest asked King Pedro the meaning of this new demonstration of faith, the king replied, "This is no novelty, Father. We wear the sign of the cross because we are Christians and in our hearts we profess the faith of the cross." Others reminded the priest that Dona Beatriz had wanted to remove the cross from the square in Kibangu, and that by wearing the sign in a new place, breaking the older custom, they were reemphasizing their dedication to it and their opposition to Dona Beatriz' teaching.

If King Pedro was relieved that Dona Beatriz had left, she had not gone far. Once away from the court, she resumed her preaching with vigor and the energy that kept her going through long hours of walking and the emotion of preaching.

As befits a saint, Saint Anthony was now beginning to heal the sick, an instantly recognized miracle that could only strengthen her clams. Dona Beatriz claimed that she was able to cure infertility. If women would devote themselves only to Saint Anthony and to no other saint, or to any other supernatural being, whether in a nkisi or an image of a saint, or anywhere else, they could have children, even if they had been sterile for a long time.

Sterility was indeed an unwelcome curse in eighteenth-century Kongo. Families depended on having many children, and women married in their late teens or early twenties to ensure that they had large families so that when they were too old to work they would have someone to support them. As in all other parts of the world, it was not easy actually to have a large family. One out of every four babies died before its first birthday, and half of the babies born to any family would not survive into adulthood.[1] These were facts of life, and one had to accept them. But the inability to have children only made the situation worse and more or less guaranteed that the couple would have a difficult later life.

[1] These data are adduced from the study of baptismal statistics from the Kingdom of Kongo at the time; for a complete analysis and explanation, see Thornton, "Demography and History."

Men would abandon and mistreat wives who could not bear children, and infertile women went to great lengths to relieve their problem. There were many folk remedies for it, most of dubious value, but they continued because of the desperation of those who sought them. Ngangas specialized in problems with fertility, and religious cures as well as medical ones abounded.

Consequently, when Dona Beatriz announced that she could heal the infertile, she found an immediate following. Women who sought treatment for infertility, or just those who wanted more children, tied small ropes and threads on Dona Beatriz' hands and feet as a sign of their faith. This practice paralleled that of both Portuguese and Italian Christians who even today tie gifts of money and messages to the statue of Saint Anthony when he is carried in procession.

But as in the case of so many European Christian customs, the Kongolese found other meanings in it. In Kongo it was also a common practice in those days to wear chains or ropes on one's hands and feet on feast days and other special occasions. According to their interpretation, these cords that bound them made them slaves of the Madonna. It is also common today to tie or bind nkisi, as a way of ensuring that the power is held in, and thus the binding of Dona Beatriz had a second significance.[2]

Kongolese Christians had yet another reason for tying up Saint Anthony's hands and feet. In Kikongo, the verb *kanga* meant to tie or bind, and is used in this context today when referring to tying up the nkisi. But Kongolese Christians also used the verb *kanga* to mean to save in a Christian sense, as in the phrase *o Dezu ucucanga* or *o Nzambi Mpungu ucucanga* ("Jesus saves you" or "God saves you") in a dictionary that the Kongolese cleric Manuel Robredo and his associates prepared for Capuchin priests around 1648. In the catechism, Jesus was called Mukangi, the Savior, and the first line of the Salve Regina asked God to save Mary with the words *o Deos cucanga*. Although *kanga* was probably not used in any part of the Salve Antoniana as we know it, either in

[2] On this custom, see APF:SOCG 476, fol. 336, Bernardo da Gallo, "Conto delle villacazione missionale, ò sia relazione delle Missioni di Congo et Angola dové missionó lj anni," 12 October 1710.

its meaning of to tie or to save, the relationship to the original prayer was probably not lost on those who knew both.[3]

By playing on these two meanings of *kanga*, Dona Beatriz' devotees were expressing both a general hope for the kind of salvation of Kongo and all the people that her Salve Antoniana promised, and a more specific request for children.

After leaving Kibangu and heading north, Dona Beatriz went first to the camps of Manuel da Cruz Barbosa at Mbuli to preach among this group of colonists, where her original message had not yet spread. Da Cruz Barbosa had not been aware of Dona Beatriz' earlier activities in the Mbidizi valley, and was initially puzzled by her teaching and the stir it created among his subjects.

He therefore wrote Father Bernardo to inquire after the matter, and reported on Dona Beatriz' teaching and activities. The priest's reply was typical: "If you want to denounce the Christian Faith, and Christ, and consequently God as well, and to adore a demon in place of God, you have only to submit to that woman and to believe her diabolical insanity."

Da Cruz Barbosa lacked Pedro's indecision, and perhaps his sensitivity as well. No sooner had he received Father Bernardo's reply to his inquiry than he wrote straight to the king demanding authorization to seize Dona Beatriz and cut off her head. But Pedro would not have it, and replied to his second in command to let her proceed and that she could go wherever she wished. He would discuss his decision more fully, later, when there was more time.

Pedro had a hard time making decisions, especially ones as important as executing Dona Beatriz. A more decisive man, someone like his second in command, would not have hesitated. But perhaps a more decisive man would also have failed in the larger mission that Pedro had taken upon himself, that of restoring the kingdom. That would take patience, discipline, and a willingness to put the common good above one's own. In the long run, per-

---

[3] Biblioteca Nazionale da Roma Vittorio Emmanuele, 1896, MS Varia 174, "Vocabularium latinum, hispanicum et congoese," fols. 51v, 116v (meaning "to tie"); *Doutrina christãa* ch. 5, no. 1, and ch. 3, no. 8 (meaning to "save" and "to deliver").

haps Pedro's hesitation would be better for Kongo. In the short run, his decision allowed Dona Beatriz to build her movement into a force Pedro would have to reckon with.

Dona Beatriz, having the freedom to go where she chose, decided to travel to Bula to see King João, around late September or early October 1704. Now that she had built up a following in Kibangu, Dona Beatriz was reaching out in the lands that lay under the jurisdiction of other rulers, just as she had explained that Saint Anthony had done when seeking a medium to possess.

King João's possessions lay south of the Zaire River, along 100 kilometers of twisting riverbank. The land was etched by the valleys of the Mpozo, Lufu, and several of the minor rivers, tributaries of the great river, creating fantastic sharp cliffs and twisted hills. Much of the upland country was forested and uninhabited, but the nature of the country made it as much a natural stronghold as Kibangu was.

It would take a traveler like Dona Beatriz four or five days, going at her leisure and preaching along the way, to follow the Lufu River from Kibangu to Bula. Its capital, Lemba, lay near the Lufu's confluence with the Zaire and benefited from traffic that flowed along the larger river to the coast. Dutch, French, and English merchants based in Malemba, capital of the small northern kingdom of Ngoyo, occasionally traveled directly upriver to Lemba, but otherwise Vili merchants from the coast, based in João's domain, traveled downriver to the ocean.[4]

Dona Beatriz visit to Bula had multiple purposes. On the one hand, she knew that the reunification of the country would require the consent of João and his sister. On the other hand, she, who lived in a world of symbols and symbolism, knew that Bula contained a rich trove of ancient Kongolese royal insignia, taken

---

[4] The old site of Lemba, abandoned sometime in the eighteenth century, was visited and examined by Georges Schellings in 1950. There he found an ancient baobab tree under which, he was told, the kings rendered judgment. It was located in Matadi Territory, Palabala sector, near the village of Kunga; Archives of the Redemptorist Fathers, Leuven (Belgium), Letter of Georges Schelling to Procureur General, Kimpese, 2 August 1951. (My thanks to the archivist, Fr. Joseph Roosen, for a copy of the letter.)

during the fateful sack of São Salvador in 1678, that would seal the restoration.

Dona Beatriz announced that she was particularly interested in obtaining an important royal relic known as the Santissimo Sacramento, or Most Holy Sacrament. This relic was a brocaded bag tied with silk threads that contained a papal bull with many indulgences given to King Diogo I (1543–61). Tradition maintained that the bull had been obtained through a miracle. Before São Salvador was sacked, it had been deposited in a sort of reliquary in the Church of the Most Holy Sacrament in the city, and hence its popular name.[5]

The bag was an important piece of regalia, and if King João would give it to Dona Beatriz, she could begin the work of reunification. Dona Beatriz believed in miracles, and it would take a miracle, too, to put it in her hands. From the beginning, João and his supporters showed themselves completely opposed to the preaching of Saint Anthony.

But whatever the king thought, Dona Beatriz found followers among the common people, and she soon had a large following that accompanied her as she moved toward João's capital of Lemba in October 1704. Sensing the hostility of the king and his faction, Dona Beatriz turned to preaching God's punishments against those who would hinder her, whether they were the followers of João II or Pedro IV.

If Kibangu were threatened with a deluge of fire that would burn the mountain, Bula was threatened with a deluge of water that would drown the people when the "Little Rains" started in October. The crowd that accompanied her to João's court was growing larger and desperate, all the more so as unseasonably heavy rains began pouring down and the rivers started to rise beyond their normal limits. Kongo had two rainy seasons – the Little Rains that started in October and went until about Christ-

---

[5] The bag and its history in earlier times was described in detail by the Jesuit missionary Mateus Cardoso as he saw it displayed at the funeral of King Álvaro III and coronation of Pedro II in 1622; see "Morte de D. Álvaro III, Rei do Congo e eleição de D. Pedro II Affonso," in Brásio, *Monumenta*, 15:491–2.

mas, followed by a brief dry spell that was broken by the Great Rains from February until May. Heavy rain in the Little Rains was therefore a warning and cause for alarm.

João and his supporters were unconvinced by this demonstration of Dona Beatriz' seeming command over nature. When Dona Beatriz came before him, she explained her mission. She maintained that Pedro IV had sent her to collect the regalia, and that he was one of her followers. João, however, was not impressed. "I am a most Christian king," he declared, and "King Pedro of Kibangu is a child in the Faith, not yet grown up." He ordered her to leave his presence, and threatened to punish her for her presumption if she remained.

Dona Beatriz was undeterred and remained near the court to insist, but João sent his Jaga mercenary guards to beat her and her followers and drive them away. Dona Beatriz had to leave, and trudged off slowly to the south in the direction of São Salvador, followed by a large crowd of devotees.

Dona Beatriz' rebuff in Bula, added to her indifferent treatment in Kibangu, showed that the nobility of Kongo was uninterested in her vision of restoring the country. But her experience in both places also demonstrated that the common people of Kongo were willing and even eager to support her.

The peasants, whose building styles made them mobile, now flocked to Dona Beatriz in spite of her own noble origins. They had reason to think themselves abandoned and exploited, and looked for someone like Dona Beatriz, whose spiritual status bypassed class prejudice, to help them.

Kongolese peasants, although they possessed a simple material culture, would not normally have been an impoverished people. By the standards of the seventeenth-century world, they were not badly off. Average life expectancy, about thirty-five years at birth, was about the same as in Europe or Asia at that time, while infant mortality, which ran to about a quarter of all the newborns, staggering by today's standards, was lower than the European average. Women married fairly early, probably in their late teens, giving Kongolese a birth rate of nearly fifty per thousand, higher than Europeans, but not unlike that of people of European origin who had settled in American colonies or were just then settling in South Africa.[6]

It was the war that had overwhelmed the Kongolese peasants, ruined them, and left them desperate, not their poverty or even their normal burdens of taxes and the lopsided justice that often characterized premodern societies. The destruction of war often fell on them, and the nobility often called on their resources to fight for honor and position. They found in Dona Beatriz someone who could speak to them and perhaps take their side. Her message was heard in the villages, and it was the villagers who backed her and who believed in her.

Dona Beatriz' message fitted their own ideology of an ideal society, which was like a village writ large.[7] Kongolese villages typically had something of a communal economy. All the people worked the fields together and the product was divided equitably, "according to the number of people in each household."[8] This economy did not necessarily preclude an economic and political elite, for in theory kings and rulers were regarded as necessary, if for no other reason than to provide protection, keep wrongdoers in line, and provide support from their own spiritual gifts against kindoki of the bad type, which would otherwise disrupt the communal solidarity of the village. Rulers were expected to be rich and to receive wealth from the community, but they ought also to share it with their followers generously. They would indeed have criticized Francisco Menezes Nkanka Makaya – the man who refused to be king because he was too much like a Portuguese – for "going around and demanding things" or "eating by himself," for such a king was not the ideal ruler they imagined.

Dona Beatriz was an ideal ruler, or could appoint ideal rulers, and could use her own kindoki to combat the evil of the present

---

[6] On the demography, John Thornton, "Demography and History in the Kingdom of Kongo, 1550–1750," pp. 507–30.

[7] For a modern Kongolese invocation of this ideal society, disrupted only by the evil forces of kindoki, see Bockie, *Death and the Invisible Powers*, pp. 1–82.

[8] See Thornton, *Kingdom of Kongo*, pp. 28–38.

rulers. In the hopes for some sort of new miracle that her follow-ers had allowed themselves to believe in, the normal run of po-litical authority – greedy, grasping, violent, and arbitrary – might truely be replaced by one that was evenhanded, unselfish, and just. As such, Dona Beatriz was as much a social revolutionary as a peacemaker.

Dona Beatriz and her followers' departure from Bula was sud-den and had left them homeless, but the crowd stayed by their saint. Their movement took on the form of a pilgrimage to their holy city, and a dangerous one at that, for they were leaving stored food supplies behind, confident that somehow they would be fed by their prophet. Dona Beatriz led her followers to believe that she had miraculously obtained the purse Santissimo Sacra-mento and had it in her possession. With this holy relic allegedly in hand, she set off for São Salvador to restore the capital and the kingdom. When Dona Beatriz and her followers arrived in the abandoned capital in late October or November 1704, they had achieved what Pedro IV had been afraid to do. They had restored the kingdom, at least symbolically.

But life in São Salvador would not be easy for Dona Beatriz and her band of devotees. Soon hunger set in, for they had left their homes and stored food behind them; they planted a crop as soon as they settled in, even though the rainy season was some-what advanced. Still, it would be some time before the grain would ripen.

Pedro Constantinho da Silva Kibenga, whose camps were close to the city, saw the movement as something he could capitalize on. He immediately offered to support them, and sent them some food as a gesture of goodwill. It helped, but it was insufficient to feed all the people who came until they could reap their first harvest. The group was reduced to eating flowers, leaves, and whatever wild products they could gather. After two or three months of their suffering, the crop matured in early 1705 and the first harvest guaranteed their survival.

Even before the harvest was in, Dona Beatriz moved on with her mission. Having reoccupied the capital herself, she proceeded with her own program to restore the country. She sent a messenger to Pedro at Kibangu, informing him that he, like the other nobles, should come to the capital. King Pedro, like King João, did not answer this call, and because of this Dona Beatriz proclaimed that he and anyone else who opposed her would soon suffer. Several others had defied her (specifically referring to the heavy rain in Bula) to their cost, and the others would pay as well.

If the nobles did not answer her call for reunion, the common people did. Even in the areas under the Kinlaza champion, Queen Ana Afonso de Leão, or around Kibangu, the commoners and peasants began singing the Salve Antoniana and proclaiming openly the tenets of her preaching. Thousands of people all over the country said the Hail Mary and cried for mercy each evening. Thousands more came to São Salvador. As Father Bernardo would write later, some came to venerate Kongo's new saint, either because they hoped the country would be renewed or perhaps, like Pedro Constantinho da Silva and the Kimpanzu, because they hoped they could earn a part in the movement. Others had heard tales of miracles and wished to be healed or rendered fertile; still others, because the restoration was a festive occasion and they wanted to see their friends and socialize. But whatever the motive, they came, and soon the city was bustling with activity, such as it had not seen in nearly half a century.

The nobility of the country was afraid of the movement, at least those who were now trying to co-opt it. But it was the traditional Church that particularly suffered. Even in Kibangu, Father Bernardo found himself abused. "You do not have the will to go to São Salvador," they told him, or "you are a false deceiver." He should have paid more attention to Saint Anthony, they said, perhaps he should have listened to her. They began to call him "Little Bernardo" or *finganga* – "little priest."

Helpless to respond to these charges, Father Bernardo took every opportunity to harass the king and his officials, hoping to shame them into more vigorous action. He began to greet them using the Antonian cry for mercy, or quoting from the Salve Antoniana, "If it were not for Saint Anthony, what are we to do?" When they asked for confession, he told them to go to Dona Beatriz and get her permission, "for I would not want to go against her will." Thus shamed, the king or his nobles declared themselves as Catholics, but Father Bernardo simply said, "I have no judgments to make, as to whether you are Catholics or not, until the end of this has been seen when I can state definitely what you are, but for the moment I cannot say with certainty."

Along with his protests of being a good Catholic, and his refusal to go to São Salvador to meet with Dona Beatriz, King Pedro was concerned about her obvious influence. She proclaimed publicly that she had obtained the Santissimo Sacramento in Bula, and the king wanted to know if that was true. To satisfy himself, King Pedro sent some emissaries to the city and demanded that they see the purse with the Santissimo Sacramento for themselves. But they were immediately rebuffed by Dona Beatriz. "If the king wants to see the purse," they were told, "he should come in person to the capital to see it; otherwise I will not give it, or send it, nor show it to anyone."

In late November or early December, Manuel de Cruz Barbosa decided to go to the city himself and ask, in the king's name, to see the purse. Again, the royal emissary was rebuffed. After a fruitless mission to Dona Beatriz, da Cruz Barbosa was abused and then threatened by troops loyal to Pedro Constantinho da Silva Kibenga, who was daily moving closer and closer to Dona Beatriz. Shamed and humiliated, da Cruz Barbosa had to flee from the city.

Now Dona Beatriz made a public announcement to answer both the king and his officials. No one could see the purse, she informed them, because it was put away in the ruined chapel of the old Capuchin hospice in São Salvador, and was being guarded by angels. These angelic guards made sure it could not be seen or known about; moreover, even visiting the ruined hospice would be fatal.

Da Cruz Barbosa did not believe this for a minute, and suspected she had hidden the purse in the chapel somewhere. So he arranged for spies to enter São Salvador by night. They entered the city undetected, went to the ruined chapel, searched the whole area thoroughly, but came back empty-handed.

Now that he had investigated the situation thoroughly, da Cruz Barbosa, as the king's majordomo, sent a report to Pedro in Kibangu. He was confident that Dona Beatriz did not have the purse and had failed to obtain it during her visit to Bula. She had made up the story to win supporters, and all her announcements about angels guarding the purse were simply "lies and deceit."

But, his report continued, the king should be aware that every day Dona Beatriz gained more and more followers in São Salvador. He had visited her and seen that it was filling up and her power was growing. She had won the protection and support of Kibenga, who would use the situation to his advantage. Finally, da Cruz Barbosa urged the king to come with all his forces and occupy the city, and quickly, too, if he did not want to lose his chance at restoring the kingdom.

On reading his subordinate's report, King Pedro decided that he must act. He saw that Dona Beatriz' message was winning more and more popular appeal, and Kibenga was using it as a force to be reckoned with. It was near the end of December 1704, and the king decided he would leave Kibangu for the capital as soon as the New Year arrived.[9]

Dona Beatriz was now where she wanted to be, undisputed mistress of the royal capital and on the way to fulfilling her mission of restoration. Wild rumors of her powers spread widely throughout the country. Some said she had transformed those who defied her into beasts. She built a small house for herself directly behind the ruins of the cathedral, and began preaching from there. To assist in this work, she began to commission her "Little Anthonys."

The Little Anthonys were to be Saint Anthony's missionaries to all parts of the country. Each would be possessed, much as Dona Beatriz was possessed, by a saint. In Saint Anthony's new revelation of Heaven, all the saints were subordinate to Saint Anthony, and therefore, although they were as much saints as Dona

---

[9] For Beatriz' travels and events from her departure from Kibangu until the end of the year, see da Gallo, "Ultime," fols. 296v–301.

Beatriz herself, they were still Little Anthonys in recognition of their lower status.

They often traveled in pairs, and moved rapidly throughout the country. Their preaching was linked to that of Dona Beatriz, but soon took on local patterns that altered her message. They were rejected, as Dona Beatriz was, by much of the Kongolese nobility, although some, especially those of the Kimpanzu faction, like Kibenga, supported them.

Little Anthonys began leaving São Salvador in January 1705 headed for the provinces. Shortly after that, Father Bernardo decided to leave Kibangu, partly to get away from the problems of the place and partly to fulfill his duties as a priest and perform the sacraments in other parts of the country. But he was also caught up in the times, and his decision to go to Nsundi, the province north of Kibangu, was also partly an intelligence mission, to see how other parts of the country were faring in this new propaganda. If the Little Anthonys were there, the priest decided, he would try to bolster the Duke of Nsundi against them.

The dukes, as members of the Kimpanzu faction might easily decide to support Kibenga, who was also a Kimpanzu, and hence might be supportive of Dona Beatriz and her messengers. At least this was what she may have hoped.

In fact, however, Duke Domingos was not so bound by family or factional ties that he had any interest in Dona Beatriz or Kibenga. He had recently taken over as ruler and did not consider himself automatically a party to anything that other Kimpanzu faction members did. Nsundi was an independent force in Kongo's affairs.

Consequently, when the first Little Anthony arrived in Nsundi, Duke Domingos would not receive him. Indeed, he would not even allow his Captain General to receive him unless Father Bernardo met him first. Father Bernardo received the Little Anthony, but rebuked him and ordered him to leave. But official disapproval of the Antonians did not necessarily mean they were not accepted by the ordinary people. Domingos later told Father Bernardo that he was very glad the priest had come, because he was afraid that without a priest he could not have stemmed the flood of support the Little Anthony won among the commoners, and even some of the nobility.[10]

But the scorn of the official church was hardly enough to stop the movement that Dona Beatriz had started. Commoners in Nsundi, as in the area around the capital, were flocking to see the messenger and resurrected saint. The general support of the masses was to some degree seconded by many of the Kimpanzu of the province who, although they valued their independence, could still see a future for a fellow Kimpanzu like Kibenga to be king.

While Father Bernardo was traveling to Nsundi, Pedro decided he could wait no longer to bring his forces out of Kibangu and move toward São Salvador. Da Cruz Barbosa's recent report, and suggestion that he could lose his kingdom if he did not come down, had convinced the king that for better or worse he could delay no longer. He made a public display of piety, going to the chapel near his palace and praying to the Madonna, Saint Francis, and Saint Anthony to protect him and guide him through this dangerous undertaking. He explained to all present that he was going down the mountain not to obey the commands of the "false Saint Anthony" but to restore the True Church.

To give his action fuller significance, he took up the crucifix from the altar and carried it with him. Bearing his holy standard, and starting in a heavy rain that marked the outset of the Great Rains, the royal army and a portion of the people of Kibangu began the rough descent from the mountain on 24 February 1705. The party traveled some distance to Mulumbi, where it joined with colonists who had occupied the place under Manuel da Cruz Barbosa. Once joined with da Cruz Barbosa, however, King Pedro did no more. From his camp, for the next year, he and his forces watched the now clearly rebel followers of Kibenga and their allies, not far away.[11]

---

[10] Da Gallo, "Ultime," fols. 301–301v.
[11] Da Gallo, "Ultime," fols. 301v–302.

Shortly after his descent Pedro sent to Father Bernardo in Nsundi to return and buttress him in his new location. The priest replied that he was glad the king had finally taken the matter in hand, but told him that he wanted to remain in Nsundi at least until Easter. After that, the priest moved down the Inkisi valley to see what was taking place in the other, smaller provinces that lay there.

His journey was only partially successful – at Mpangu, Nsundi's southern neighbor, the marquis treated him badly and did not allow him to stay, possibly because of Antonian teaching or because the priest was perceived as being too close to King Pedro. Whatever the cause, Father Bernardo soon feared for his life and had to flee under cover of darkness.

Farther south still, at Mbata, Father Bernardo found the situation more complicated. The two rival dukes, one supported by Kibangu and the other an independent faction that included some of the eastern regions, made any negotiations difficult. Attitudes had hardened – just a few months before he visited, Miguel Ngoma Mpasi, King Pedro's longtime ally, had been killed by his own followers for the simple reason of having gone too near the lands of his rival. The priest performed Miguel Kilau's marriage ceremony, but the duke died not long afterward, even though he was a young man. The dissension continued even after the death of both contenders, kept alive by their supporters and no doubt by Kibangu interests as well. Invoking clerical neutrality, the priest managed to visit both new dukes, however. While he was in Mbata, Father Bernardo received another urgent message from King Pedro, begging him to return to his side.

Pedro was now facing a major crisis, for his decision to move was also putting pressure on his followers in the colonist camps to renew their obedience. This was not a problem for the loyal majordomo, da Cruz Barbosa, but it would be important for the ambitious Pedro Constantinho da Silva Kibenga. When the king came to Mulumbi, he had called on Kibenga to join him and swear public allegiance. Kibenga had refused, and then declared himself a rebel.

Kibenga's rebellion had an extra bite for King Pedro, not just because his erstwhile ally, a man whom he had deliberately cultivated with honors and position, had deserted him. King Pedro had also married Kibenga's niece, Hippólita, and she was now torn between her loyalty to her husband and to her family. To this she had added some personal twists of her own. Since Dona Beatriz had visited Kibangu, Hippólita had been attracted to her, and in the interim the queen had become an Antonian. She would never be able to reconcile these conflicts when her uncle defected from the king, for her faith and her family inclined her toward Kibenga and away from her husband.

When Father Bernardo returned in August, he compromised Pedro's cause by refusing to stand unequivocally on the king's side. Instead of joining King Pedro, the priest built a small hospice for himself between the two camps. Again invoking clerical neutrality, he offered to work for reconciliation. But on the whole, the priest was a poor negotiator. Far too arrogant and hotheaded himself, he contributed little to reconciliation.

While this standoff developed near São Salvador, Dona Beatriz continued her work in the capital. Her first Little Anthonys had gone to Nsundi and failed, but more were going out to see if they could promote the religious fervor of São Salvador in other parts of the country. They now began to focus their attention on other areas where the Kimpanzu faction was welcome or was in control, such as Soyo, the Kimpanzu's traditional champion, or the lands still controlled by the Kimpanzu de Nóbrega line at Luvota and Mbamba. Kibenga had been friendly to Queen Suzanna and was also related to both the Kimpanzu and the princes of Soyo, so the possibility of finding political support there was growing stronger.

During Lent, in early March 1705, two of the Little Anthonys arrived in Mbanza Soyo. They were taken before the prince, António III Baretto da Silva.

"We have been sent by a person recently risen from the dead, into whom Saint Anthony has entered," they told the astonished prince, and "we are charged with advising you that according to the will of God, the Kingdom of Kongo is to be restored.

"All the great men of the country," they continued, "are to

gather together at São Salvador." The Prince of Soyo was "particularly enjoined to be present."

After allowing them to speak a bit longer, as their claims became more and more revealing, Prince António ordered them driven away, threatening them with harsh punishment should they continue their preaching in his domains.

If the Prince of Soyo was uninterested in Dona Beatriz' style of restoration of Kongo, however, there were those who received the Little Anthonys with much more favor. Rebuked in Mbanza Soyo, they moved down to lands in Soyo's south and beyond its southern border, where Kimpanzu pretenders were lodged. There they joined other Little Anthonys arriving from São Salvador.

Kongo's south coast was dry, almost arid. There were years when it never rained, although humidity was often stiflingly high and the tropical heat was close to unbearable. Most of it was under the Duchy of Mbamba, the largest in surface area of all of Kongo's major provinces, and the smallest in population. Most of the people lived either on the coast or in the far inland areas where higher elevations brought cooler temperatures and more rain. Along the coast the villages were often perched on hills and other elevated areas to catch the sea breeze. Fishing and salt-making were the principal occupations of its inhabitants, although in 1705 unusually heavy rains (the same rains that had threatened to flood Bula and gave weight to Dona Beatriz' threats) had ruined the salt production. The villages were surrounded by stout palisades, intended to prevent marauding lions from molesting the people at night. It was quite different from the areas farther north, where people often slept outside their houses on warm nights without fear. In the south, the people always went indoors to sleep.

The politics of the area had further contributed to its poor condition. Luvota was one part of Mbamba where Queen Suzanna de Nóbrega, although over ninety years old and blind, still more or less ran the affairs of the area, with the uneasy support of the princes of Soyo.

The Marquisate of Nseto, also in Mbamba, had the worst of the situation, for it was forced to pay tribute to three overlords: the

Prince of Soyo as well as both contenders for the control of Mbamba, Manuel de Nóbrega and Pedro Valle das Lagrimas, who held Mbamba on behalf of Queen Ana Afonso de Leão. The people suffered from constant war and were ripe for the Antonian message. Queen Suzanna, unlike the rulers of Soyo or Nsundi, allowed the Little Anthonys to circulate in her lands. Her son Manuel had temporarily left his charge as shadow Duke of Mbamba, and gone to the São Salvador region to be with Kibenga, who, since announcing his open break with King Pedro, was moving closer to Dona Beatriz and was cultivating relations with his Kimpanzu relatives.

Virtually every village in Nseto received a Little Anthony from the capital – in Samba there was one, while another Saint Anthony (not Dona Beatriz) was stationed at Ita. Saint John, who made rounds of the various settlements from his base in the village of Nsukulu, collected offerings of tobacco and takula, the wood used as a dye that could be sold at a profit. Another village nearby contained Saint Ursula.

Saint Lucy, who was also operating in the area, died and was laid out in a catatonic state, in the way that people always laid out the bodies of the dead. There she remained for a week, but after that she came back to life. Now she died and was reborn every week.

Saint Lucy sometimes worked with Saint Isabel, yet another resurrected saint. Saint Isabel conducted religious services, baptizing babies, hearing confessions, and giving absolutions with the Latin words *In nomine Patris et Filii et Spiritus Sancti*.

In addition to these spiritual exercises, and the usual ones of the Antonian movement – repeating the Salve Antoniana and crying for mercy – the Little Anthonys distributed their own particular type of nkisi. These were little cast-metal statues of Saint Anthony, intended to replace the cross and other symbols of Christian worship that Dona Beatriz had declared to be objects of misdirected kindoki.[12] Although the cult of Saint Anthony had

---

[12] On the geography of the Antonians in southern Soyo, see da Lucca, "Relazioni," pp. 231–5.

statues already in churches, these little statues represented something a little new. Archaeologists have recovered a tiny statue of Saint Anthony fixed to a Portuguese coin dated 1698, in a cemetery in eastern Kongo.[13] Locally manufactured statues of Saint Anthony, called *Ntoni Malau* were to become commonplace in Kongo in the eighteenth century, and many are in private collections and in museums in Kongo and all over the world even today. While there may be no connection to the Antonian movement itself, the custom of producing religious objects in Kongo seems to date from this time.[14]

In accordance with the Antonian creed as enunciated in the Salve Antoniana, the Little Anthonys told the people that baptism served no purpose in God's eyes, at least not that given by the Church. They were therefore wary when Father Lorenzo da Lucca, the Capuchin priest stationed at the hospice in Soyo, arrived on an annual tour to baptize children late in June 1705.

Father Lorenzo was on his way to the de Nóbregas' lands, and expected little trouble outside of the usual problems of overland travel. He had learned from long experience that the Kongolese had deep respect for priests and rarely presented them with real obstacles to travel. They might delay them to enjoy their services, or to demand payment for carrying their goods, but they rarely prevented a priest from performing his duties, even in this war-torn region.

Therefore the Tuscan priest was surprised when the teacher and catechist who accompanied his small mission train returned from a trip ahead to report that the people of Nseto did not want to see the priest or bring their children to him to be baptized. Kongolese always wanted their children baptized. Priests were exhausted by these demands; whenever they traveled, people would come from miles around to wherever a priest had stopped to bring their children to be baptized. Just a few weeks earlier,

[13] Olivier de Bouveignes, "St. Antoine et la pièce de vignt reis," *Brousse* 3–4 (1947).

[14] See Robert Wannyn, *L'art ancien du métal au Bas-Congo* (Champles, Belgium, 1961), pp. 40–3 and plates XXXIV and XXXV; and J. F. Thiel, *Christliches Kunst in Afrika* (St. Augustin, Switzerland, 1987), pp. 96–7.

on mission in the small Marquisate of Kiondo, near Mbanza Soyo, Father Lorenzo had been mobbed by women shouting "*Nganga, nganga, santa mungwa*" ("Father, Father, holy salt"), as the Kongolese called baptism because of the priest's putting a tiny bit of salt on the newly baptized's tongue. Sometimes a priest had to baptize more than 1,000 children, one at a time, in a day. Priests had left the country having baptized as many as 50,000 or more children in the course of their residence.

If the priest refused or excused himself, he was threatened and indeed forced to perform this sacrament. Kongolese rarely were married in the Church, except for the highest nobility. They scarcely ever sought to confess their sins, and few indeed heard the Last Rites. But baptism was different. This sacrament they had to have. It was the symbol of their Christianity.

The teachers of Soyo were among the most numerous and best organized of the country. Most of them were members of the nobility, and some saw the position, as did others in the service of the Church, as a political opportunity. Prince António himself had served for much of his youth in the local church, as altar boy, sacristan, and teacher. These people were not impressed with the Antonian message, and were greatly concerned about the arrival of the Little Anthonys. The teacher accompanying Father Lorenzo spoke to these concerns when he informed the priest that the people of Nseto had "been listening to the preaching of a black man who, under the shadow of devotion has been teaching many heresies and falsehoods."

"But," he went on, "many believe him and make a great show of devotion and obedience on their knees before him." The teacher's explanation had its effect, for Father Lorenzo asked for more details.

"He teaches that they ought not to adore the Cross, as it was the instrument of Our Lord's death. Instead, he has them adore a tin statue of Saint Anthony." Father Lorenzo then informed the teacher that he had been present at the interview of the Little Anthonys with the Prince of Soyo, and asked if he could help him identify them.

"By God," the teacher replied, "he was sent by a person who

had risen from the dead. He was one of two ambassadors sent from São Salvador by this resurrected person who calls herself Saint Anthony."

Father Lorenzo recalled that he had met the same person a few days before, in the Marquisate of Funta, in the southernmost regions of the Prince of Soyo's domains. There he had heard people singing devotions and following a person around, but he had assumed it was just the local teacher doing his job well. He had later heard, however, that the real teacher in the area had ordered this leader imprisoned, but he had escaped, although one of his tin statues of Saint Anthony had been left behind. Now, in Nseto, Father Lorenzo was encountering him again, and this time learned the details of his mission.

Father Lorenzo was determined to imprison what he considered an imposter, and so he sent a message ahead secretly to the Marquis of Nseto and set out the next day to go there himself. He and the *mwene musambi*, an official sent from Mbanza Soyo to oversee the prince's interests in the region, took thirty of his assistants, many armed with muskets, and crossed the Mbidizi River into Nseto, reaching the village where the Little Anthony was residing around midday. This small army entered the town on pretext of other business, and in a short time had arrested the Little Anthony and presented him to the priest.

Father Lorenzo recognized him as one of the two ambassadors who had visited the prince some months earlier and who, he was told, called himself Saint Anthony. Now, captured, the man was on his knees before the priest. Asked his name, he told them he was called Saint Anthony, but he was not really Saint Anthony.

"I know," the priest told him, "that you are not Saint Anthony, but why do you preach these falsehoods?"

Saint Anthony, offended, replied, "In these lands there are diabolic and superstitious things, and I have come here to seize them and burn them."

"Why have you burned them," asked the priest, "if the bush here is full of diabolic things?" He then ordered the man closely guarded.

Several of the teachers of the area were pleased that Father

Lorenzo had arrived. They had worked against the Little Anthony, and he in turn had placed them under his excommunication, using his own powers of kindoki to pronounce the curse of kumloko. They were unconcerned, they told Father Lorenzo, because they had a Missionary Father with them who had the power to absolve their excommunication with his own kindoki (which they hoped was stronger).

Obviously, the impact of the Little Anthonys was more thorough than could be resolved by arresting one of them. The teachers were sure that he possessed some power, whether diabolic or divine, that required the missionary to help them. The common people were likewise uncertain.

The teachers went out to find the ruler of the area and to gather the children for baptism, since parents had earlier refused to have their children attended to when the Little Anthony was at large. After a time the teacher returned with a great mass of people, who asked the priest for a benediction.

"Now that I have come here," the priest told them, "I would not like to leave without baptizing the children," as they had not sent them to him when he was some distance away.

The people, however, while wanting to be blessed by the official Church, were still not convinced that Saint Anthony's message was false. They hoped that Father Lorenzo's blessing on them was also a recognition of the status of the new form of Christianity, which they understood as a powerful tool against the visible wicked kindoki of their time, and the harsh conditions it had brought about.

They told Father Lorenzo, "We have no children to baptize because they are with their mothers in the fields." Father Lorenzo knew that they were putting him off. Such activities had never interfered with his missionary work before, and just a day or two earlier people had stopped work to come to him. He now suspected that the Little Anthony had made a bigger impression than he had suspected earlier.

Now the priest decided it was important to take matters firmly in hand. Pointing to the small group of armed men he had with him, he threatened to burn down their village if the children were not brought at once.

Just then, an old man, who was the nkuluntu, or village leader, arrived. "It would not be good to burn down the village," he told the priest, adding that he would get the children to come. He then ordered the women to bring their children for baptism, but without success. Finally, he told the priest that he had some children of his own to baptize, but the people could not afford to pay the customary fee.

Again, Father Lorenzo was unconvinced. Priests often charged no fee at all, or simply sought their subsistence. He told them he would baptize the children without a fee, at which point six children were brought.

"Where are the rest?" he asked the people, who were still milling around. "There are no more," they told him. Again this was clearly untrue. Typically, even in lightly populated rural areas, a priest would have a hundred or more children to baptize at any given stop.

"Where are the others?" Father Lorenzo demanded.

"There are no others" came the reply.

"It is not possible that as many women as live here would have no children," the priest replied.

"They are all sterile" was the answer.

Finally, stubbornness won out. Father Lorenzo insisted he would not leave until the children were brought, and eventually they began coming. By the end of the day the people had brought eighty-two children to the tree where the priest sat and did his work. But his troubles were not over.

Although the people continued to return to the official Church's sacraments, they still hoped that the Antonian movement with its promise would receive some official support. Therefore a delegation of the more important village leaders went to Father Lorenzo and asked if he would not set the Little Anthony free before he left. Father Lorenzo replied that he would if he found the man innocent.

But the delegation was not entirely satisfied with this answer;

they were suspicious that Father Lorenzo would go back to the old ways once he was away from them. They told him that they could easily free the Little Anthony by force if they wished.

Father Lorenzo then made a public announcement that anyone seeking to free the prisoner would fall under excommunication of the Church. Placing the prisoner in the midst of his armed men, the priest moved off.

Much like his colleague Father Bernardo, Father Lorenzo was convinced that the possessed saints were in league with the Devil. He did not view their movement as a political trick or even as insanity. When Father Lorenzo heard that Saint Lucy was regularly dying and being reborn, he concluded that the Devil himself brought Saint Lucy food secretly while she appeared dead.[15]

Father Lorenzo may have won the victory at that spot, for that moment. But the incident shows the strength of the movement that Dona Beatriz had started. Within a few months of the start of her preaching, she had won the support of large masses of common people, living a great distance from São Salvador, whom she had never visited personally. Two Little Anthonys, unarmed and apparently unaccompanied, had managed to get a whole district to stop baptizing their children. No doubt they were responding to the call in the Salve Antoniana that baptism served no purpose as God would know the intention in their hearts.

Political authorities might try to use the movement. They might, like a number of Kimpanzu leaders, allow Dona Beatriz or her Little Anthonys to circulate in their domains. They might feed and support them, as Kibenga had done when Dona Beatriz' hungry followers arrived in São Salvador, but they would not ultimately control the forces that had been unleashed by Dona Beatriz's teaching and preaching.

The political authorities had an important role to play in the spread of the movement, as Father Lorenzo himself soon discovered. All throughout the rest of his travels across Nseto, and even beyond its southern border on the Loze River, he met with resistance and even with people mocking him. Indeed, at the small

---

[15] Da Lucca, "Relazioni," pp. 218–22.

village of Mayenga, one particular woman gave Father Lorenzo special trouble, finally prompting him to ask her if she was crazy or possessed. In response, she and the other women who were with her simply "laughed shamelessly." Not even local authorities were prepared to support him. But when he crossed into Nsulu, south of the area, the situation changed dramatically. This was the area under control of the Kinlaza duke of Mbamba, Pedro Valle das Lagrimas. There was no mocking of priests there, but only an orderly visit, with many baptisms and uneventful performances of the Mass. The Antonian movement was becoming involved in the politics of the kingdom; as such, it was becoming more of a player in the forces of disunity and its kindoki was potentially tending toward the dangerous sort.[16]

[16] Da Lucca, "Relazioni," pp. 235–41.

7

Saint Anthony in Sin and Glory

KING PEDRO'S DESCENT FROM KIBANGU and his establishment at the camp of Mulumbi might have made life much more difficult for Pedro Kibenga, but it did not affect Dona Beatriz. She was in command of São Salvador, and thanks to Kibenga and his Kimpanzu allies, she was secure in her position. Now Kimpanzu nobles crowded around her. Kibenga's own wife led a number of other highborn ladies in constantly sweeping the path that led to her house by the cathedral.

When she ate, Dona Beatriz was surrounded by followers, noble as well as peasant. Wealthy Kongolese often wore cloaks and mantles across their shoulders and upper bodies, and these were put before the saint as a tablecloth. It was a great honor to receive any food from her hand, and even to eat the crumbs that fell from her mouth. When she drank, her adherents would place their hands under the cup to catch any stray drop that might fall, so that they could be blessed by drinking it. To encourage this sort of devotion, Dona Beatriz occasionally deliberately let water or palm wine fall into these outstretched hands.

Dona Beatriz' position in São Salvado was made stronger every day as more and more people came from the countryside to the ruined city, covering the hillsides and the valleys near the old capital with their houses, filling the air with their songs and praise of the new saint. They learned the Salve Antoniana along with the new Hail Mary that Saint Anthony introduced (although its text is no longer known).

Dona Beatriz performed many spiritual exercises in the cathe-

dral, preaching or leading the people in prayer and song. Many
Church leaders had gone over to her, and a number of teachers,
interpreters, and catechists were among her closest adherents. Although the ordained clergy, either Italian Capuchins or mulattoes
from Angola, remained steadfastly opposed to the movement, it
was the teachers who provided Kongolese Christianity with its
doctrine, and had the respect of the people. Many remained with
the orthodox Church, of course, but the conversion of many to
Antonianism strengthened the idea that the Church accepted her
as a saint.

Apollonia Mafuta, Dona Beatriz' predecessor and now her follower, came to São Salvador along with the leader. There she
began her own practice, paralleling and supporting Dona Beatriz'
movement but independent of it as well. Mafuta took the name
of Old Simeon on instructions she received from another vision
of the Madonna, sent her own ambassadors out to the provinces,
and created her own chapel in one of the other churches of the
capital. There she dressed three stones as altars, one dedicated to
Saint Isabel, one to Saint Ursula, and one to Saint Anne. She said
Mass, heard confession, and did other spiritual exercises. When
giving absolution, she did so with the Latin formula: *In nomine
Patris et Filii et Spiritus Sancti.*

When Dona Beatriz went to preach, she arrived before the congregation, sang the Salve Antoniana, and then mounted the dais
at the altar to conduct Mass after her fashion, and to preach.
When she was finished, she left through the sacristy and took the
path to her house. Before going in the house, however, she went
to a small grove of trees, where her followers came up to her and
reverently kissed her feet. The house itself, besides serving as her
sleeping and personal quarters, was fitted out with a special place
on the floor where she slept in penance; it also had a front room
where she had a picture of the Virgin Mary, candles, and many
of the ties that were used to bind her symbolically.[1]

Trees and forests represent the Other World in Kongolese theology, and thus her standing at the border between the cleared

[1] Dona Beatriz' house is described in da Gallo, "Ultime," fols. 312v–313.

or cultivated area of the city and this small wild and uncultivated place symbolically linked her to the worlds of the living and the dead. It was for this reason that Kimpasi society houses were built on the edges of woods, and the imagery undoubtedly influenced her. Her status as a prophet and incarnate saint was reinforced by such symbolism.

Dona Beatriz spoke in elevated language resembling the secret language of the Kimpasi, with many obscure phrases which many could not understand but which people believed was evidence of her great wisdom. As with many prophets and saintly people, and especially mystics, she was credited with sanctity precisely because she had mastered arcane theological matters without study and at a young age.

"The Missionary Fathers preach the gospel and teach us many things about the Faith," Dona Beatriz's followers maintained. "This is not impressive, because they study very well and then do not preach anything except what they have learned." This was not the same as the achievement of "a simple woman, without any education whatsoever, much less a formal education in the Church," who could "preach such sermons and speak such words that cannot be understood, except perhaps in part – that this is remarkable, admirable!" For them, this was the best evidence that she was in fact Saint Anthony.

This knowledge could be transferred, as Dona Beatriz argued when she commissioned the Little Anthonys. They, too, became learned people upon their possession by their specific saints, without further study. Using these new ministers, Dona Beatriz let it be known that there would be a new order in Kongo.

Her attempt to create an order of nuns did not meet with the same success as her work with the Little Anthonys, many of whom were male. She recruited some young girls and gathered them to study and engage in religious practice; but many of her male followers sensed an opportunity in this that was different from her own purpose. The girls were soon surrounded by Little Anthonys, Guardian Angels, and other male followers. As news of the impending scandal was carried back to the girls' mothers, their parents intervened and the experiment was stopped.

In addition to the theology of her new movement, Dona Beatriz promised a new era of wealth in her sermons. She told the people that the trunks of the trees that had been cut down but not uprooted all around the city would soon turn to gold and silver. Under the stones of the city were mines of gold, silver, and jewels. Silks, clothing, and luxury goods of European origin were hidden in various places, and could be discovered.

To prove her point, Dona Beatriz revealed the location of some of these treasures. People went to various places in the city at her direction and dug up packages which were found to contain *nzimbu*. These were little shells, found around Luanda Island and the southern coast of Mbamba, that were used as money. Although the other treasures of gold, silver, silk, jewels, and imported luxuries were not found, these smaller miracles greatly helped to boost Dona Beatriz' reputation as a saint.

With wealth came power. Dona Beatriz' followers, especially her noble ones, had always seen her movement as a potential source of political gain. Dona Beatriz was becoming more explicitly political as her influence rose. Everywhere, the cry for mercy seems to have changed – subtly, from *tari* (mercy) to *yari* (power).

"Up to this point there has been no king in Kongo," she announced to her followers, "but if all the pretenders were to gather in the church, the one who was standing in the doorway would have a wreath placed on his head by an Angel who was to come from Heaven – that one would be the King of Kongo."

She believed that the present kings knew this, and that is why the Kimpanzu and Kinlaza were in competition. When the Angel selected someone from the rival factions, Dona Beatriz would declare herself to be on their side; she would let her followers know and they would all go over to the new king.

A new history was needed for a new kingdom, and Dona Beatriz provided some novelties. Now that she was actually exercising power in São Salvador, and actively planning to help in the selection of a new king, her teaching was beginning to include more politics. She was still very much a religious teacher, but the ideology of politics in Kongo often used religious symbolism.

Dona Beatriz was less interested in the origins of the monarchy, as partisans of a more conventional political solution, such as Pedro IV, were. The past of the kings themselves was irrelevant, since the choice of the next king would be through a divine miracle. Nor was she particularly concerned about the fine points of the country's constitution or the relationship between rulers and ruled. Perhaps this is because she envisioned the new Kongo as being something of a theocracy in which she, as Saint Anthony, and her specially appointed Little Anthonys would be the real force, and the kings and other secular rulers their servants.

For her, therefore, the origins of religion were what counted. One of her concerns was the foreign origins of Christianity. In her early teaching in the Mbidizi valley, Dona Beatriz had insisted that Kongo needed black saints, and that the Capuchins had wrongly denied that there were black or, rather, Kongolese saints. Her earlier explanation concerning the origin of Jesus, Mary, and Saint Francis in ancient Kongo, and assigning Kongolese nationality to them, had provided a satisfactory origin tale for her purposes.

At São Salvador, she elaborated on the question of race, albeit in a way that fitted Kongolese conceptions. Dona Beatriz informed her followers that Europeans had their origin from a clayey white stone called *fuma* in Kikongo. Kongolese or blacks had their origin, on the other hand, from a tree called *nsanda* in Kikongo, whose bark could be pounded and made into thread from which cloth was woven.

This history of the origin of humanity had readily identifiable symbolism in Kongolese thought. White was the color of the dead and of ancestors to the Kongolese. Ancestors were often thought of as dwelling in lakes, streams, oceans, or other large bodies of water, and hence were conceived as being on the "other side" of these bodies. The rock fuma was both white in color and usually found in streambeds or on the banks of bodies of water. Europeans, in addition to being pale in color, came from across water and could thus be readily identified with the ancestors, even if their present humanity was unquestioned. Europeans had introduced Christianity into Kongo, and in 1705 almost the only Europeans that anyone in Kongo saw were priests. All these matters suggested a connection with the Other World of the ancestors. Furthermore, no one doubted that the priests possessed the kindoki they claimed to have, although they might question, sometimes even violently, whether it was used with good or evil intention.

Nsanda tree bark produced a black cloth, of course, and black was the color of the living, of This as opposed to the Other World. The opposition between black and white, as Dona Beatriz saw it, was not primarily a racial matter but was also the opposition of the two worlds of religious thought. The tree was regarded as sacred – a nsanda tree shaded Lusunzi's stone at Kibangu. Musanda trees produced a cloth that was associated with childbirth. In fact, Dona Beatriz taught, it was the same cloth that was used as swaddling by the Baby Jesus. It was therefore closely associated with the living and with This World. Anyone who wore it, she explained, would never lack for silver, gold, or other precious commodities.

Dona Beatriz had her followers make cloth from this tree, and then wear it as a sort of crown. She herself crowned her most favored male supporters with this cloth; she was the only woman who wore one, probably because as Saint Anthony she was a man, in spite of her appearance. Those who were blessed with wearing the crown formed a special group, her Angels.

As a final flourish on the color scheme, Dona Beatriz also indicated that takula wood, whose bark produced a red dye used often in marriage and other rite-of-passage ceremonies, was the blood of Jesus Christ. It was a twist on the usual interpretation of communion wine, which connected to the color red, the color of transformation in life states (and hence its use in childbirth, marriages, and the like).[2]

Dona Beatriz' followers began to build a new political order based on her teaching. Outside São Salvador, this was developed

[2] On takula in the Antonian movement, see Colombano da Bologna to Propaganda Fide, 15 May 1706, APF:SRC Congo, 3, fol. 358v, published in Filesi, "Nazionalismo."

mostly by the work of her Little Anthonys; they fanned out in the areas under control of the Kimpanzu faction, who had openly declared themselves adherents of the new creed. This increased both the numbers and security of her followers, but it also had the consequence of delivering the movement in many subtle ways to the political leaders who had continued the civil war.[3]

As the Antonian movement's political character became more manifest, so, too, did the strength of the reaction against it by rival sections of the nobility. Once it became identified with the Kimpanzu, the Kinlaza leaders were anxious to add extirpation of heresy to their long-standing vendetta against the Kimpanzu. Although the movement continued to have a strong peasant following throughout the country – in large measure because the poor could see the benefits of the end of war and were willing to accept Dona Beatriz' preaching of an age of miracles – in Kinlaza areas such beliefs became dangerous even to peasants.

In response to the popular dimensions of the movement, Kinlaza nobles felt strongly obliged to take direct action against it. As much as it was feared because of its political dimensions and its alliance with the Kimpanzu, it had the potential to become a social movement that would upset the nobility as a group, which added a sense of urgency to the nobles' attack.

Because of this sense of urgency, Pedro Valle das Lagrimas decided to go on the offensive against the Antonians in the late dry season of 1705. He took up a great cross, and bearing it, he and a body of his soldiers moved eastward from his base at Mbanza Mbamba. He crossed Mbamba, and then up the Mbidizi valley to Mbanza Mpemba, where his brother served as marquis. Together the two declared a sort of crusade against the Antonians, rounding them up wherever they could be found, expelling the Little Anthonys who had rooted themselves in the villages, and returning the people to Catholicism.

The two brothers carried their campaign to Mbanza Nkondo, where their aunt, Queen Ana, was based. There the three united their forces and joined the Capuchin priest Father Giovanni Maria

---

[3] Da Gallo, "Ultime," fols. 303v–306.

da Barletta, who had recently come to staff the chapel at Nkondo, in continuing their cleanup operations.

Their efforts were not without resistance. Although the armed forces faced little difficulty in routing the Antonians out of the areas they controlled solidly, they faced more problems where Kimpanzu forces could intervene. Just as Duke Pedro Valle das Lagrimas was moving up the Mbidizi valley, some of the people in his possessions near to Nseto, where the Kimpanzu and the Antonians were the strongest, revolted. Several villages and their leaders declared themselves for the Antonians, and made common cause with the Kimpanzu. Supporters of Manuel de Nóbrega and his mother, Queen Suzanna, supplied armed assistance, and the district was lost to the Kinlaza.[4]

Driving the Antonians out of São Salvador, where the Kimpanzu had concentrated the bulk of their forces and where Kibenga had his own resources, would clearly not be as simple as the campaign to rid areas that the Kinlaza controlled firmly.

At this point, King Pedro and his loyal followers were seeking to do by conciliation what the queen and her supporters were to advocate doing by force. Since he had joined the majordomo da Cruz Barbosa at Mulumbi in February, Pedro had been seeking to return Kibenga to his service – but to no avail, especially when the former Captain General publicly declared himself a rebel. Father Bernardo, after his return from Nsundi in August, had sought to reconcile the two, although without much success.

King Pedro was disappointed that the priest was not automatically on his side. He sent Father Bernardo messages entreating him to be loyal, but the priest insisted that his role as missionary and representative of the Church did not allow him to take sides in affairs of this sort.

To make matters worse, Father Bernardo began writing and corresponding publicly with Kibenga, hoping to persuade him to recognize Pedro as king again. Pedro heard of this correspondence, and many of his supporters suggested to him that the priest was abandoning him.

[4] Da Lucca, "Relazioni," pp. 263, 274.

Pedro then sent Father Bernardo a cup of palm wine, a *mbungu*, elaborately garlanded with palm leaves. Such a cup is regarded in Kongolese etiquette as an invitation to a serious discussion, likely to produce a decision. A ritual exchange of greetings and statements of intent is likely to precede such meetings, and formal conclusions, witnessed by the participants, will follow.[5]

Father Bernardo recognized the seriousness of King Pedro's entreaty; coming from the king himself, it was, he noted, "an honor accorded almost no one." But the priest did not want to be pinned down. He sent messages saying that he liked the palm wine, but he wished that the king would not embarrass him with such important gifts. He made light of the offer, remarking that the palm leaves were not such an important gift after all, ignoring the cup which, of course, was the message.

Father Bernardo's actions were rooted in the long-standing Capuchin tradition of neutrality in disputes among the Kongolese nobility, and in a deeper concern that Kibenga's embracing of the Antonians posed a greater danger to the Church than the civil wars had. This was a critical point, since the priest had publicly declared the Antonian movement heretical, and Kibenga was flirting with ecclesiastical censure by supporting it.

But the priest still tried to reassure Pedro. "I found you to be the acclaimed King of Kongo when I arrived," he wrote him, "and so you remain as far as I am concerned until death, you and no other will be king." Indeed, Father Bernardo's correspondence with the Vatican makes it clear that he was a vigorous partisan of Pedro as king, and believed that only restoration through him would safeguard the Church. In his strong advocacy of a new crown to replace the lost one, Father Bernardo proposed personalizing it. He suggested that it be gold, set with precious stones, and inscribed with a Latin motto, paraphrasing Christ's statement to Peter: "You are Peter and upon this cornerstone [the famous Latin pun on Peter's name as word for rock] I will build the church of my lord." He went on to tell Pedro that "even if

---

[5] On the significance of *mbungu*, see Wyatt MacGaffey, *Custom and Government in Lower Congo* (Berkeley and Los Angeles, 1970), pp. 103–10.

the rebels would declare another king, I would have to recognize you and not the other as king."[6]

This stalemate and exchange of letters went on for the rest of 1705 and early 1706. Finally, beginning on Holy Saturday of 1706, Pedro decided to move in on the city and on Kibenga's forces. He left Mulumbi with his army and moved to the mountain of Evululu, only a day's journey from São Salvador. This forested area would be secure from any threat that Kibenga's forces could mount, and could be made into an impregnable base for future operations. As it was within striking distance of the city, Pedro paused there to regroup his forces, plant crops, and build a base. He hoped that the threat would bring Kibenga to his senses, but it had no effect. Pedro would remain in Evululu for the next three years, cautiously waiting for the opportunity to strike decisively.

Again the king wrote to Kibenga, offering him a full pardon if he would submit and obey him as a subordinate should. He should not be fooled by Dona Beatriz and her followers, Pedro reminded him, but should reform himself and come to his senses. He did not want to make war, King Pedro declared, "because it was precisely because of continuous wars that our kingdom has already been destroyed," and then added, in an obvious reference to the Antonians, "and the Faith has been destroyed also."

King Pedro believed that he spoke for everyone when he said that the "Kongolese do not want any more embarrassments, tired as they are from having to remain like beasts in the woods and fields: while relatives, wives, and children on all sides are outraged, killed, stripped naked, sold, and slaughtered." It was indeed just such an array of possibilities – killing, rape, looting, sale as slaves – which formed the core of discontent that had driven common people into adherence to Dona Beatriz, and which had led to the religious fervor arising from her original message.

---

[6] Da Gallo, "Ultime," fols. 302–303v. On da Gallo's partisan support of the king to Rome, see APF:SOCG 476, "Conto della villacazione," fols. 332–332v, and 335v. The inscription was to read "Tu es Petrus, et super hunc Petram angularem edificabo ecclesiam domini mei" (Matthew 16:18).

Early in 1706 Dona Beatriz made new announcements about Saint Anthony's mission in Kongo. Events were happening fast, she told her followers, and in order to keep up, she would have to visit Heaven frequently. She announced that she would die every Friday and go to Heaven, dining with God and "pleading the cause of the blacks, particularly the restoration of the Kingdom of Kongo" before Him. However, each Monday she would return to life and bring the news from on high down to her followers at São Salvador. Her house next to the cathedral was specially built to accommodate her during these visits to Heaven. It comprised three rooms, but only the two outer ones had doors; the middle one apparently had no door at all but could be secretly accessed by her closest supporters, and it was in this middle room that she went during her visits to Heaven.[7]

Events in her personal life were to make this new doctrine of greater significance than before. About the time she arrived in São Salvador, perhaps in late 1704, Dona Beatriz formed a close relationship with a man named João Barro. He became her principal Guardian Angel, to be known as Saint John, when she gave these honors out. Unlike Kibenga and the other highborn followers who received honors, Barro was her personal companion.

Twice Dona Beatriz became pregnant with Barro's child, but each time she aborted, using local medicine. However, in mid-1705 she conceived again, and this time the abortion medicine failed to work. The pregnancy created a problem for Dona Beatriz because ever since she had begun commissioning her Little Anthonys, she had wished them to lead lives of chastity, perhaps along the lines of the Capuchin clergy, the most visibly chaste religious figures in Kongo and a group whom, in spite of her theological positions, she respected greatly. She wished to set a model of chastity herself for her Little Anthonys, and for the order of nuns she was trying to create.

The events had an important impact on Dona Beatriz' ideas about her teaching and mission. There is no reason to believe that from the time of her possession until she came to reside in São

[7] Da Gallo, "Ultime," fols. 312v–313.

Salvador, Dona Beatriz did not fully and firmly believe she was possessed by Saint Anthony and that he spoke through her. She was probably not literally possessed for the entire period, but mediums are capable of being possessed for fairly long times, interspersed with periods of normal consciousness. She was therefore aware that she was still Dona Beatriz as well as Saint Anthony, but that even when she was not possessed her knowledge came directly from the saint.

She believed the saint could protect her, but she was no stranger to matters of this world, and had been married twice, after all. She had become pregnant by Barro, and in this the saint had not protected her. She had begun to doubt her mission, perhaps even the reality of what had happened to her. However, she was not so convinced of this that she was prepared to denounce herself, and because her followers were prepared to accept what she had said at face value, she now was forced to engage in subterfuge to keep her mission going.

Obviously, it would be difficult for her to be a model of chastity when she herself was pregnant, and consequently she hid the pregnancy from her followers. Being both tall and young, she was able to go for some time without the pregnancy being obvious. But as she neared the end of her term it became harder to conceal. She cut down on her public appearances, and her sojourns in Heaven at the end of every week may well been intended to keep her out of the public view as well as give her time for complete rest from the rigors of pregnancy.

By February or March 1706 she had decided that if she did not want her pregnancy to become common knowledge, she would have to take herself away from São Salvador. So she began to preach a variation on her weekly trips to Heaven. It would now be necessary for her to spend an extended time in Heaven, and she told her followers that "in order to further their cause with God and in order to handle their problems well, it would be necessary for her to remain in Heaven for a long time."

"Have patience in times of tribulation, and have courage and constancy in the Faith until death," she urged them. It was a deliberate deception on her part, perhaps the first time she announced something that she was convinced had not really happened to her, at least in her possessed state. Then she left them, quickly descended the mountain of São Salvador, and went back to the Mbidizi valley – where she had been born and had begun her ministry – to visit her family. Apollonia Mafuta, now Old Simeon, joined her there.[8]

It was then the end of the Great Rains, the best growing season that stretched from about January until the beginning of May. The harvest was being taken in, and the fields of the area's many villages were covered with stacks made from the chaff of the corn. She, Barro, and a girl of about eleven who served her took refuge in these refuse stacks, and there she gave birth to her son, named António in honor of the saint who had possessed her body.

The birth of her child coincided, quite by accident, with the campaign of the Kinlaza to clean up the Antonian movement. Valle das Lagrimas and his aunt, Queen Ana, had chosen this moment to send envoys to King Pedro to enlist his support in the campaign and to join their forces against Dona Beatriz, Kibenga, and the Kimpanzu.

The envoys' route just happened to pass through the very area where Dona Beatriz and her newborn son were living. As the ambassadors were walking at this fateful moment in early May 1706, they heard the voice of a baby crying from among the stacks of harvested grain. The envoys sent one of their number ahead to investigate and to hold anyone until the main group arrived. The scout discovered that the crying baby was none other than Dona Beatriz' baby. Thus, with no effort at all, Dona Beatriz, Barro, and the child fell into the hands of the Kinlaza leaders.

"Barro," the Kinlaza envoys asked the man, whom they recognized, "why have you left São Salvador? Where are you going?" they wanted to know. "And why do you have that woman with a child with you?"

"It is true," he replied, "I am indeed the Guardian Angel of Saint Anthony." Not only that, he told them he was only tem-

---

[8] Da Gallo, "Ultime," fols. 306v–307.

porarily in the area and that the woman was, in fact, Saint Anthony herself.

"Saint Anthony!" the astonished envoys repeated. "Saint Anthony here among these peasant houses and harvest stacks! Saint Anthony with a baby in arms, nursing it to quiet its crying?"

This was quite a revelation. "Tell us whose son is that baby?" they demanded.

Barro replied, "It's Saint Anthony's baby."

"Saint Anthony's baby?" they asked sarcastically. "But if she is Saint Anthony, how can she manage to have children?" Pointing out an obvious discrepancy, they continued, "Since when did Saint Anthony, who is a member of the Franciscan order" – and hence celibate – "have children? Tell us, then, did she have this child with you?"

"No," Barro replied.

"How can this be?" they pressed him, sensing that they were onto something very important.

"Ah, Ah!" he replied. Then, echoing the catechism that urged believers to accept many elements of religious teaching on faith and not to question them, he continued, "These are Divine secrets which cannot, nor must not be questioned."

They then turned to Dona Beatriz and asked her whose baby it was she was holding. "I cannot deny it; it is not mine," she answered them, "I do not know where it came from; I only know that it is something from Heaven."

"You had better come with us," they told her.

Raising their swords, they shouted "Ola," and without further hesitation ordered their servants to place Dona Beatriz and Barro under arrest. "We'll see if they're saints, and if their wickedness extends to the inscrutable secrets of God!"

Without further hesitation they bound their captives and took them directly to Evululu, where they presented them to King Pedro. Shortly afterward, the king managed to arrest Apollonia Mafuta and imprison her with the others.

Pedro was unsure what to do with his prisoners. He did not necessarily consider Dona Beatriz a capital enemy, even after her

alliance with Kibenga. He recognized that she was politically naive and that her program had too many Otherworldly dimensions
for her to be a genuine partisan. He also realized that her pregnancy had altered both her attitude toward her mission and her
future as a charismatic leader. He was certainly aware that his
own wife, Hippólita, had become her follower and was her partisan among his own court. It might be better not to deal with
Dona Beatriz than to risk a rupture within his court about her.

Pedro was therefore inclined toward mercy and, as was his
general approach, toward some sort of reconciliation. Finally,
however, he realized that as long as she was at large in Kongo,
she and her following represented a serious and popular coun-
terargument to his own plans for a negotiated, noble-led restoration of Kongo.

Taking all this into consideration, the king consulted with his
trusted associate, da Cruz Barbosa, on the matter, and decided
that since Dona Beatriz was either a religious leader or a heretic,
it was beyond his authority to punish or even to try her either
way. She had not, after all, violated the laws of the country.
Therefore, he decided that the best course was to send her under
armed escort to Luanda, where the bishop of Kongo and Angola
resided. The bishop had the authority to try her on religious
grounds, and in any case, in Luanda she would be out of Pedro's
hair.

A few days later, at the end of May, Father Bernardo came to
visit Evululu. He was short of provisions at his temporary hospice
between the camps of the rival kings, and had recently received
two visitors, Fathers Lorenzo da Lucca and Giovanni Paolo da
Tivoli, who had come from Luanda with orders to reopen the
hospices at Nkusu, east of São Salvador, and at Queen Ana's
capital in Nkondo. So, while in the country to collect provisions,
Father Bernardo took the opportunity to visit the king and discover what was being done about the two prisoners who he heard
had been recently captured. He was anxious that the king adhere
to what he thought were the Church's interests in the matter.

He met first with da Cruz Barbosa, whom he considered a lev-
elheaded person much less given to what he deemed King Pe-

dro's irresolution, and learned of the king's plan to send the prisoners to Luanda.

Father Bernardo did not like this idea at all, and frankly told the majordomo so. There were many dangers in it. What if the followers of Saint Anthony were able to free her on the long trip to Luanda, especially as the route would pass quite close to Luvota, the Kimpanzu stronghold? It was impossible to keep the trip a secret since Antonian spies were everywhere, even in the king's household. If they did get to Luanda, then what? The bishop might punish her, perhaps with a rebuke and explanation, as was required in matters of this sort, and return her to Kongo. In this case, her followers would surely believe that the bishop had in fact blessed her and the movement would gain even more strength.

But what if the bishop took the advice of the king or his advisors and decided to keep her there? She might still easily be freed, for Father Bernardo did not think that Luanda was particularly secure. On the other hand, if the bishop sought to exile her, so that she would be sure not to return to Kongo, would this be the solution? Then, Father Bernardo believed, the rumor would spread in Kongo that she had been sent to Europe or to the pope to be recognized as a saint. None of these would be satisfactory from the priest's point of view.

Father Bernardo reminded the majordomo what the consequences of leniency had been in the past. "Remember when there was one man preaching, and he was captured and let go?" he asked. "The next thing that happened was that the old woman, Apollonia Mafuta, started her career, and when she was also detained and released, Dona Beatriz began preaching." No doubt leniency was not working, it was only making matters worse.

Instead, Father Bernardo argued to da Cruz Barbosa, why not try Dona Beatriz right there in Kongo? Forget about ecclesiastical law or the powers of the Holy Office of the Inquisition to examine heresy. Could she not be judged and condemned under Kongolese law? Da Cruz Barbosa agreed. He had never been even slightly convinced by the claims of Dona Beatriz, and had wanted to be rid of her from the very beginning. It was he, after all, who had offered to behead her as soon as he heard her preaching and had asked Father Bernardo about her status.

The two men agreed that the best way was for Father Bernardo to take the matter directly to the king. Da Cruz Barbosa promised he would do all in his power to support the priest in a call for swift and sure punishment that would end the movement and its prophet.

About mid-June, Father Bernardo went to the king to persuade him that he must try Dona Beatriz in Evululu and condemn her. The king received the priest with great joy, and arranged for him to meet Dona Beatriz.

Together, the king and priest interviewed her. Both were anxious to learn as much as they could about her in a meeting on their terms, unlike their meetings of two years earlier, which had been more on her terms.

When she was brought before the pair, the king's first question concerned her remarkable teaching. Had she simply made up the stories about her sanctity, her possession, the knowledge that she claimed to have about Otherworldly things, about going to Heaven every week, and so on? he asked her. If she confessed to this, he could inform the priest that she was simply a trickster, perhaps naive, perhaps politically motivated, but ultimately someone who could be exposed and dealt with as the Church felt appropriate. She would, presumably be charged with blasphemy, and might be punished in much the same way that traditional ngangas were punished, through penances and short imprisonments.

But Dona Beatriz responded that she had not made these things up, that they had happened to her. Her pregnancy, her flight from the city, and her deception of her followers had shaken her self-confidence, but had convinced her only that she had sinned and let her followers down, not that she was a fraud.

Pedro then asked her if she had met with Father Bernardo again after the first meeting he had arranged in 1704, or if they had had any further discussions between them. She denied that this had ever happened as well.

Finally, the king asked her if she believed that he had sent her to Bula to obtain the purse that held the papal bull Santissimo Sacramento. There were rumors that he had sent her, spread either by her followers to connect her mission to royal approval, or by Pedro's detractors to suggest that he was manipulating her. To his relief, she answered that he had not sent her, that she had gone on her own.

After answering these questions, Dona Beatriz said that "all the virtue under which I have worked and lived, would have been enough to repopulate São Salvador and were given to me by God." However, she continued, "I lost the virtue by reason of my sins, which have reduced me to the state in which I now find myself." She clearly felt that the birth of the child and her failure to remain chaste had caused her downfall, and just as clearly she believed she had been on a divine mission as the vehicle for Saint Anthony.

The king then sent for Apollonia Mafuta so that she could also be interrogated. However, Mafuta was old and had never been in a good state. Even when Father Bernardo first met her on the slopes of Kibangu in 1704, he had thought she was harmless because she was just crazy. Now, with the trauma of her captivity, she was in a truly dismal condition and was unable to speak. They saw she could offer nothing in any case, and the interview ended.

Father Bernardo decided that rather than return to his hospice, he would stay at Evululu to see what would happen. The Feast of Saints Peter and Paul was to come up on 28 June, and he used this as a pretext to remain in the royal camp, since Pedro was accustomed to celebrate the feast of his patron saint with great pomp and would like the services of a priest.

Meanwhile, in accordance with their plan, da Cruz Barbosa came to the king, and then the royal council met. Father Bernardo did not attend the meeting, so that decisions would not be made according to the law of the Church but only according to Kongolese law. This would eliminate any embarrassment for the priest, should he condemn someone without having Church authority for doing so.

The council discussed the matter of Dona Beatriz fully; in the end, the majordomo's reasoning prevailed and the council sentenced Dona Beatriz, João Barro, and Apollonia Mafuta to death by burning. The deliberations were secret, but in making their announcements the royal council found them guilty under Kongolese law and did not involve the Church at all.

A short time after this meeting, Father Bernardo's two companions and visitors, Fathers Lorenzo and Giovanni Paolo, came to Evululu to celebrate Saints Peter and Paul's Day. When they learned of the sentence they thought it best that they leave the day after the feast, to avoid embarrassing themselves by association with what might prove to be a difficult situation. But Father Bernardo persuaded them to remain for a more opportune time. This was a very tricky situation, and Father Bernardo needed all the companions he could get.

The king sent gifts to the two new priests and invited them to see him. Father Bernardo took the opportunity to take them to the king and to hold them until after the sentence against Dona Beatriz was carried out. Father Giovanni Paolo, however, was sick from his journey and in considerable pain, so Fathers Bernardo and Lorenzo went together to see the king on 29 June. He gladly received them, on the great plaza that could be found in front of all Kongolese palaces, where people assembled to hear the king make proclamations or pronounce judgment. Accompanied by all the principal officers of state, he embraced both the priests then led them inside the building, where they remained with him for some time. Afterward, they were assigned houses near the palace to spend the night. Thus, he chose to honor them in a way he had refused some years earlier to honor Father Marcellino.

The next day, 30 June, the three priests and the royal council, including da Cruz Barbosa and Dom Bernardo, the *vuzi a nkanu* (or chief judge) in Kikongo, as well as others of the royal council convened to pass official sentence against Dona Beatriz and her companions. Dona Beatriz was brought in covered in chains, still wearing her crown of nsanda cloth and carrying the child in her arms. Mafuta, because she was considered insane and thus harmless, was tied by a simple cord. The priests were not sure whether she was truly possessed by the Devil, and tried to ask her questions, but got no response that they could understand.

Then the majordomo, who convened the council, told the prisoners that the next day they were to be put to death by burning at the stake, with no chance of appeal. The priests appealed to Dona Beatriz that they "yield themselves up to the hands of Blessed God and conform to the Divine Will, and to admit everything in a good confession."

At this point Dona Beatriz, now feeling shame for what she had come to perceive as her great sins, asked, "Could I be baptized again of my own free will, in hopes that the sacred washing would purge the wounds of so many sins that I have committed?" In Kikongo, baptism was normally called *kudia mungwa* or "eating salt." In the mid-seventeenth century, however, the Capuchins had officially declared this usage misleading and had sought to replace it with *lusukulu lua nkisi*, meaning "holy washing," although the new usage had never won popular support (indeed, *kudia mungwa* was still the term used for baptism in the early twentieth century).[9] By using the Capuchins' preferred language, Dona Beatriz emphasized her new submission to the Church and recognized their specific ideas of orthodoxy.

Since she was already baptized, "this could not be done, but she could return to a state of innocence by means of Holy Confession."

---

[9] In very recent years, Father J. de Munck quoted the tradition of the Nkanga Mvemba: "utete wadia mungwa muna wene wa Kongo" (right at first he "ate salt" in the kingdom of Kongo) in his *Kinkulu kia nsi eto a Kôngo*, p. 46. Redemptorist missionaries have generally not shied away from employing the term, although it is not normally used in official church publications in any denomination. Instead, the verb *-bota* is used – for example, in the narrative of the same book de Munck says, when referring to the first baptisms in 1491: "Ntinu Nzinga Nkuwu wabotama mu lumbu kia 3 dia Mayi 1491" ("King Nzinga Nkuwu was baptized [plunged in water] on the 3rd day of May 1491"); *Kinkulu . . .* , p. 15; see also Diawaku dia Nseyila's Kikongo paraphrase of Jan Vansina's *Kingdoms of the Savanna* – *Bimfumu biankulu bia Nzanza*, p. 25 – in referring to the same event: "Batunga nzo ya Nzambi yobotukulwa, mu Juni, ntinu a Kongo" (They built a church and in June, the king of Kongo was baptized).

This provided an opening for a full disclosure of the Antonian movement from the inside, and both Dona Beatriz and Barro made complete statements, which provided Father Lorenzo and Father Bernardo with the information to report on the movement to Rome and, ultimately, for modern historians to use.

Father Lorenzo gave her a stern lecture. "The Devil has used you and your followers to annihilate the honor of such a great Saint as Saint Anthony," he told her, and "now it has become necessary to hardly speak of this saint." After this the prisoners were returned to prison to await their execution.

That night the king put out a general order to the population. They were to bring wood into the public plaza to prepare the pyre on which the condemned were to be burned. It was late in June, deep in the dry season, and the countryside had no lack of dry wood.[10]

[10] Da Gallo, "Ultime," fols. 307v–310.

8

Facing the Fire

SUNDAY, 2 JULY 1706 – execution day. Early in the morning Father Bernardo rose and said Mass to a small group. Then around midday Dona Beatriz and Apollonia Mafuta were taken to Father Lorenzo for their last confession. The priest was convinced that Mafuta was not sufficiently sane to receive the sacrament of confession and, moreover, that she could not be held culpable for her preaching. As a result, she would be spared the flames.

This would not happen for Dona Beatriz. She was now thoroughly convinced that she had committed grave sins, not about her mission but about her pregnancy and her subsequent flight from São Salvador. She had decided that this betrayal warranted death, and was prepared to die.

"My death will be a penance for my sins," she told Father Lorenzo, "and well I deserve it." She went on, "What does death matter to me? This has to come to everyone at some point. My body is nothing more than a bit of earth, it is of no account. Sooner or later it will be reduced to cinders."

Continuing to feel sorrow and speaking fervently, she said, "It is better to die now, since I recognize my errors, than to live on that I might easily return to my old faults through the influence of the Devil, and damn myself."

She was now speaking rapidly and emotionally, and the priest was touched deeply. Soon all were weeping as he sought to console her. "Put yourself in God's hands," he exhorted her, "and hope for pardon from His infinite mercy."

At his suggestion she willingly accepted the idea of making a public abjuration so as to relieve her followers of whatever loyalty they felt to her. She was then returned to prison.

A bit later Dona Beatriz' infant son was brought out to Father Lorenzo to baptize. She informed the priest that she wanted to name him António, but Father Lorenzo would not agree to that. It would not do to keep the memory of the heresy, as he saw it, alive. He had already noted that it would be hard for them to make use of Saint Anthony in their mission, for some time to come anyway, and he had always been a popular saint. He decided that the baby should be named Jerónimo.

A bit later, Barro, her Guardian Angel who had also been condemned to burn, was brought in to make his confession. Father Lorenzo had to leave to say the main Mass of the day for the king and his followers, and Father Bernardo heard Barro's confession, similar though less touching than Dona Beatriz'. Barro, too, agreed to a public abjuration of his sins.

Father Lorenzo's Mass was well attended, and afterward the two priests met with King Pedro to lay out what they thought would be appropriate for the execution in the eyes of the Church. They were anxious that both the condemned be given the opportunity to confess their sins and to make a public abjuration. The priests also wished to be present at the execution and to play some official role so that the Church would be represented. This, they thought, would relieve the Antonian movement of its religious content and make it easier for Dona Beatriz' followers to be won back to the Church. Those at Evululu who still doubted could be convinced by this.

Pedro was in an ugly and indignant mood, however, and would not agree to their plan. "It is well known," he told them sharply, "that everything those miserable people taught is false," and for that reason there was no need for any abjuration.

Nor did he not want the priests to be present at the execution. There was likely to be a large crowd there, many people had participated in the bringing of wood for the fire, and the word of the execution was spread far and wide. Even though most who attended were from Evululu and likely to be supporters of the king more than of Saint Anthony, Pedro could not be sure how the day would go.

"I cannot be sure if you will be safe from the great crowd of people," he told them, and he did not wish to risk their being injured.

Father Lorenzo wished to debate this point. "Abjuration is an obligation of the condemned," he informed the king, "and it absolutely cannot be put aside." The Church had a strong interest in maintaining its side in what had been a religious issue. Besides, he noted, "our assistance will be a comfort to these young people, and will help them in this moment to remain resigned to the Divine Will."

Pedro suspected that the priests' insistence was not simply to comfort the condemned. He was particularly suspicious of Father Bernardo, who had constantly exhorted him to seize and execute Dona Beatriz even when he felt he had important reasons of state to tolerate her teaching. He disliked the priests' haughty attitude, and now felt that his resolve to conduct the execution had been challenged. He wondered if they were really only anxious to ensure the execution was carried off, and whether this was why they insisted on being present.

"Father," he said passionately, "if perhaps you think that I will not carry this out, because I want to spare them from death, remove any such thought from your mind, because I swear by that God which gave me the government of this kingdom" – and at this point he snatched the royal staff from the hands of his standard bearer who was nearby – "and who made Himself flesh and came to die for us on this cross" – he gestured to the silver crucifix at the end of his royal staff – "that nothing else will be done to these culprits, except that which has been determined, that is, to die by being burned alive!"

While impressed by the king's conviction, Father Lorenzo still wanted to make his point. He personally had not doubted Pedro's certainty, at least in part because he had a firmer opinion of the king's resolve than Father Bernardo had, who had known him earlier when he had indeed vacillated on the question of Dona Beatriz' arrest and even on her condemnation quite recently. Instead, Father Lorenzo was anxious that the Church play what he considered the proper role.

"With regards to the order for death," the priest continued, conscious of the fine legal points that had led to Dona Beatriz' civil conviction in which the Church had not been involved, "we have no role to play, being prohibited from it by Canon Law. But with regards to assisting the condemned," he went on, "this is our obligation, because this is customary in all of Christendom."

Pedro accepted this argument, and said the priests could play a role in the execution. He then turned and went back to the palace, leaving the two priests standing in the public square, waiting to see the end of the affair. The king had other business to attend to and had decided not to be present at the execution.

Shortly thereafter, the execution ceremony began. Two heralds bearing bells entered the square. These were the double-ended bells that royalty alone were allowed to keep, a sign of royal authority. The bells were clapperless and were beaten by a stick, producing a dolorous tone which all knew meant that serious government business was being transacted. A crowd had already formed, and it grew rapidly around the square.

The crowd began to sing a song appropriate for the occasion. Then Dom Bernardo, the *vuzi a nkanu* (principle judge), came out into the square, leading Dona Beatriz and Barro. It was he who had taken the blame for allowing Lusunzi's sacred stone to fall into the hands of the Capuchins, and whose own son had been accidentally burned on Saint James' Day in the same year. He was a tall man dressed in a long black mantle that went from his shoulders to his feet and wearing an *mpu*, the cap of authority similar to a Turkish fez, equally in black. He had a stern countenance, which now took on an appropriately threatening air.

Dona Beatriz followed this grim leader, trembling with fear and dread, still holding her baby. She and Barro were directed to sit on the bare ground near the platform where the sentence of death would be announced. She could not help but see the great piles of wood that had been prepared.

At that moment it occurred to Father Lorenzo that they intended to burn the child along with his mother, and he decided this was not right. He ran from the plaza back the short distance to the palace to see if the king would remit the sentence on the child.

Pedro's palace at Evululu, like the one in Kibangu, was surrounded by the triple enclosure with all the gates and porticos that were typical of Kongolese palaces. Father Lorenzo, who had only recently come to Evululu, did not know his way through the maze and rushed wildly from gate to gate until at last he reached the innermost enclosure.

There he saw the king, surrounded by his councillors, receiving various petitions. King Pedro was in the midst of this business, standing under a large umbrella and speaking with several petitioners who, following custom, were lying flat on the ground, having covered themselves with dust. Some others were kneeling at a distance, while others still sat on the ground waiting their turn.

The priest hesitated, not wishing to interrupt the business at hand and displease the king. But after a brief pause he decided that time was precious if he were to save the baby's life.

"Your Highness please excuse me, if I interrupt your speaking," the priest said as he advanced toward the king, "but the business which I must deal with cannot wait a bit." Father Lorenzo was a far more tactful priest than some of his predecessors, such as Father Marcellino, who had held up court business two hours trying to excuse a Spaniard from royal customs.

"Do not take as presumption the ardor with which I come forward in wishing to meet when Your Highness is engaged in the business of his kingdom," he said carefully. "I am here to ask for a boon, which is nothing other than the life of an innocent baby, which is the son of Dona Beatriz, called Saint Anthony, who is supposed to be burned along with his mother.

"It does not seem reasonable to me," the priest continued more calmly, "that an innocent creature should pay the penalty for a crime he did not commit." He continued, having now been assured of the king's attention, "It would seem to be too great an act of cruelty."

"What fruit does a rotten and infected plant produce?" the king responded. "In Italy, if a child is born of a heretic or a Jew of perverted habits, and their crimes and perversions merit death, what do you do with the child?"

"The child," Father Lorenzo answered, "because of its innocence is not capable of the defects of the father, and would be pardoned, as you can read in the stories of many people who were criminals. For all of them the children were pardoned, as being innocent of the crimes committed by their parents."

Then, dramatically, Father Lorenzo took in his hand the crucifix which he wore around his neck and said, "By this Son of God, crucified for the love of us, I beg for the life of this innocent one."

King Pedro was touched and, removing his mpu, replied, "And I, for the love of that crucifix, grant life to the son of that trickster. For that, however," he added, seeing an opportunity, "for the love of the same crucifix, Your Grace ought to do a favor for me, when I ask it."

Father Lorenzo thanked him for sparing the child's life and added that "in the matter of a favor for you, it would depend upon my decision, since I cannot fail to perform my duties." Then, contented, he excused himself and hurried back to the square.

While Father Lorenzo was pleading for the life of her child, Dona Beatriz sat unknowing in the square. Dom Bernardo had begun a very long discourse on the sentence, beginning with a lengthy list of titles and authorities of the king and their explication, and then continuing to an equally long and solemn speech on justice and its application to this case. He spoke sonorously, carefully, and clearly, as if lecturing a group of students. But he faced a crowd whose growing excitement and impatience made his speech incongruous, a paradox.

A message came through the throng to Dona Beatriz. Her child's life was to be spared, and she should give the baby up to one of the waiting officials. She was anxious about it and held back, but Father Lorenzo arrived by her side and comforted her. "You have nothing to fear for him," he assured her.

Dom Bernardo's speech continued as the baby was removed and the two priests prepared for what they hoped would be the religious part of the ceremony. However, the vuzi a nkanu was conscious of this and covered what he considered relevant from both a religious and legal perspective. Although Dona Beatriz was condemned according to Kongolese law, this law included ample provisions for crimes of a religious nature, and in this the vuzi a nkanu had an excellent command, explaining in detail and with many asides the nature of the crimes, the reasons they were to be considered heinous, and the logic for applying the death penalty in this particular form.

Finally, he reached the end of his speech. Addressing Dona Beatriz, he said, "For having fooled the people with heresy and with lies, under the false name of Saint Anthony, the king and his Royal Council have condemned you to death by fire" – then turning briefly to Barro, as if by an aside – "with your concubine."

At that point Dom Bernardo turned abruptly to leave the square, and the two priests moved forward to begin their part of the final preparations. Dona Beatriz, on their cue, rose and began to make her abjuration.

But this was not to take place. The crowd, whose impatience had been sorely tested by the lengthy legalistic speech, finally broke loose. No sooner had the vuzi a nkanu turned to depart than the first ranks of the crowd burst forward, and their noise and the sea of their bodies made the performance of any additional function out of the question. The mob fell upon the two condemned people and began to assault them, pummeling them, throwing them to the ground, and abusing them "like so many dogs," Father Bernardo recalled later. It seemed impossible that anyone could survive the beating, especially a young woman.

Barro grabbed Father Bernardo's habit, having lost his nerve in the assault, and now begged the priest to spare his life. But that was impossible, and it was only with great effort that the priest was able to free his habit from the man's terrified grip. It was obvious that the priests not only were unable to perform a formal function of abjuration, they were even unable to provide the services that the Church expected for those about to die.

Dona Beatriz and Barro were dragged along the square, sometimes trying to rise, sometimes being carried along, sometimes trampled underfoot, to the gallows. The officials had managed to tie them up tightly along the way, and they were badly bruised and bloodied by the time they reached the place.

Both were roughly thrown onto two carefully stacked squares of wood, side by side. Then more wood from the piles nearby was thrown rapidly on top of them, covering both. The wood was quickly lit and, dry as it was, burned furiously. Father Bernardo, in his official report of the affair, noted that "in the time it takes to say a prayer, they gave up their souls, one speaking the name of Jesus and the other the name of the Virgin Mary." He could not help but add, sarcastically, that "the poor Saint Anthony, who was accustomed to dying and reviving, this time really died and never again revived."

King Pedro had studiously ignored these proceedings outside the palace, although the sounds of the tumult from outside worked their way into the royal compound. As it happened, this day was an important one for him: later in the afternoon he would receive an ambassador from the Queen of Matamba, Dona Verónica Guterres Ngola Kanini. Matamba, a powerful kingdom that lay south of Kongo, was Christian like Kongo and was ruled by a dynasty founded by the famous Queen Njinga, for which reason the ruler was sometimes still called Queen Njinga.[1] Pedro also had to attend to the embassy that had come from Queen Ana and Pedro Valle das Lagrimas, the same ambassadors who had captured Dona Beatriz a bit earlier.

That afternoon, Pedro began the ceremony of feeding his court before receiving the ambassadors officially. This was a special Kongolese ritual in which the king personally placed food in the mouths of his most honored subordinates. They sat patiently, sometimes for hours on end, to receive a bit of nfundi, the boiled corn meal that everyone ate as a staple, or perhaps some mwamba, the stew that accompanied the nfundi, from the hand of their king – a great honor. He had chosen to do this in the

---

[1] For her kingdom and reign, see Fernando Campos, "A data da morte da Rainha Jinga D. Verónica I, *Africa* (São Paulo) 4 (1981): 79–104; 5 (1982): 171–204; 6 (1983): 89–128. Queen Verónica ruled from 1681 to 1716.

presence of the ambassador from Matamba and the other ambassadors, as a way of emphasizing his command over his subordinates.

In the midst of this ceremony the two priests, Fathers Lorenzo and Bernardo, entered the court. Seeing them, King Pedro immediately ceased his feeding, entrusting the task to the vuzi a nkanu, and went to speak with them. Their appearance had reminded him that Dona Beatriz was dead, and that another struggle lay ahead of him. He was perfectly aware that the movement Dona Beatriz had started was not likely to disappear with the death of its leader.

At first they discussed a variety of issues, but eventually, the feeding having been completed, the king dismissed everyone but a few close councillors and turned to the priests. He was deeply concerned that his taking a final step in the matter of Dona Beatriz had now forced him into a showdown with the remaining Antonians and their Kimpanzu supporters. War was likely, and he was very unsure of the outcome.

In a dramatic gesture, he threw himself at the feet of the Capuchins, his voice shaking with uncertainty and fear. He begged them to pray to the Lord for his success in the war that would surely come. "Today, the false Saint Anthony has done her part." If the war went badly, it would be not only to the king's disadvantage but also to the detriment of the Capuchins and the Church in general; consequently, they had an interest in the outcome.

The astonished priests tried to do their best to console the king. They reminded him that God had helped King Afonso when he stood facing his brother in battle two hundred years earlier, sending him the miraculous heavenly apparition that still decorated the royal arms – God would not forget Pedro now either. "Confide in Blessed God," they said, "and He will help you."

Pedro was comforted by this, and he and his close associates became encouraged, feeling stronger that their fateful decision to burn Dona Beatriz would come to a good end.

That night great celebrations started at Evululu. Not just the royal council but the population in general began to sing songs in praise of the king and the priests. They had faced the Antonians and now were prepared to take the next step. Sleep was banished, and the merrymaking lasted all night.

The next morning, royal officials decided that to avoid the problems they envisioned might arise if any remains of Dona Beatriz or Barro could be used as relics, they would carefully reburn all that was left of Sunday's holocaust. Meanwhile, King Pedro, having not slept all night because of both the celebration and "keeping an eye out for his Antonian enemies," came to a simple Mass dressed as a soldier, animated and full of joy.

That afternoon, to put a new and less somber face on the whole proceeding, King Pedro staged an nsanga, a military review and dance. A multitude of people participated, dressed for war, often painted, and carrying a variety of weapons, and the priests said Mass for the crowd. It was simultaneously a celebration of the death of Dona Beatriz and a challenge to the remaining Antonians and all their supporters that Pedro intended to finish with them.

Indeed, Pedro had reason to feel uncertain, for the Antonian movement was not going to die with its leader. On the one hand, although much of the movement had relied on the charismatic personality of Dona Beatriz and the acceptance of the basic tenants of her teaching that Saint Anthony was the highest of saints, "the second God," and that she was his incarnation, she was not necessarily indispensable for its continuation. The Little Anthonys were not simply ordinary people commissioned by her, they had undergone the process of death and resurrection as saints. Just as Kimpasi society initiates were reborn and retained their status as new people long after the original initiation had finished, so, too, the Little Anthonys kept their status.

Furthermore, Dona Beatriz' whole movement had addressed death and rebirth, and who was to say that Saint Anthony might not be reborn. Now that her mortal remains were totally obliterated, the saint might not be in Dona Beatriz' body anymore – after all, before coming to Dona Beatriz had Saint Anthony not tried several other people? Thus, the Antonians in Evululu could say that while the "form" of Saint Anthony had died, Saint Anthony himself remained. Others were asserting that Dona Beatriz had not died but was even now alive in Kongo or somewhere else. King Pedro had to be cautious about proceeding directly against any such talk because his own wife, Hippólita, had become a believer and there were many among his entourage who would listen to these new postexecution theories. Dona Beatriz was dead but, in more ways that one, her spirit continued to guide its movement and would not cease to do so until many more had died.

If it was not enough to know there were believers among his own close clients and followers, King Pedro was also aware that the Kimpanzu and Pedro Kibenga had made a firm commitment to the movement, and their rebellion was armed, occupying São Salvador, and perfectly capable of defying him with or without Dona Beatriz.[2]

Pedro Kibenga had indeed settled in São Salvador as his colonists had gone over to the Antonian movement. There he had reconstructed the palace, not of stone as the older palaces had been, but in the complex of buildings, chambers, and enclosures that were characteristic of upper-class Kongolese dwellings and the palaces of the pretender kings. In his elaborate audience chamber, Kibenga had placed his throne and decorations befitting a king.

The floor before the throne was covered with a rich Dutch carpet. To the left of it was a pillow covered in white cloth on which was placed a sword and a pistol; on the same side there was also a buffalo tail, or nsesa, a royal emblem. Above these he placed a picture of the Virgin Mary. On the opposite wall was a richly ornamented bow and arrows, and below them, a simple backless chair covered with white silk on which was placed a rosary with a book.

But Pedro Kibenga was also in a quandary of sorts. Although he controlled São Salvador, had thousands of subordinates, a good army, and at least the nominal support of the Antonians, he could not be king. He was widely rumored to be epileptic,

[2] On the execution and related events, da Gallo, "Ultime," fols. 310–313; da Lucca, "Relazioni," pp. 266–76.

which was considered to make him ineligible for the office. But such a sickness need not be taken literally; epileptic seizures were thought to be symptoms of kindoki, inflicted either by evil persons from outside or, more likely, from harboring evil thoughts and intentions within. Kibenga's reputation as a ruthless pursuer of power had touched him, and even though Dona Beatriz had moved toward him, he had not been exonerated from the suspicion. Even if he never had a seizure that people witnessed, the rumor would circulate based on a perception of his personality.

He was in power without doubt, even if he was not king, and he had the support of the Antonians, but it was an uncertain support. When news of Dona Beatriz' execution reached São Salvador, there was considerable denial, or claims that the movement could live on without her. Rumors spread that she had been seen in the treetops around the city. Another woman, others said, had been possessed by Saint Anthony and was in the city preaching that they should not give up hope, that others would be the "Mother of Virtue."[3]

For the more down to earth, however, there was a surge of anger against King Pedro. Antonian hostility toward the king might serve Pedro Kibenga well, but he was not strong enough to move against him in his fortified mountain of Evululu. As crucial as the Antonians were to Kibenga's movement, many of his followers were not Antonians, and he was thus in a position opposite King Pedro. In Pedro's camp the majority were not Antonians, but the minority was well enough placed to cause him trouble and hurt his policy. In Kibenga's camp the majority were Antonians, but not enough that he could abandon the Church safely.

The paradox of his situation was brought home quickly. Within a few days after Dona Beatriz' death, he heard news that Dom Diogo, a local commander, had captured two priests, and they were coming to São Salvador. The pair, Father Lorenzo and his

---

[3] Lorenzo da Lucca to Holy Father, 5 October 1711, in APF:SOCG 578, fols. 676–676v, published in Filesi, "Nazionalismo."

companion, Father Giovanni Paolo da Tivoli, had left Evululu on the 7 July, on their way to Nkondo. The death of Dona Beatriz had ended, for the time being, the crisis in Kongo, and they were hoping to reestablish their presence in Queen Ana's territory and also in Nkusu, east of her lands.

However, Dom Diogo, with a detachment of fifty soldiers based at the village of Nsuku, had seized their small caravan and taken its goods. The older Church servants had either fled or were captured and bound, destined for sale as slaves. Only the two priests and a handful of children, mostly youthful servants and students, remained together.

The countryside was thickly populated, and the night was lighted by the fires of many houses and villages. It was also a major center of Antonian worship in the heart of the Mbidizi valley, very near to Dona Beatriz' own hometown. The priests could hear their cries in the night: "*Tari, Tari, Nkadi a Nkema, Jesu!*" (in the Antonian transformation of Kikongo, the word for Devil, *Nkadi a Mpemba*, was changed to *Nkadi a Nkema*), and "*Maria, Tari, Tari!*" The priests overheard discussions about their being burned in retribution for the burning of Dona Beatriz.

Pedro Kibenga, recognizing the significance of the capture of the priests, sent his nephew Dom Álvaro with orders to restore the priests' property and bring them to São Salvador. The local commander, however, was unwilling to part with the profits of his capture; perhaps too, he was closer to the Antonians in the area than his colleague from the capital. Álvaro, unwilling to take action directly, returned to São Salvador to seek advice and reinforcements. Emboldened by the dispute, however, the priests declared Diogo excommunicated, and found enough local support that they began baptizing children in the area, to the chagrin of the Antonians.

Indeed, the night after Álvaro left, Diogo's men began a mobilization. Rumors were afoot that both Kibenga and King Pedro were sending armies to Nsuku because of the mistreatment of the missionaries. The drummers shouted, "Look, look at what the king and the Captain General are doing, we would sooner die than run away, and then we will deal with the missionaries who have started this war!" Another crier proclaimed an order to bring wood to burn the priests.

The orders were not carried out, however, and Dom Pedro, another nephew of Kibenga, was sent with orders to bring the parties of the dispute to court to settle it there. Diogo, confident that he could make his claims good, accompanied the envoy peacefully.

The entry of the party into São Salvador demonstrated clearly to Pedro Kibenga how deep a rift there was in the capital between him, who was skeptical to say the least about the Antonian movement, and the devotees of Dona Beatriz. The priests had shown this clearly by performing baptisms all along the route in defiance of the Antonian prohibition, and were now singing hymns. The schoolteachers of the vicinity had welcomed the priests, as had a number of highly placed nobles.

A huge crowd greeted the priests in the city, people crowded along the road, and others even climbed on top of the houses to see better. A great many wore the Antonian crown made of nsanda cloth that marked them as Little Anthonys and shouted their Antonian mottoes loudly. But a great many others stood silently – which the priests took as a sign of their adherence to a more orthodox version of the Faith.

Pedro Kibenga paid the priests the respect of coming out to the second gate and portico of his palace, and conducted them to the audience chamber, where they were seated on chairs in his presence. From Kibenga's perspective, the Church's noted neutrality in political disputes had worked to his advantage, for Father Bernardo had refused to side with the king even during Kibenga's rebellion. He now hoped that he could use it again to solve the problem he faced, both with the king and with the Antonians.

The urgency of the problem was brought home during the interview, for as Kibenga spoke with the priests a great tumult broke out on the plaza outside his palace. Cries of "Tari, Tari, Jesu ye Maria" filtered into the audience chamber. There was a popular riot outside, and Kibenga was visibly shaken, for as Father Lorenzo subsequently wrote, "his normally black face became blanched" at the sound of their voices.

Father Lorenzo, thinking that the Antonians were to win this day, turned to Father Giovanni and said, "We're betrayed!" under his breath in Italian, so as not to be understood. But it was not to be, for as it turned out, Kibenga had the situation well enough in hand to be able to continue his interrogation of Álvaro concerning the capture of the priests and the possibility of the restitution of their goods. He was also prepared to keep them in a well-guarded house while they stayed in São Salvador.

The next day, Kibenga summoned the priests to him, who made their own report on the execution of Dona Beatriz, her abjuration, and their views on her movement. They berated him for having followed her and being fooled by her teachings. He listened to their lecture, for he had brought them to São Salvador precisely to galvanize opinion. To this end, he invited the priests to say Mass the next day to his immediate followers, so as to remove any suspicion that he harbored Antonian sentiments.

The next day was 25 July, Saint James' Day, the most important holiday in the whole of the Kongolese year. As a day commemorating Afonso's victory over his brother in the sixteenth century, it was to be an important day for reassessing the fate of the traditional Christian faith and the role of the Antonian movement in São Salvador. Crowds began to assemble in a festive mode, both Antonians and the orthodox mingling together.

When Father Lorenzo came to say Mass in the palace, he spotted Antonian crowns among the revelers, and demanded that the wearers throw them to the ground. They, in turn, took up the challenge and called for action against the priest. To meet their challenge, Father Lorenzo took up his crucifix and held it aloft:

"How is it," he shouted, "that even within the walls of the palace, Your Excellency allows a Diabolic congregation, gathering together Devils that give such offense to the God who created them?" Hoping that Kibenga or important officers could hear him, Father Lorenzo continued, "Are Heresiarchs received even within the enclosure of the Princely Palace? Are these Demons incarnate allowed?" On and on he shouted, hoping for either popular or official support.

Kibenga's guards managed to disperse the crowd on behalf of

the priest, although no arrests were made, and took Father Lorenzo into Kibenga's private quarters, where the prince was devoutly praying.

"Excellency, Christ, tortured by these heretics cries 'Justice!'" he shouted, still holding his crucifix up. "The Holy Faith, trampled down by these wicked ones, cries 'Justice!'

"Oh, I wish that I would die this very day, than to see the revenge of this betrayed Christ! Are we to leave such terrible villainy against the Holy Faith unpunished?" Then, in a more historical mode, Father Lorenzo reminded Kibenga of the great early Christian king of Kongo. "Where are you, Afonso the First, King of Kongo, who for love of the Faith buried your own mother alive! Come, O Afonso, come to avenge the injury that these perverse people have done to the Holy Christian Faith in this city!" Father Lorenzo was tapping into the widely believed tradition that Afonso had buried his own mother alive because she refused to remove a small idol from her neck. Even in the twentieth century, the motto "Don Funsu Mvemba Nzinga wazikidi ngw'andi a kimoyo kakwikila nkanka a Ntinu Nkangi" (Dom Afonso Mvemba Nzinga buried his mother alive to support the faith of the Savior King) reflects this tradition.[4] While not true at all,[5] the tradition established Afonso's reputation as champion of the

---

[4] This statement is found in the motto of the clan Vuzi dia Nimi, quoted in Cuvelier (ed.), *Nkutama*, p. 70, and elsewhere in varied form.

[5] A definitive seventeenth-century account of Kongo's traditional history, Mateus Cardoso, *História do Reino de Congo*, ed. António Brásio (Lisbon, 1969), ch. 23, fol. 33, notes that Afonso's mother, Dona Leonor, was buried in a Christian manner in the royal cemetery. This tale of matricide is also not to be found in Cavazzi's monumental *Istorica Descrizione de' tre regni di Congo, Matamba, ed Angola* (Bologna, 1687), based on traditions current in midcentury. This suggests that the story was not true as, indeed, contemporary accounts also make no mention of the dramatic events. It is first mentioned about 1690 among people close to Manuel I in Soyo; Biblioteca Nacional de Madrid, MS 3165, da Pavia, "Viaggio," fol. 92, and also in APF:SOCG 576, fol. 321v, da Gallo, "Conto delle villacazione." Something that relates to the civil war period caused this tradition to surface and then remain a part of Kongo mythology from that time on.

Church, and reinforced the idea that kings were free to create the law they wished and possessed their own form of kindoki, as indicated by their power to kill even the most precious of persons at will, in the interests of the people and the state.

This tumultuous entry had its effect, and Kibenga had his men clear the plaza of people. He had invited those he considered most important and worthy to join him at Mass. But Father Lorenzo, who was to say Mass that day, made significant changes in the usual order of the service. Midway through the consecration of the host, he abruptly interrupted the service and declared all the Antonians heretics and they were henceforward excommunicated. But he assured the notables present that this did not apply to them, that the Lord would aid them in their struggle. "Remember," he told them, recalling the festival day, "that Afonso the First, your king, defeated an entire army of enemies of the Holy Faith with only a few soldiers." He continued in this encouragement, addressing Kibenga especially.

At this exhortation, all present fell to their knees as a means of expressing their agreement.

Kibenga acted quickly on his decision to accept the Church. By afternoon, criers had declared all the Antonians excommunicated all over the city. But at the same time, Kibenga caused the war flags to be prominently displayed. Reconciliation with the Church would not mean reconciliation with King Pedro.

Celebrations of Saint James' Day then took on a more traditional form, focusing on the Church of São Miguel, where King Afonso's remains were buried. The church, ruined for many years, had fully mature trees growing within its walls and around the graves, but the people cleared what could be cleared, decorated the church, and celebrated there, although without the clergy.

No amount of celebration, however, could patch up the differences between Kibenga and the Antonians. Kibenga knew that his break with them could not be complete, since many high-ranking nobles who were now resident in São Salvador were devotees of Dona Beatriz, some even having become Little Anthonys.

But Kibenga also had some firm supporters who were devoutly orthodox, such as Queen Dona Ilaria, the wife of the long dead King António I, the last great Kinlaza king of Kongo, killed in battle at Mbwila in 1665. In addition, the Kimpanzu candidate Manuel de Nóbrega, who came from Mbamba to the capital, had been persuaded to remove the Antonian crown and rejoin the orthodox.

At the same time, the Church itself was under pressure from King Pedro either to return Kibenga to loyalty, peacefully if possible, or to abandon their mission in São Salvador. Finally, bowing to this pressure and their sense that they could not have much independent influence there, Father Lorenzo and his ailing companion, Father Giovanni Paolo, left the capital on 8 August.[6]

The next year, 1707, brought a further hardening of the situation from a military standpoint and further confusion from a religious one. Father Bernardo decided after Easter to visit São Salvador voluntarily; he met a great deal of hostility along his route by Antonians still very much uncowed by Kibenga's official condemnation of the year before. In the countryside where Antonian sentiments were much stronger, for Dona Beatriz' movement was always popular among the common people, the priest was accused of practicing his kindoki for evil purposes, undoubtedly because of his association with the nobility. To the spiritual charge was added a more prosaic one of being a spy for King Pedro. But if Father Bernardo was not well received among common people, more nobles were prepared to stand behind him. He discovered the hidden central chamber in Dona Beatriz' house near the cathedral, and concluding that the chamber had been put there to hoax the people, openly displayed it, although without winning much new popular support for his efforts. A group of nobles led by Dom Daniel, son of the former Kimpanzu king Daniel (who died in 1674), ceremoniously surrendered their Antonian crowns to the priest.

Father Bernardo, for his part, was prepared to accept any noble

---

[6] Da Lucca, "Relazioni," pp. 287–99.

who wished back to communion, and lifted Father Lorenzo's blanket excommunication of the Antonians from all but three of Kibenga's noble followers. These three, however, were still a break in the ranks of Kibenga's nobles, and he continued to play to the remaining Antonians in subtle ways whenever he could. In October he won a major coup through this policy. Dona Hippólita, the wife of Pedro himself, fled from Evululu and took refuge with her uncle Kibenga.

Now encouraged, Kibenga began military operations on a small scale against the king. A raid seized some sixty people from lands held by King Pedro's colonists, and a more extensive attack destroyed all the villages loyal to Queen Ana north and west of the Mbidizi River. At the same time, Manuel de Nóbrega launched a much stronger attack in Mbamba against the queen's nephew, Pedro Valle das Lagrimas.

The last effort failed, however, and Valle das Lagrimas' armies pursued de Nóbrega back to his own protected town. An army from Soyo intervened on behalf of Valle das Lagrimas, and a bloody battle ensued in which de Nóbrega and Valle das Lagrimas both suffered significant casualties. But the latter won the day, and de Nóbrega decided to abandon his town without defending it. In mopping-up operations, though, Valle das Lagrimas injured his foot badly by falling into a pit trap hidden in the fortifications.[7]

If Kibenga's hopes were set back by the defeat of de Nóbrega, his important ally in Mbamba, 1708 brought him another disaster. Kibenga, working through spies and traitors, laid careful plans to take one of King Pedro's strongholds, Tadi dia Nsundu, defended by Rafael Nzinga a Mvemba, the king's half brother. But at the last moment, he was betrayed and not only was unable to capture the fort, but his troops were badly mauled in the following encounter.

While Kibenga was seeking to improve his situation, Soyo suddenly underwent a civil war that had to figure in any calculations.

[7] Da Gallo, "Ultime," fols. 312–314; da Lucca, "Relazioni," pp. 325–6.

Soyo had been a player in the royal politics of Kongo since the civil wars began in the 1660s. Its armies were typically pro-Kimpanzu, but the Kimpanzu themselves were not a unified voice anymore. King Pedro was half Kimpanzu, as was Kibenga, who was also directly related to the princes of Soyo. Prince António Baretto da Silva had been outright hostile to the Antonian movement, was lukewarm to Kibenga, and had even abandoned the Kimpanzu de Nóbregas in their fight for Mbamba, helping to defeat them. But for all that, Kibenga might still be able to win the princes over, at least as a backup, for their hostility to the de Nóbregas did not automatically translate into support for King Pedro.

Soyo's policies toward Kongo were totally overturned, however, when Prince António was overthrown by a party upset by his policy toward Kibenga and the Kimpanzu, as well as by his trying to maintain his own inner circle in power at the expense of his more distant relatives. The revolt broke out shortly after Saint Peter Apostle's Day, 28 June 1708, in Kiova, Soyo's eastern-most province. Malcontents rose up and sacked the mbanza, then moved westward against the capital, taking Kionza along the way. On 11 July the prince assembled the people of the capital area and extracted and oath of allegiance, then moved his army against the rebels.

When the battle was joined, in an open field between Ngwela and Kitombo, however, Prince António's supporters deserted him, leaving him to defend himself with only a few slaves of his personal bodyguard. Wounded by an arrow and a musket ball, Prince António clutched the large wooden cross that was set up in the public square, saying fervently, "It is here that I want to die!" His wish was granted by a nobleman, who told him that "you never wanted to listen to my advice, now take the punishment."

Although Father Bernardo heard that the rebels were also Antonians, his assessment may well have been based on their pro-Kimpanzu bent in politics rather than any overt ideas they had. They did, however, invade the princely city and sacked many of

Blessing the weapons before battle. (From "Missione in Practica" ca. 1750)

the churches, finally arriving at the Capuchin hospice. There, the leaders demanded *"Tubena ntu'anganga muculuntu"* (show us the head of the Father Superior!).

While one group of rebels was sacking churches, the other took over the offices of state and elected Amador da Silva as the new prince. He was the son of Prince Paulo da Silva, who had defended Soyo from the Portuguese invasion of 1670 and had won a hero's victory at the battle of Kitombo, although it had cost him his life. Amador was neither Antonian nor anticlerical. He saved the priests from the angry mob but was dead within a day and a half, apparently the victim of poison. The electors then chose Paulo Generoso da Silva e Castro as prince.[8]

---

[8] APF:SOCG 594, fols. 441v–443, Francesco da Troyna to Clement XI, August 1714, is the principal eyewitness account of the revolt in Soyo. Other information is found in da Gallo, "Ultime," fol. 313; da Lucca, "Relazioni," pp. 365–8; APF:SRC Congo, 3, fol. 293, Colombano da Bologna to Propaganda Fide, 10 December 1710.

Although Prince Paulo was able to consolidate his position as ruler, Soyo was effectively unable to participate in Kongo's affairs, either in the south in the struggle over Mbamba, or at the capital. On the whole, the events turned out well for King Pedro, who saw his hand strengthened considerably.

At about the same time, Queen Ana Afonso de Leão died, rumored to be at an age of one hundred years, but probably not much over eighty. Her nephew Álvaro succeeded her on the throne, and promised to be more willing to back King Pedro unconditionally if need be.

The stage was now set for King Pedro to move at last to defeat Kibenga and reoccupy the capital. Pedro had spent many years trying to avoid a war, but at last had to accept it. At least, from his point of view, he would be waging it from a position of strength.

9

The War for Peace

KING PEDRO LAUNCHED his final assault on Kibenga's positions at São Salvador on 15 February 1709. Twenty thousand troops from Pedro's territories and those of the late Queen Ana, now headed by her nephew Álvaro, moved against the city. The king went into battle unarmed, carrying only a crucifix from the altar of the royal chapel at Evululu, which he had borrowed from Father Bernardo. The battle had much of a religious crusade about it, for if Pedro and his crucifix represented the orthodox, then the cries of the Antonians, "Tari, Tari, Jesus ye Maria" sounded constantly from the rebel army.

King Pedro wanted the battle to be the last one, and was anxious to reconcile as many of his enemies as possible. Even before this last war began, he issued a proclamation declaring a pardon to anyone who would join him. He had never wanted to fight, but three years of fruitless negotiations had ultimately forced him to.

Kibenga, for his part, fought dispiritedly, having neither the religious zeal to go down fighting alongside the Antonians, nor the faith to fight as an orthodox Christian. When the battle began going badly for him, Kibenga decided to avail himself of the royal pardon. His intent was mistaken by Pedro's soldiers, however, and he was shot dead. When they realized that the body was that of their enemy, they cut off his head and hands and carried them back to the king in triumph.

Kibenga's routed army and his followers, both Antonian and orthodox, fled in all directions. A large number fled eastward but were captured by Pedro's brother Dom Rafael at his base in Tadi dia Nsundu. Others moved northward toward Bula, hoping that King João, enemy of King Pedro, would protect them despite his disdain for both Antonians and the Kimpanzu. Wary of seeking his help directly at his capital, they took up residence in Tadi dia Bossa and sought to get the various factions of the divided Bula nobility to support them.

João took advantage of what he saw as an opportunity as refugees streamed into his outlying territories throughout the dry season of 1709. Pedro's troops had been mobilized for some time and had fought a battle, which they tried to follow up in pursuit wherever possible. João mobilized an army in Bula and marched southward to see what he could gain from his overextended rival. On Saint Francis' Day, the soldiers of Bula met those of King Pedro head-on. The two principal contenders for the Kongo throne met head-to-head in battle, but Pedro's troops prevailed. Pedro was so elated that he wrote to Father Bernardo in Angola on 28 March that Saint Francis was truly the protector of Kongo, and he renamed his home base São Francisco de Kibangu, in honor of the victory. For a time, it appeared that João might recognize Pedro as king, and in 1715 he in fact briefly did so. But in the end, João thought the better of it and reproclaimed himself as rightful King of Kongo in 1716.[1]

While events in the north were being resolved, another group of refugees fled eastward from the cataclysmic battle at São Salvador toward Soyo, where the unsettled affairs promised some hope. Pedro's Antonian queen, Hippólita, took refuge in Soyo's province of Kiova on the south bank of the Zaire, where the movement that overthrew Prince António in 1708 had originated. Also, the great wilderness between Kongo and Soyo, called Mfinda a Nkongo (the Forest of the Hunter) provided another refuge for those fleeing from the capture of São Salvador. There they beseeched Soyo's leaders to intervene in Kongo on behalf of the Kimpanzu if not for the Antonians.

Paulo Generoso da Silva, the new Prince of Soyo, decided to

---

[1] APF:SRC Congo, 4, fol. 163, João II to Propaganda Fide, 10 October 1716.

ignore the Kimpanzu and sent his own ambassador to São Salvador to deal with King Pedro. But Pedro was unwilling to receive them, arguing that Paulo's ancestor had killed the king's father and, moreover, Soyo had in his view been a constantly disruptive force in Kongo. In any case, on 26 April, Prince Paulo died, poisoned by his enemies. His successor, Jerónimo de Almeida da Silva, had been a leader in the movement that overthrew Prince António in 1708. He was sympathetic to Queen Hippólita in Kiova and to the refugees in Mfinda a Nkongo, and cooler toward King Pedro. But he was not prepared to go to war over the issue.[2]

Finally, a last important group of refugees fled the capital through Mbamba to Luvota, Manuel de Nóbrega's stronghold, where they would be safe. However, Pedro was anxious to maintain better relations with this group since he badly wanted to mend fences with the Kimpanzu. He received a number of Kimpanzu nobles graciously, giving them the pardon that Kibenga himself had sought unsuccessfully. Manuel Makasa, Kibenga's youngest brother and one of his principal lieutenants, was singled out for special favors. Just as Pedro had once granted broad titles and favors to Kibenga himself when he was a refugee in Kibangu, so he showered honors on Manuel Makasa. Pedro gave his own daughter to Dom Manuel as a bride, and eventually named him Prince of Kongo, with the promise that he would succeed Pedro as King of Kongo.

It would take longer, however, before the rivalry between the Luvota-based Kimpanzu Manuel de Nóbrega and Queen Ana's Kinlaza cousin Pedro Valle das Lagrimas over Mbamba would be resolved, in spite of King Pedro's reconciliation. The Antonians, led by a range of resurrected saints whom Father Lorenzo had met entrenched in nearly every village of Luvota when he passed in 1705, had their best refuge here. In 1714, Valle das Lagrimas

---

[2] On the final battle and its aftermath, see da Gallo, "Ultime," fols. 313–313v; APF:SOCG 576, da Gallo, "Conto," fols. 332v–333; APF:SOCG 576, fols. 314, Pedro IV to Bernardo da Gallo, 28 March 1709; Pedro Mendes, p. 355. On the later events, APF:SOCG 604, fol. 69, Lorenzo da Lucca letter, 1715; APF:SRC Congo 4, fol. 163, João II letter, 10 October 1716.

began a long war that devastated the countryside one more time. After more than a year of fighting, his forces were victorious, and in 1715 they cut off Dom Manuel's head as a sign of their triumph. The victory was not decisive, however, for Mbamba province was divided between the two parties: Valle das Lagrimas remained in control of most of the province subsequently known as Great Mbamba, for the Kinlaza and those generally loyal to the rulers of Nkondo who succeeded Queen Ana. Mbamba Luvota, on the other hand, remained the core of a Kimpanzu faction that succeeded from the descendants of Suzanne de Nóbrega. Although both factions ultimately recognized Pedro as king, the division of the province was permanent. Given Pedro's reluctance to press for complete victory, the Antonian movement probably lived on much longer in these provinces than it could have in São Salvador or the Mbidizi valley, where the king was anxious to put an end to heresy as well as rebellion. The Antonians had a strong local organization that could outlive Dona Beatriz and at least the tacit support of the elite.

King Pedro died in 1718, leaving his compromise settlement of the kingdom intact, and Manuel Makasa, true to the agreement, succeeded him as Manuel II, ruling from the restored capital of São Salvador. Although João II never ultimately acknowledged Pedro as his ruler, Manuel's successor, Garcia IV Nkanga a Mvemba came from Bula faction, where he had ruled the Marquisate of Matari. He was probably from among those nobles formerly loyal to João II who had given their allegiance to Pedro IV in 1701. When other lines took their turn, no one from "Great Lemba," as Bula was known by midcentury, made an independent claim on the throne, and its constituent marquisates became more or less independent – Manga went one way, while Matari and Sumpi went another, and Bula itself remained as a rump under a grand prince. Pedro IV's own descendants remained in Kibangu, claiming the title of prince but not pressing claims to be King of Kongo.

Tradition held that a half century after Pedro's death, he arranged for a rotation to take place between the Kimpanzu and the Kinlaza, which effectively meant that the throne passed between the powers of the Mbidizi. In the east, the faction once headed by Queen Ana Afonso de Leão from Mbanza Nkondo, which came to be known as the "Lands of the Queen," supplied the Kinlaza kings, while in the west, those descended from Queen Suzanna de Nóbrega at their base in Luvota presented Kimpanzu candidates.[3] But the rotation was hardly secure and peace was not really restored. At least one major war, waged in Mbamba in the 1730s, disturbed this peace, perhaps between Kinlaza partisans of Garcia IV and the Kimpanzu of Luvota,[4] but the tale of continuing war was best told by the growing human hemorrhage of the slave trade.

The elite of Kongo fought its wars and made its peace in the years following Dona Beatriz' preaching. But for thousands of the commoners who had come to São Salvador originally to seek Dona Beatriz and had then been caught up in the politics of civil war, there was a different fate. As in all the battles of the war, thousands were made prisoners and sold. In the case of Antonians, the sale was easiest to justify because they had forfeited whatever claims they might have on royal mercy by their adhesion to heresy.

We have no record of how many people were enslaved on that day, or the subsequent follow-up actions when many more were

[3] Scholars are virtually in the dark concerning events in Kongo after 1720. Much of history of the post-Manuel epoch can only be inferred from the catalogue of the politics of the country in Cherubino da Savona's description of the state of affairs around 1759–65, Cherubino da Savona, "Breve ragguaglio del regno di Congo . . . ," in Carlo Toso (ed.), "Relazione inedite di P. Cherubino Cassinis da Savona," *L'Italia Francescana* 45 (1974), with original pagination fols. 42–45. Garcia IV was known to be a Kinlaza from da Savona's description, and his location in Matari is known from a tradition concerning his tomb recorded in Cuvelier (ed.), *Nkutama*, p. 72: "Wavinga don Grasia Nkanga a Mvemba, mwana'a Nlaza. Yandi wele mu kiandu ku Kongo" (He [D. Grasia Nkoko a Mvika] was succeeded by Don Garcia Nkanga a Mvemba, a child of the Nlaza. He went to the throne of Kongo).

[4] The war in 1733 is known only obliquely from the account of Angelo Maria da Polinago in Archivio di Stato, Parma, Carteggio Franesino-borbonico, Estero, Roma, 436, 16 August 1733.

rounded up. Given the size of armies in those encounters, and the likely rate of enslavement, however, it is safe to say that there were probably more than 5,000 people captured. Most were male, but there were many females within the group, especially since Dona Beatriz' message had appealed to all; and the civilian population was more likely to be Antonian than were the followers of Kibenga, who could expect military protection in defeat.

To this number must be added another group, probably not exceeding 2,000, who were captured shortly after the taking of São Salvador in Pedro's victory over João on Saint Francis' Day. Because Pedro was fighting defensively, he faced an army primarily of soldiers and their immediate support group, including the women who followed every army. There were few civilians vulnerable to enslavement among this attacking army; at São Salvador a large civilian population of Antonians could be enslaved even if they were noncombatants.

Prisoners captured in these wars designated for export were sent out over perhaps the next year through the various time-honored routes – south to Portuguese Angola, or to Vili merchants who carried them on to Soyo and especially Kabinda.

The first of these captives were probably reaching the coast by May 1709, joining those already captured and exported in the skirmishes of 1707 and 1708, but the bulk probably arrived for shipment to the Americas well into the next year, and indeed for several years beyond that, so that perhaps another 5,000 people were exported from the wars of 1714–15, many of whom were Antonians. Of those who were purchased by *pombeiros* sent out by the Portuguese merchants of Luanda, virtually all were exported to Brazil. Father Lorenzo da Lucca returned to Europe via Brazil after his term of service and witnessed the horrors of the crossing in 1708, when hostilities were still climbing toward the climactic battle in 1709. On 7 July, Father Lorenzo, preparing for the trip, said Mass for the travelers at the church of Nossa Senhora do Cabo on the "island" (actually a narrow penninsula) of Luanda. Standing before not only many Portuguese and Luso-Angolans but a great multitude of Africans about to be sent into slavery in Brazil, he prayed for good luck on the voyage.

Father Lorenzo had traveled widely in Kongo and Angola. There were among that multitude of prisoners those, especially the ones from Kongo, who had seen him before, heard him say Mass. Perhaps their children were among the thousands he had baptized. Some had also worn the Antonian crown, already captured in Mbamba by armies of Pedro Valle das Lagrimas or raiders from King Pedro's camps – the next year there would be thousands waiting to embark in Luanda after King Pedro's victories.

Following Mass, the captives were formed into a great review and carefully counted by fiscal officials of the Portuguese crown in order that the proper taxes be paid. Then some of the slaves, eventually reaching the number of 742, were loaded onto the ship, also called the *Nossa Senora do Cabo*, that carried Father Lorenzo. Including the sailors, more than 800 people boarded the fragile wooden sailing ship for the transatlantic voyage.

Just after noon the sails were unfurled, and a favorable wind carried them from the island to the ocean. Suffering began quickly. Long ocean voyages were a severe hardship for anyone who undertook them in those days, but as Father Lorenzo noted, in a few days the ship was "transformed into a great hospital."

"I do not know how to describe it," he wrote in a letter to his home province that year, "I will only say that extreme confusion reigned. Those blacks were to be found crouched down amidst filth and discomfort." The discomfort was a product of the incredible crowding, it was "almost impossible to change places." Thanks to the lack of space, "it is virtually impossible to put food in one's mouth, and the food there is badly prepared. Sleep is brief," he recalled, "because one is barely able to close one's eyes."

The complete lack of toilet facilities soon made the smell aboard ship unbearable. Given the situation, Father Lorenzo was undecided whether it could best be compared to Hell or Purgatory. "It is not a tableau of Hell," he finally decided, "because the suffering is temporary. Therefore, in the place of that term, I will use Purgatory, which seems better. I assure you," he continued in the letter, "those who have endured this suffering with patience will have found the means to extirpate their sins and acquire great merits for their soul."

Father Lorenzo's unwilling co-passengers did not suffer the pain in silence. "One cried out on one side, another on the other," he wrote, "There were those who cried and lamented, while others raged." Those who raged had many people to blame – the rulers who had forced them into military service (or perhaps the officers who had lost the war), or maybe the bandits who had seized them, the specific cruelties of their capture, the harsh and uncaring supervisors on their journey to the coast, and now the avaricious powers that had loaded them into this latest place of suffering.

Many if not most regarded the whole experience as the product of the worst sort of kindoki, and as a result rumors spread that they were in the end to fall into the hands of the most dreadful of ndokis – cannibals who would eat them or grind them up to make powder for guns. A conspiracy of ndokis and their vast network of both willing and unconscious agents, driven by evil intentions ranging from the corrupt rulers to wicked bandits to greedy merchants, was, many of the masses crammed into the fetid hold of the ship believed, the ultimate cause of their suffering. It was against exactly this sort of evil kindoki, in all its forms, that Dona Beatriz had preached, and it was against this background that she had won her followers.

Father Lorenzo became sick himself and spent much of the last part of his voyage in a state of semiconsciousness, finally arriving, shocked and drained, at Bahia, Brazil, on 10 August after thirty-four days at sea.[5]

Probably a larger number of the prisoners captured in the war to restore São Salvador in 1709, however, did not cross the ocean like those who traveled with Father Lorenzo to Brazil the preceding year. Instead, they ended up with the Vilis and, through their trade network, being put into the holds of Dutch, English, and

---

[5] On the trip, da Lucca, pp. 347–8. On the beliefs of the slaves (not specifically found in this source), see John Thornton, *Africa and Africans in the Making of the Atlantic World, 1400–1800*, 2nd ed. (New York, 1998), pp. 153–62.

French shipping bound for the Caribbean, the Spanish Indies, and
North America. There were many Vilis in São Salvador even before the great battle, and their networks were in place, ready to
take advantage of the commercial opportunities that came with
every battle of the civil wars. Vilis knew well whom to contact
on either side, depending on who was victorious, and were well
enough connected to stay out of harm's way once battle was
joined.

From the battlefields at São Salvador, the site of King João's
defeat, and the fields of Mbamba where Valle das Lagrimas over-
came Dom Manuel, the Vilis carried their captives north, across
the Zaire River to various ports – Malemba, Kabinda, or Loango,
but especially to Kabinda. It was here that English and Dutch
shippers, who dominated the northern trade in those days, would
acquire the slaves, carrying them in all directions to destinations
in America, under conditions very similar to Father Lorenzo's
floating Purgatory bound for Brazil. Indeed, the voyages of the
northern traders were longer – ten weeks to two months in general – than the month-long voyage of Father Lorenzo's companions. The longer the voyage, the worse the conditions by the time
it ended.

The newly enslaved carried by Dutch ships went largely to
Dutch possessions or to those they served regularly. For example,
the *Rosenburgh* carried 390 people to St. Thomas in the Danish
West Indies in 1709; the *Joanna Magtelt* carried 650 people from
the coast to Curaçao in 1711; and the *Guntersteyn* took 600 un-
fortunates to Surinam in 1716, returning for 538 the next year,
and yet another 596 in 1719.[6]

English shippers took their share primarily to the islands of the
Caribbean, especially Jamaica and Barbados, which served as central markets for transporting them to other English colonies,
whether the smaller islands like Antigua, Nevis, or Montserrat,
or the large mainland colonies of South Carolina and Virginia. In
May 1709 Captain Hereford of the *Elizabeth Hannah* brought 200

[6] For these ships, Johannes Menne Postma, *The Dutch in the Atlantic Slave
Trade, 1600–1815* (Cambridge, 1990), Appendix I.

people to Jamaica "from Angola," the English term for all of central Africa. They were "in miserable condition having suffered from a want of provisioning,"[7] a product of the long voyage and attendant shortages. A Bristol-based ship, the *Joseph*, landed 280 more Kongolese in Jamaica in November of that same year to the great delight of the sugar producers, for they were sold quickly thanks to "the planters having lost abundance of Negroes by the Small pox."[8] Given their weakness, no doubt many who had come with Captain Hereford in May on the *Elizabeth Hannah* were among those dead of the pox.

The English merchants sought to negotiate the problem of the Church's opposition to their taking Catholic slaves to Protestant ports in hauling off their share of the prisoners of war. They received some relief, for the formation of the South Sea Company in 1713 to deliver slaves to the Spanish Indies under a special contract, called the *asiento*, gave merchants a license to import slaves into Spanish possessions. An English ship that left Soyo in September 1714 gave written notice that its cargo would be delivered in the Spanish Indies, Captain Joseph Grew showing a license from the Spanish officials to this effect the same month: while yet another ship the same year gave Cádiz as its destination. But others were not able to meet the Church's demands and traded illegally. António Etona, head of the village of Masomo at the mouth of the Zaire, invited English shippers to set up a temporary factory there. Among the shippers was Thomas Harney, who surreptitiously sent three canoes full of captives in August 1714 to his ship the *Anna Galley* at Kabinda.[9]

---

[7] Public Record Office, T70/8 Abstracts of Letters, fol. 46, Col Peter Beckford and Mr Lewis Waltry, 28 May 1709. Voyages from central Africa generally took less than two months, so these people would have been purchased in late March or early April, and were thus probably enslaved in the storming of São Salvador on 15 February.

[8] Public Record Office, T70/8 Abstracts of Letters, fol. 50, Daniel Motet, Jamaica, 24 November 1709.

[9] These transactions were noted by Father Giuseppe da Modena, "Viaggio al Congo, fatta da me Fra Giuseppe da Modena . . . ," fols. 373–4 and 376–7, published with original foliation in Calogero Piazza, "Una relazione inedita sulle Missioni dei Minori Capuccini in Africa degli inizi del Settecento," *L'Italia Francescana* 48 (1977): 209–92, 347–73. Monari gave the

Harney's slaves were surely not bound for the Spanish Indies or any Catholic country or he would have been willing to present his papers as others did. Instead, he probably took them to Jamaica or Barbados, the principal destination of Kongolese slaves in the English New World – perhaps his was the unnamed ship with 120 slaves "from Angola" that arrived in Jamaica on 15 November 1714.[10]

The Jamaican slave markets were also regularly visited by smaller ships from England's North American colonies – Virginia, Maryland, and South Carolina – which were just beginning to import large numbers of Africans, but there was not yet a large enough demand to justify sending many whole shiploads directly there. In fact, of the 5,226 Africans brought into Barbados between May 1713 and May 1714, some 1,500 were re-exported to other colonies.[11] In 1708, Governor Nicholson of Maryland could write that up to his day the vast majority of slaves in that colony, a major importer of the period in North America, still came in small lots from the West Indies. It would be another decade before North America became an importer capable of absorbing whole shiploads of Africans.

British traders dealing in Kabinda, Soyo, and Malemba bought more than 65,000 slaves in the decade following Dona Beatriz' execution and Pedro's restoration of São Salvador, followed by nearly 90,000 in each of the next two decades, although the pace of British purchases fell off dramatically around 1740. French merchants, who had not been nearly as active as the British earlier on took up much of the slack, so that total exports from West-Central Africa remained high.[12] In the earliest part of the half

---

names of the English captains as Giuseppe Grue and Thomas Arnae; my version is just my best guess of what the English form might have been.

[10] Public Record Office, T70/8, fol. 88v, John Stewart and John Wright, Jamaica, 15 November 1714.

[11] Public Record Office, T70/8 Abstracts of Letters, fol. 80, Patrick Thomesone, Barbados, 8 June 1714.

[12] Statistics on exports come from David Richardson's estimates based on shipping records, "Slave Exports from West and West-Central Africa, 1700–1810: New Estimates of Volume and Distribution," *Journal of African History* 30 (1989): 1–22.

century following Dona Beatriz' death most of these exports came from the continuing fighting in the Kongolese civil wars, either skirmishing between rivals and major wars over succession – as in about 1730 – or increasingly uncontrolled banditry that inevitably accompanied a failure to maintain public order.

Toward the end of this half century, and in the next half century, however, slaves coming from farther inland – up the Zaire River, in the lands north of the river, or inland beyond the Kwango where the Lunda empire was shaping – supplied as many and eventually perhaps even more than the Kingdom of Kongo itself. But war and dissension in Kongo continued, and the last quarter of the eighteenth century witnessed a situation as chaotic as that in the times of Dona Beatriz.[13] The prisoners of those wars fed the slave trade mightily, especially the trade to Saint Domingue/Haiti on the eve of its great slave revolution of 1791, as France became the leading buyer of central Africans.

North America was among those regions that received many Kongolese slaves in the years following Dona Beatriz' death. Kongolese began arriving in force around 1720 and most came to the coastal lowlands of South Carolina that were just being brought under intensive rice cultivation and generating the incomes and demand necessary to arrange the direct shipment of slaves from Africa. At the same time, a smaller wave of Kongolese arrived in Port York serving the southern part of Virginia and the James River valley. Nearly 60 percent of the more than 10,000 people brought from Africa to serve on South Carolina's rice and indigo estates in the 1720s and 1730s were shipped from Kabinda, the vast majority from Kongo. More than 40 percent of the roughly 8,000 workers brought from Africa to labor on the James River's tobacco estates in the 1730s hailed from Kongo.[14] In 1720, the

---

[13] A detailed vision of Kongo in the late eighteenth century can be drawn from the 300-page manuscript of letter reports from Rafael Castello de Vide, missionary in 1781–8, Academia das Ciências, Lisbon, MS Vermelho 296, "Viagem de Congo . . ."

[14] On Kongolese in this period in America, Peter Wood, *Black Majority: Negros in Colonial South Carolina from 1670 Through the Stono Rebellion* (New York, 1974), and Alan Kulikoff, *Tobacco and Slaves: The Development of Southern Cultures in the Chesapeake, 1680–1800* (Chapel Hill, N.C., 1986), esp. pp. 320–3.

French ship *Néréide* landed in Biloxi, 294 slaves that had been
acquired at Kabinda, the first Kongolese in French Louisiana (although not until the end of the century would large numbers of
Kongolese live in that territory).[15]

South Carolina therefore became the Kongolese center of North
America. At that time, Brazil was the only region that had a
greater percentage of Kongolese among its people. This prepon-
derance of people from one region would have a significant influence on the development of the colony.

The Kongolese brought their language and their culture with
them, but most notably and particularly, their Catholic faith. In
the 1720s, when they began arriving in large numbers, quite a
few may have had contact with the Antonian movement, and
they certainly brought with them the attitudes that had fueled
Dona Beatriz' movement, if not its specifics. It is no wonder, then,
that they might have chosen to express their consternation at their
enslavement in this strange land in religious terms.

The fate of Catholic slaves arriving in a Protestant English colony was not lost on its Spanish neighbors in Florida, who sought
to intrigue with the enslaved for their own ends. English settlers,
always anxious, even paranoid, about the Spanish threat to their
south, reported numerous rumors in the 1730s of mysterious per-
sonages, sometimes believed to be Jesuit priests, meddling under
cloudy circumstances in their coastal districts. Among the promises that Spanish Florida held out to enslaved South Carolinians
was the possibility of freedom and, perhaps specifically for the
Kongolese, rejoining a Catholic community. The background of
the African workers in South Carolina was not lost on the English
settlers. An anonymous English reporter observed that many Carolinians from Africa were Catholics, converted "in Angola," he
believed by Jesuits, those sinister agents of the Counter-
Reformation who troubled the English mind of the time. In reality, of course, the Catholics were from Kongo and maintained
in the Faith by Capuchins.[16] Not surprisingly, an increasing num-

---

[15] Gwendolyn Midlo Hall, *Africans in Colonial Louisiana: The Development of
Afro-Creole Culture in the Eighteenth Century* (Baton Rouge, 1992), p. 384.
[16] For a fuller explication of this document and linkage to Kongo, see
Thornton, "African Roots."

ber of African "deserters" fled, singly or in small groups, to Florida.[17] The Spanish authorities chartered a town, Santa Teresa de Mose, to receive such deserters and used them to help defend their frontier.[18]

In 1739, a Kongolese known in America as "Jemmy" led a major breakout from South Carolina which was to become one of the bloodiest uprisings in colonial North America. A group of twenty slaves, mostly Kongolese, gathered near the Stono River around dawn of 9 September, a Sunday and thus a "free" day for them, when supervision was at its lowest. They proceeded to Stono Bridge and there raided Hutchinson's store to capture arms and powder. Some, perhaps most, had probably served in the wars in Mbamba five years earlier and knew well how to use such weapons. Mbamba Luvota had also proven the last haven for the Antonians after Pedro IV's victory, and some of the older men may well have seen the wars between Pedro Valle das Lagrimas and the Kimpanzu of Mbamba Luvota twenty-five years earlier, when Antonianism was widespread in Kimpanzu territory.

The Stono rebels posted the heads of the storekeepers on the front steps of the building as an announcement of their seriousness. From there the group, which grew as it went along, attacked and burned houses, killing their residents and sparing only anyone, like the keeper of Wallace's Tavern, who was "a good man and kind to his slaves." Not all the slaves supported this breakout – some hid their masters or aided their escape, others were forced to march along so that they would not spread the alarm. But many – perhaps from the thousands of Kongolese enslaved in the colony who found themselves stirred by martial music played on the rebels' two drums – joined the march.

"Liberty!" was their cry, a word that, to those Kongolese who

---

[17] On these desertions, see the information culled from runaway advertisements and the notices of Anglican priests of the Society for the Propagation of the Gospel, in Michael Mullin, *Africa in America: Slave Acculturation and Resistance in the American South and the British Caribbean, 1736–1831* (Urbana and Chicago, 1992), pp. 43–4, 187.

[18] On Santa Teresa de Mose, see Jane Landers, "Gracia Real de Santa Terese de Mose: A Free Black Town in Spanish Colonial Florida," *American Historical Review* 95 (1990): 9–30.

still thought in Kikongo as they spoke in English, was *lukangu*,[19] whose root, *kanga*, also meant "salvation" to a Christian. Playing on the verb *kanga*, which ironically means also to bind or tie up, had been a characteristic of the Antonian movement, and the un-translated word for salvation in the Salve Regina had inspired the first lines of the Salve Antoniana. Later, too, revolutionary Haitians from Kongo would play on the same verb in their famous chant, "Kanga bafiote, Kanga mundele, Kanga ndoki la, Kanga Li" (meaning "Tie up [or free, or save] the black men, tie up/free/save the white man, tie up/free/save the witch, tie them up!")[20] But for many, no doubt, it meant nothing more than that they were fleeing their masters and would not be stopped before they reached Florida.

By the time the rebels were met with a force raised by the planters, they numbered close to a hundred and were flying standards, although the encounter proved indecisive. More than a dozen rebels were killed in the exchange of fire, but most escaped and moved onward. For the next week there were sporadic encounters between groups of armed rebels and colonial forces of one or another type. The planters, fearful that this was the beginning of a general rebellion of their slaves, were relieved to see that the danger had passed, although they continued to fear well through Christmas that another outbreak would start. Some of the rebels probably did eventually make it to Florida, as many who ran away in smaller groups had done earlier, although there is no documentary proof of this.[21]

[19] As in the seventeenth-century (1648) dictionary of Joris van Gheel, Biblioteca Nazionale da Roma Vittorio Emmanuele II, Rome, Fundo Minori 1896 MS Varia 274, 1896 "Vocabularium congoense, hispanicum et latinum," fol. 51v, giving various definitions of the Latin *liberare* and its derivatives, specifically *liberatis lucangú*. However, the word *libertas* is translated by another Kikongo word, *lusarilú* (the abstract nominal form of the applicative of the verb, *sala*, meaning to work or be engaged), while the act of freeing a slave "liberta a esclavo, hecho libre" is rendered *forrú eiácalá*, borrowing its verb from the Portuguese term for this act and adding the Kikongo word for man (*yakala*). These seem to convey the meaning of "liberty" less well than the derivatives of *kanga*.

[20] Thornton, " 'I am subject of the King of Congo,' " pp. 210–13.

[21] For the history of the revolt itself, I have followed the careful reconstruc-

The revolt, news of which was widely published in North America, led to a strong reaction against the importation of workers from central Africa, or "Angolans." Coinciding as it did with a precipitous decline in British shipping visiting the region in the face of strong French competition, the great era of Kongolese importation to North America drew to a close, although still as many as one in eight Africans arriving in the British colonies of the continent were central Africans. Kongolese returned to North America in great numbers only in the 1790s, when renewed British involvement in the trade brought them once again to South Carolina. At the same time, the other great importing center of North America, Louisiana, was obtaining Kongolese captives along with thousands of other central Africans through French and English shipping interests.[22]

Dona Beatriz had sought to end the wars that fed this trade in humans by attacking the kindoki, the relentless greed that fueled it. Greed for goods, greed to rule, greed to command – all these had led to the motivations of those who caused the wars, headed the bandit gangs, carried off the prisoners, captained the ships, supervised or owned the plantations. Many were Christians, some were good Christians, but as Dona Beatriz had taught in the Salve Antoniana: "Prayer serves no purpose, it is the intention that God takes."

tion of events in Wood, *Black Majority*, pp. 314–20; for the linkage to Kongo, see Thornton, "African Roots."

[22] On Kongolese in shipping of North America in the late eighteenth and early nineteenth centuries, see Joseph Holloway, "The Origins of African-American Culture," in Holloway (ed.), *Africanisms in American Culture* (Bloomington, Ind., 1990), p. 7. For Louisiana, see Hall, *Africans in Colonial Louisiana*, pp. 275–315.

Appendix: A Recovery of the "Salve Antoniana"

This is an attempt to render into the original Kikongo Dona Beatriz' version of the Salve Regina. It is given only in an Italian translation in Bernardo da Gallo's account of Dona Beatriz' movement.[1]

ORIGINAL ITALIAN TEXT

Salve voi dite, e non sapete il perche. Salve recitate, e non sapete il perche. Salve bastonate, e non sapete il perche. Iddio vuole l'intenzione, l'intenzione Iddio piglia. Nulla serve il casamento, l'intenzione Iddio piglia. Nulla serve il battesmo, l'intenzione Iddio piglia. Nulla serve la confessione, l'intenzione Dio piglia. Nulla serve l'orazione, l'intenzione Dio vuole. Nulla servono l'opera buone, l'intenzione Iddio vuole. La Madre et il figlio nella ponta di ginocchio. Se non era S. Antonio, come havevano da fare? S. Antonio è il pietoso, S. Antonio è il remedio nostro, S. Antonio è il restauradore del regno di Congo, S. Antonio è il consolatore del regno del cielo. S. Antonio è lui la porta del cielo. S. Antonio tiene le chiavi del cielo. S. Antonio è sopra gl'Angioli, e la vergine Maria. S. Antonio è lui il secondo Dio . . .

[1] Archivio "De Propaganda Fide" (Rome), Scritture Originali nelli Congragazione Generali, vol. 576, fol. 304v, as published in Teobaldo Filesi, "Nazionalismo," p. 495.

ENGLISH TRANSLATION OF ITALIAN TEXT

Salve you say and you do not know why. *Salve* you recite and you do not know why. *Salve* you beat and you do not know why. God wants the intention, it is the intention that God takes. Marriage serves nothing, it is the intention that God takes. Baptism serves nothing, it is the intention that God takes. Confession serves nothing, it is the intention that God takes. Prayer serves nothing, it is the intention that God wants. Good works serve nothing, it is the intention that God wants. The Mother with her Son on her knees. If there had not been St. Anthony what would they have done? St. Anthony is the merciful one. St. Anthony is our remedy. St. Anthony is the restorer of the kingdom of Kongo. St. Anthony is the comforter of the kingdom of Heaven. St. Anthony is the door to Heaven. St. Anthony holds the keys to Heaven. St. Anthony is above the Angels and the Virgin Mary. St. Anthony is the second God ...

PROPOSED ORIGINAL IN KIKONGO

The vocabulary comes from Mateus Cardoso's 1624 catechism[2] in Kikongo which was widely used in the Church in Kongo, although in Dona Beatriz' day it was probably known in the second edition published by the Capuchins in 1650;[3] and from the Kikongo dictionary of about 1648 compiled for the Capuchins by

---

[2] I would like to extend a special thanks to Hazel Carter and François Bontinck, who read earlier drafts of this proposed translation and suggested changes. I am especially grateful to Carter for her grammatical interventions, as she is, indirectly, my teacher through her course in Kikongo, *Kongo Language Course: Maloongi Makikoongo: A Course in the Dialect of Zoombo, Northern Angola* (Madison, Wis., African Studies Program, 1987) that I followed in studying the language. I would not dare hold them responsible for any errors, grammatical or otherwise, that appear in the text that follows.

[3] Mateus Cardoso (ed.), *Doutrina Christãa* (Lisbon, 1624), cited by chapter and verse to aid consultation of the modern critical edition of François Bontinck and D. Ndembi Nsasi, *Le catéchisme kikongo de 1624. Réedtion critique* (Brussels, 1978). Bontinck's introduction also gives all the relevant information on the later edition.

the canon (and later Capuchin himself) Manuel Robredo.[4] The orthography I have chosen is intended to show phonemes, and thus does not indicate the tone bridging or elision typical of most modern orthographies of the language, although seventeenth-century texts like the catechism and the sermon found in the dictionary[5] showed both features through word division. I have opted for one letter one sound (e.g., using "k" for "c" and "qu"), except that I have followed "Vocabularium" in using the "bh" for an bilabial "b," which today is uniformly a "v" sound (e.g., *vanga* for *bhanga*). I have shortened second vowels in words beginning with "mu" in the catechism, as this vowel was rapidly being assimilated into a nasal, and, indeed, "Vocabularium" chooses to use the apostrophe (i.e., *mucua nzabi* versus *m'cua nzabi*). In accordance with seventeenth-century usage, I have used "r" where modern Kikongo often uses "d," but this "r" is to be pronounced as in the international alphabet rather than as in English. Speakers of Kikongo will also note the use of the *ku-* in the infinitive and nominal form of verbs, a form that was lost sometime in the mid-eighteenth century.

The seventeenth-century Kikongo version of the "Salve Antoniana" follows on pages 218–20.

[4] Biblioteca Nazionale Centrale, MS Varia 274, "Vocabularium," MS copy belonging to Joris van Gheel, composed ca. 1650. There is a modern edition of this dictionary by J. Penders and Joseph van Wing, *Le plus ancien dictionnaire bantu* (Brussels, 1928), but it has modernized the orthography and changed the presentation of the work from a Latin to Kikongo to a Kikongo to French and Flemish version.

[5] "Vocabularium," fols. 125–25v (a sermon devoted to confession), also reproduced with a modernized orthography and French and Flemish translation in Penders and van Wing, *Dictionnaire*.

Salve[6] nubhobha[7] yo kenuzeye ya nki[8] ko.
Salve nusamba[9] yo kenuzeye ya nki ko.
Salve nulweka[10] yo kenuzeye ya nki ko.
Nzambi a Mpungu ozolele nsi a moyo.[11]

[6] I have kept the word *salve* in original Latin, since it is found untranslated in the Salve Regina in the catechism, *Doutrina Christãa* V, 1. Perhaps this untranslated word is the trigger that causes the first part of the prayer, since a Kikongo speaker would not know the meaning of the term.

[7] The Italian verbs are conjugated in second person plural familiar, but Kikongo lacks a familiar form of verbs, and one must assume that da Gallo's translation uses this form as appropriate to exhortations of superiors to inferiors in Italian rather than reflecting anything special in the Kikongo, which here simply uses second plural in present indicative. In present-day Kikongo the form would probably be *nuvovanga*, the current present tense, but in the seventeenth century this form was the usual present, as indicated in Brugiotti's grammar of 1652, and the usage in general in the catechism.

[8] The Italian gives "non sapete il perche" (you do not know the why), a somewhat awkward phrase; but if rendered in Kikongo, it seems to fit a literal translation of this phrase. In the catechism, questions of reason and definition are often given with *ya nki* (the reason is . . .) as their starting phrase, perhaps Beatriz' own starting point. For example, see *Doutrina Christãa* I, 3, when in answer to the question "Why do you say by the Grace of God?" [Quiâquiûma bobelebo, munâ sambu za Zambianmpungu?], the student replies "Not because of my merits" [Yanquî boque mu mifûnu miameco]. This pattern continues with a different question phrase after I, 7, where "Porque dizeis homen que crè . . ." [why do you say someone who believes . . .] is "Quiansûcu bobelebo muntu üacuiquî" and the reply is "Porque todo fiel christão . . ." [Because every faithful Christian] is rendered as "Yanquîbo onço Christão . . ." and this pattern continues through the remainder of the "why . . . because" questions and answers. The *ya nki* seems an appropriate, if somewhat strange, way to render "and you do not know the why."

[9] Although *kusamba* (infinitive form) is regularly used to mean "to pray," the term is also used to mean "recite," as in "recite the Rosary and Hail Mary," *Doutrina Christãa* XV, 5; clearly the usage intended here.

[10] "Vocabularium" 74v, "percutio.is: herrir. culuéca" (to beat). The Italian *bastonate* with its implication of beating with a club or stick would require a compound in Kikongo, which seems inappropriate here. In a letter to me of 4 November 1993 concerning an earlier attempt at translating this, François Bontinck suggested the beating in queston referred to flagellation of penetinents, a practice noted in Kongo.

[11] This expression is apparently not found in modern Kikongo, at least in dictionaries. It is, however, well attested in seventeenth-century sources:

Nsi a moyo kabonga o Nzambi a Mpungu.

Kukazala[12] kekubhanga mfunu[13] nkutu ko, nsi a moyo kabonga Nzambi a Mpungu.

Kuria mungwa[14] kekubhanga mfunu nkutu ko, nsi a moyo kabonga Nzambi a Mpungu.

Kufungisa[15] kekubhanga funu nkutu ko, nsi a moyo kabonga Nzambi a Mpungu.

Kusamba kekubhanga mfunu nkutu ko, nsi a moyo kazolele o Nzambi a Mpungu.

Kubhanga owote kekubhanga mfunu nkutu ko, nsi a moyo kazolele o Nzambi a Mpungu.

O Ngudi yo Mwana bhana makungulu mandi.

Ke S. Antonio ko, bari tubhanga nki?

S. Antonio nkwa kiyari.[16]

S. Antonio uzooloelo[17] weto.

"Vocabularium," fol. 49, "Intentio npitú nssia moyo"; fol. 119, "voluntas.tis nissia moio"; "voluntarie ianssia moio mússia moio." *Doutrina Christãa* III, 8, in Lord's Prayer, "seja feita a tua vontade" [Thy will be done] "ubua ensiacua monho." The term *nsi*, which might mean "land or country," is also used to mean "below" or "underneath," but has an idiomatic usage here. In his letter of 4 November 1993, François Bontinck has proposed that it might render "the deepest of the heart," as in Latin one would say "ex intimo corde."

[12] In *Doutrina Christãa*, both *kusompa* and *kukaza* are used to mean marriage, in which kusompa is clearly derived from the Kikongo original (to borrow, in exchange for bride wealth), and kukaza comes from Portuguese *caza*: XVI, 2. Here it is referred to in general advice to Christians; "especially marriage" is given as *yacubaza enayaucaza*. In the list of sacraments in IX, 4, *unganga üacucazâla* is given for *matrimonio*. The term actually means "priestly marriage." Given the context, I have preferred the Portuguese loan word here in a more generic form.

[13] "Vocabularium," fol. 98, "servio.is cubhanga múfúnu. pr npanguiri *id* cubhanga pr. npanguiri cusiruila pr. nsiriuiri." I have chosen the first option, since the term clearly means "serving a purpose" and hence the addition of *mfunu* seems appropriate.

[14] *Doutrina Christãa* IX, 4, Cudiâ munguâ" given for *Baptismo*.

[15] *Doutrina Christãa* IX, 4, "Cufunguna given for *Penetencia*.

[16] "Vocabularium," fol. 21, "clemens. m'cuaquiari. m'cuantantu. m'cuaqimgunda. pl. acua *id*." I have chosen *quiari* from among this list since the cry of the Antonians was consistently given as forms of this noun, *Tari, Sari* in the sources.

[17] "Vocabularium," fol. 90, "remedium ÿ uzooloelo. pl. *id* qdo scat medicamentium: quilonguianú" cf. "remedio. as cuzoolola. pr. nzolloele cuz-

S. Antonio mwauluri[18] o Wene[19] wa Kongo
S. Antonio mfyauri[20] o Wene wa Mazulu[21]
S. Antonio ebhitu[22] dia Mazulu
S. Antonio nkwansabi[23] a Mazulu
S. Antonio osundiri Anjos[24] ye Msundi Maria
S. Antonio i Nzambi a zole . . .

eolola pr. nzeoleole." In Kikongo, as in Italian, the concept of medicine has substantial religious significance, so a term with a medical application seems appropriate.

[18] "Vocabularium," fol. 91v, "restario.as. cúaúlúla pr. iaúluiri" and "resturatio Lúaulúlú". I have coined this term (not found in a seventeenth-century source) by following the common practice of converting a verb into a person performing the action of the verb by adding *mu*-as a prefix and changing the last vowel to-*i* as described in Brugiotti's grammar: e.g., *mucangui* (savior) from the verb *canga* (to save). For morphophonetic reasons, I have converted the last "l" in the stem to an "r."

[19] "Vocabularium" supports *utinu*, meaning kingdom, derived clearly from *ntinu*, meaning king. But *Doutrina Christãa* XII, 6, uses "Oüene üa mazûlu" to mean "Kingdom of Heaven," which seems to be appropriate in the context.

[20] "Vocabularium," fol. 24, "consolator. múfiaúri."

[21] *Doutrina Christãa* XII, 6, uses the plural form *mazulu*, which I follow here; the Italian uses the singular, but this is probably simply idiomatic, "Kingdom of the Heavens" not being the normal rendering in Italian.

[22] "Vocabularium," fol. 78v, "porta. d. ebhitú. p. mabh-."

[23] "Vocabularium," fol. 21, "claviger. quimzabi p. Iuzabi m'cuanzabi. pl acuanzabi." I have preferred the second of these two since it seems likely that da Gallo would have translated this version of "keybearer" as "carries the keys of heaven." *Nzabi* seems to be borrowed from Portuguese *chave*, meaning "key." The concord is to class 1/2 from the pluralization of the term in the "Vocabularium" rather than from *nzabi*.

[24] I have preferred a Portuguese plural for this word. "Vocabularium," fol. 10, gives "angelis i. anjo [Spanish regloss] anjo." No plural is given in this text, suggesting that the word was not "naturalized" in Kikongo.

Index

Note: There are no entries for Dona Beatriz Kimpa Vita, Kongo, and Saint Anthony as they are referred to throughout the book. All Kikongo names are treated as additional first names, e.g., Pedro Mpanzu a Mvemba is listed under Pedro. Kongolese with European-style surnames are alphabetized under their surnames, e.g., Ana Afonso de Leão is under Leão, Ana Afonso de, except the Princes of Soyo who are indexed under their first names, like kings.